Understanding White-Collar Crime

Unlike other books of its kind, *Understanding White-Collar Crime: An Opportunity Perspective* uses a distinct theoretical perspective in its coverage of white-collar crime. Using the opportunity perspective, or the assumption that all crimes depend on offenders having some sort of opportunity to commit an offense, allows the authors to uncover the processes leading up to white-collar crimes and offer potential solutions to this rampant issue, without being reductive in their treatment of the topic. With this second edition, Benson and Simpson have greatly expanded their coverage to include new case studies, substantive materials, and an annotated appendix of online resources to make this a core book for courses on white-collar crime.

Michael L. Benson is Professor of Criminal Justice at the University of Cincinnati. He is a past president of the White-Collar Crime Research Consortium. He has published extensively in the areas of white-collar crime, intimate partner violence, and life course criminology. With Francis T. Cullen, he authored *Combating Corporate Crime: Local Prosecutors at Work,* which received the Outstanding Scholarship Award in 2000 from the Crime and Delinquency Division of the Society for the Study of Social Problems. The second edition of his book *Crime and the Life Course: An Introduction* was published in 2013 by Routledge. He is currently working on a book on emotions in crime and criminal justice.

Sally S. Simpson is Director of the Center for the Study of Business Ethics, Regulation, and Crime (C-BERC) and Professor of Criminology and Criminal Justice at the University of Maryland, College Park. She is the Principal Investigator (with Peter C. Yeager, Boston University) on a Bureau of Justice Statistics grant to build a federal white-collar offending statistical series and is working with Mark Cohen (Vanderbilt University) and colleague Tom Loughran on a project funded by the National Institute of Justice to study the public willingness to pay for white-collar crime control. She has authored/edited five books and over 70 articles, chapters, and reports—many on the subject of white-collar/corporate crime. In 2013, Simpson was awarded the Gilbert Geis Lifetime Achievement Award by the White-Collar Crime Research Consortium. She is a Fellow of the American Society of Criminology and, in 2008, was named Distinguished Scholar by the Division on Women and Crime, American Society of Criminology. Simpson has served as President of the Association of Doctoral Programs in Criminology and Criminal Justice, is former Chair of the Crime, Law, and Deviance Section of the American Sociological Association and past president of the White-Collar Crime Research Consortium. Recipient of the Herbert Bloch Award from the American Society of Criminology, in 2010 Simpson was named Woman of the Year by the President's Commission on Women's Issues at the University of Maryland.

Criminology and Justice Studies Series

Edited by Shaun L. Gabbidon, *Penn State Harrisburg*

Criminology and Justice Studies offers works that make both intellectual and stylistic innovations in the study of crime and criminal justice. The goal of the series is to publish works that model the best scholarship and thinking in the criminology and criminal justice field today, but in a style that connects that scholarship to a wider audience, including advanced undergraduates, graduate students, and the general public. The works in this series help fill the gap between academic monographs and encyclopedic textbooks by making innovative scholarship accessible to a large audience without the superficiality of many texts.

Books in the Series

Published:

Biosocial Criminology: New Directions in Theory and Research
Edited by Anthony Walsh and Kevin M. Beaver

Community Policing in America
Jeremy M. Wilson

Criminal Justice Theory: Explaining the Nature and Behavior of Criminal Justice
Edited by David E. Duffee and Edward R. Maguire

Lifers: Seeking Redemption in Prison
John Irwin

Race, Law and American Society: 1607 to Present
Gloria J. Browne-Marshall

Today's White Collar Crime
Hank J. Brightman

White-Collar Crime: An Opportunity Perspective
Michael L. Benson and Sally Simpson

The New Criminal Justice: American Communities and the Changing World of Crime Control
John Klofas, Natalie Hipple, and Edmund McGarrell

The Policing of Terrorism: Organizational and Global Perspectives
Mathieu Deflem

Criminological Perspectives in Race and Crime, 2/e
Shaun Gabbidon

Corrections
Jeanne Stinchcomb

Community Policing
Michael Palmiotto

A Theory of African American Offending
James Unnever and Shaun Gabbidon

When Crime Appears: The Role of Emergence
Jean McGloin, Christopher Sullivan, and Leslie Kennedy

Voices from Criminal Justice
Edited by Heith Copes and Mark Pogrebin

Crime and the Life Course, 2/e
Michael L. Benson

Wrongful Convictions and Miscarriages of Justice
Edited by C. Ron Huff and Martin Killias

Human Trafficking: Interdisciplinary Perspectives
Edited by Mary C. Burke

Race, Law and American Society, 2/e: 1607 to Present
Gloria J. Browne-Marshall

Research Methods in Crime and Justice
Brian Withrow

Understanding White-Collar Crime

An Opportunity Perspective
Second Edition

Michael L. Benson, Ph.D.
School of Criminal Justice,
University of Cincinnati

Sally S. Simpson
Department of Criminology and Criminal Justice,
University of Maryland

 Routledge
Taylor & Francis Group

NEW YORK AND LONDON

Second edition published 2015
by Routledge
711 Third Avenue, New York, NY 10017

and by Routledge
2 Park Square, Milton Park, Abingdon, Oxon, OX14 4RN

Routledge is an imprint of the Taylor & Francis Group, an informa business

© 2015 Taylor & Francis

First published by Routledge 2009.

Library of Congress Cataloging-in-Publication Data
Benson, Michael L.
  [White-collar crime]
  Understanding white-collar crime : an opportunity perspective / by Michael L. Benson and Sally S. Simpson. — Second edition.
    pages cm. — (Criminology and justice studies series)
  Revised edition of the authors' White-collar crime : an opportunity perspective, published in 2009.
  Includes bibliographical references and index.
  1. White collar crimes.   I. Simpson, Sally S.   II. Title.
  HV6768.B465 2015
  364.16′8—dc23
  2014026980

ISBN: 978-0-415-70402-1 (hbk)
ISBN: 978-0-415-70403-8 (pbk)
ISBN: 978-0-203-76236-3 (ebk)

Typeset in Adobe Caslon and Copperplate Gothic
by Apex CoVantage, LLC

Printed and bound in the United States of America by Sheridan Books, Inc. (a Sheridan Group Company).

In memory of Gilbert Geis—scholar, teacher, mentor, and friend.

CONTENTS

ILLUSTRATIONS

PREFACE TO THE SECOND EDITION

Since the first edition of this book was published, white-collar offenders have been busy. New scandals and schemes have emerged with regularity and significant consequences, such as the apparent cover-up of the defective and deadly ignition switch on cars manufactured by General Motors as well as the incredibly long-running and costly Ponzi scheme orchestrated by Bernard Madoff. We've also observed the tremendous social and financial costs associated with the extensive frauds in the U.S. mortgage market. All of this activity has given us plenty of new material. Throughout this new edition, we introduce and analyze some of these recent episodes of white-collar and corporate crime, drawing from new research by white-collar crime scholars. Although we have altered the organizational structure of the book by dividing it into five parts and moving material around in some of the chapters, the general flow of the narrative remains the same.

Part I addresses definitional issues and the question of who is the white-collar offender. In Chapter 1, to supplement our discussion of the problem of how best to define white-collar crime, we have added a new section addressing the difficulties of measuring it. These two topics—the definition and measurement of white-collar crime—are, of course, intimately related. Chapter 2 explicates the groundbreaking work on the social and demographic characteristics of white-collar offenders by researchers at Yale

University in the 1970s, but it has been expanded to include data from the U.S. Sentencing Commission that permits us to compare contemporary white-collar offenders with the offenders in the Yale study. This comparison reveals that the demographic makeup of the white-collar offending population has changed in ways that mirror broader social changes in America. This chapter also includes a review of new research on white-collar criminal careers as well as new and sometimes disturbing research on the psychological characteristics of white-collar offenders. Finally, we include new material on organizations as offenders.

Part II examines various theoretical approaches to explaining white-collar crime and introduces our opportunity perspective. Chapter 3 covers traditional theories of white-collar crime and here we have added a discussion of some new methods of estimating the prevalence rate of offending among corporations. This is an important issue to get settled in light of the ongoing dispute between the advocates of self-control theory and the proponents of nearly all other theoretical perspectives about whether white-collar crime in corporations is rare or widespread. This chapter also includes an expanded discussion of the increasingly popular "choice" perspective as applied to white-collar crime. In addition to being renamed, Chapter 4 now includes a discussion comparing the routine activity concepts "suitable target" and "lack of guardianship" with the closely related but not identical concepts of "lure" and "lack of credible oversight" drawn from the choice perspective.

In Part III, we examine different forms of white-collar and corporate crime. As in the first edition, Chapter 5 presents an analysis of financial white-collar crimes but with a greatly expanded discussion of the veritable cornucopia of frauds that took place in the mortgage industry between 2000 and 2008. We also devote more time to securities offenses, especially stock manipulation, insider trading, and investment schemes. Bernard Madoff's Ponzi scheme is discussed at length, and we also address some new antitrust cases. Regrettably, in the past 5 years, there has been no shortage of the types of white-collar crime that harm people and the environment. Thus, in Chapter 6 we present new data on environmental crime cases, focusing in particular on the deadly Deepwater Horizon explosion. To deepen our understanding of this case, we draw from an emerging theoretical perspective called conservation criminology. Chapter 6 also covers the seemingly intractable problem of workplace safety both here and abroad by reviewing recent mining disasters. Finally, we have added a section on manufacturing crimes, which focuses on the manufacture and distribution of dangerous products such as the faulty ignition switch installed in General Motors cars.

Part IV takes a look at the symbolic and structural aspects of white-collar crime opportunities. Chapter 7 includes a review and analysis of new research on gender differences in the use of neutralizations. The symbolic dimensions of white-collar crime opportunities are also addressed through an analysis of the competing narratives that inevitably emerge whenever a new corporate scandal comes to light such as the General Motors defective ignition switch. On one side is a narrative that paints the individuals involved as amoral calculators who callously put profits over people, but on the other side are powerful corporate and political forces arguing that corporate executives are well-meaning people who sometimes regrettably make mistakes. These competing narratives bring to light the importance of the processes of concerted ignorance, neutralized deviance, and normalized deviance. On the structural dimensions of access to opportunities, Chapter 8 presents penetrating new research on the gender gap in white-collar offending and victimization. In regard to offending, the new research confirms what white-collar crime scholars have long suspected: that the gender gap in high level corporate frauds is exceedingly large. Women may be rising in corporate hierarchies, but they still do not hold leadership positions when it comes to large-scale frauds.

Finally, in Part V we address the problem of controlling white-collar crime and the future of white-collar crime. Effective control of white-collar crime and corporate wrongdoing remains a daunting problem for both the criminal justice and regulatory systems. Accordingly, the new Chapter 9 presents an expanded discussion of the difficulty of applying criminal law to certain white-collar offenses as well as a more focused discussion of the strengths and weaknesses of both criminal justice and regulatory systems as means of control. In the new Chapter 10, we offer a greatly expanded discussion of situational crime prevention theory as a way of thinking about white-collar crime control. We also examine how advances in computer hardware and software have created possibilities for improving the credibility of oversight. If these advances are taken advantage of, that would represent a significant advance in white-collar and corporate crime control. Chapter 11, on the future of white-collar crime, remains largely the same, because the forces that we identified in the first edition as promoting white-collar crime continue to operate. However, we do note that there is some evidence that the world is slowly coming to grips with the criminogenic effects of globalization. Increasingly, nations are responding through cooperative agreements involving transnational regulation. It remains to be seen just how far this trend will go and how effective it will be.

PREFACE TO THE FIRST EDITION

Most of us recognize that we could be victims of crime and try to take reasonable precautions against this happening. We lock our doors, avoid dangerous neighborhoods, and keep our belongings close by when we are out. These simple precautionary measures work primarily because they make it hard for offenders to get close to us or our property. They probably do help reduce the chances that we will be the victims of certain types of crime, such as burglary, robbery, assault, and larceny.

Unfortunately, these measures are unlikely to have any effectiveness against the types of crimes and criminals discussed in this book—white-collar crimes. White-collar crimes are committed in ways that are difficult, indeed often impossible, to prevent by simply blocking the offender's access to his or her target. White-collar offenders use techniques and take advantage of opportunities that are unavailable to ordinary street crime offenders to carry out their criminal intentions. Their crimes can harm victims both directly and indirectly without the victims even knowing it. Compared with ordinary street crimes, they pose significantly different risks and threats to individuals, government, and society in general.

This book is designed to help students better understand how white-collar crimes work. We take what we call an "opportunity perspective." This perspective is growing in popularity in regard to ordinary street crimes, and this book represents the first attempt to apply it systematically to white-collar crime. We assume that all crimes depend on offenders having some sort of opportunity to commit an offense and that different types of crimes have different "opportunity structures." The idea that opportunities are required for crime to occur is such a simple one that it is often overlooked in discussions about crime. Obviously, the crime of, say, bank robbery depends on banks being available to rob. Thus, when people think about the causes of crime and how best to control it, they often focus on offenders and the question of why they do it. The question of motivation is, of course, an important one, and we address it in this book. But, as we will show, the seemingly simple idea of opportunity turns out on closer analysis to be more complex than we might have thought and to have a number of important implications for our understanding of the causes of white-collar crime as well as the problem of how to control it.

Although in recent years there has been a growing number of monographs and textbooks on white-collar crime, this book has several distinguishing features that we think will make it valuable to students. First, we focus explicitly on opportunity structures and white-collar crime. Though other books have mentioned this topic, they rarely treat it as systematically as we do here. By analyzing opportunity structures, we help students understand how white-collar crimes are committed, including crimes that have physical as well as financial effects. Understanding how a crime works is the first step in developing ways to prevent it. Our analysis of opportunity structures includes both their subjective and objective dimensions. Thus, rather than simply describing the many terrible things that white-collar offenders have done, we try to give students a way of understanding the offenses so that they can do more than simply be morally outraged by them.

Second, opportunities to commit white-collar crime are not randomly distributed throughout society. Some people have greater access to white-collar crime opportunities than others. Accordingly, we discuss at length how the major demographic variables of gender, race, and social class are linked to both white-collar crime offending and victimization. In this way, we ground our analysis of white-collar crime in a broader sociological perspective.

Finally, drawing from our opportunity perspective, we present a new way of thinking about white-collar crime control. Discussions of crime control in regard to both white-collar and other forms of crime often are too narrowly focused on offenders. How can we get better at catching them, and how severely should they be punished when we do apprehend them? The opportunity perspective alerts us to the possibility that sometimes we can prevent or at least reduce particular forms of crime without necessarily doing anything directly to the offender. Rather, we can at times prevent offenses by altering some aspect of their opportunity structure. Based in situational crime prevention theory, this way of thinking about crime control is becoming increasingly popular with academicians and law enforcers. We show that it is an approach that can also be applied to white-collar crime.

Like virtually every other textbook on white-collar crime, Chapter 1 begins with a discussion of the thorny problem of how to define white-collar crime. We treat both the offender and offense-based approaches to definition and propose a partial synthesis of the two views. Chapter 2 presents a detailed analysis of what is known about the demographic, social, and psychological characteristics of white-collar offenders. In Chapter 3, we review several of the traditional theories or explanations of white-collar crime. In Chapter 4, we introduce the opportunity perspective in more detail, discussing the special features of white-collar crimes and their reliance upon distinctive techniques. Deception, abuse of trust, concealment, and conspiracy as techniques of criminal offending are addressed here. In Chapters 5 and 6, we apply the opportunity perspective to selected forms of white-collar crime. Although we do not cover every possible type of white-collar crime, we focus on a broad and heterogeneous selection of common white-collar offenses, including both property crimes and those that have physical effects too. Chapter 7 deals with the subjective or symbolic dimensions of opportunities. We discuss how white-collar offenders are adept at defining their crimes in morally favorable terms and how this contributes to their offending. Chapter 8 presents data and analysis regarding the distribution of white-collar offending and victimization by gender, race, and social class. In Chapter 9, we address the problem of how best to control white-collar crime by legal as well as extralegal means. Finally, in Chapter 10, we summarize our arguments regarding the special features and techniques of white-collar crime. Then we speculate on the future of white-collar offending and offer some thoughts regarding the policy implications of our analyses.

ACKNOWLEDGMENTS

Working in the white-collar crime field can be a challenge. There is too little funding, too few databases, and a lingering sense that our work has little impact on the broader field or social policy. Yet, there is a small group of dedicated scholars, from a variety of countries and epistemological positions, who do brilliant work toiling in these trenches. Although we may come at these problems in different ways, we all share a belief that it is important to carry Sutherland's torch, to continue to raise the issue of white-collar crime (in its many forms and permutations), and challenge the typical ways in which crime and criminality are depicted and understood across our nations. I dedicate this book to my students—the future of the field. Go out and shake things up.

Sally S. Simpson
July 31, 2014

Many of the ideas presented in this book were developed in part through casual discussions with my colleagues and students at the University of Cincinnati. In particular, talking with Frank Cullen, John Eck, and Tamara Madensen helped refine many of the ideas presented here. They certainly contributed to this book, even though they may not have known they were doing so at the time. Students in my seminar in White-Collar Crime also helped with their questions in class and their willingness to listen to lectures that were more works in progress than well-thought-out presentations. I thank my former graduate assistant Andrew Gilchrist, as an efficient fetcher and carrier of books who helped me avoid wasting a lot of time hiking around campus and prowling the university library. I also thank Andrew for putting together the annotated list of websites. Both Sally and I also give special thanks to Kathleen Brickey, who very generously made available to us data she has collected on post-Enron convictions for financial fraud in corporations and to Darrell Steffensmeier, who responded to our questions about race in the CFTF data.

Last, a word of thanks to Stephen Rutter and Margaret Moore at Routledge for their patience in waiting for us to get done.

Michael L. Benson
July 31, 2014

PART I

AN INTRODUCTION AND OVERVIEW OF WHITE-COLLAR CRIME

On December 27, 1939, in the city of Philadelphia, Pennsylvania, a 56-year-old sociologist by the name of Edwin H. Sutherland gave a talk that altered forever the study of crime throughout the world. Professor Sutherland was addressing the annual meeting of the American Sociological Association as its incoming president, and his talk was entitled "The White-Collar Criminal" (Sutherland, 1940). In his address, the professor took aim at what he regarded as a fundamental failing of the criminological theory of his day, namely, the failure to recognize and take seriously the "monstrous amount of lawbreaking by persons in positions of power" (Geis and Goff, 1983:ix). He called this lawbreaking *white-collar crime*. Prior to Sutherland's address, lawbreaking by persons in positions of power had been largely ignored by academic criminologists, who instead focused almost exclusively on the ordinary street crimes committed by the poor and disadvantaged. In the 75 years since his address, the concept of white-collar crime, though much criticized and debated, has become an established part of both criminological thinking and public discourse.

Part I of this book explicates the concept of white-collar crime and the debates that surround it. We begin by tracing the historical evolution of the concept and then introduce two different ways of defining it, called *offender based* and *offense based*. Next, we review what is known about the demographic, social, and psychological characteristics of white-collar offenders. Although Sutherland wanted to draw attention to lawbreaking by persons in positions of power, you will see that many of the people who commit what can only be called white-collar crimes are not all that powerful. Nevertheless, even though many white-collar criminals are not wealthy or powerful, they are also not like ordinary street criminals either. Rather, they are drawn from a distinctly different segment of the American population.

1

WHAT IS WHITE-COLLAR CRIME?

White-collar crime is a technical term that has migrated out of the realms of science and academia to become part of public discourse. Stories about white-collar crime are often in the news. If you were to ask the proverbial man or woman on the street, you would surely find that most of them have heard of white-collar crime. However, if you pressed them to explain just what white-collar crime is, the answers you would receive would not be very informative. Most people would probably say something about men in suits who steal money and don't go to prison and let it go at that. Yet, the problem of white-collar crime is enormously complex. It raises difficult social, legal, and theoretical issues that have important implications for society and for the field of criminology. This book is designed to help you better understand the complexities of white-collar crime so that you can think critically and analytically about this important social problem. Of course, thinking critically and analytically about a social problem may strike some readers as not terribly exciting. For those of you who are looking for a more compelling reason to keep going, we hope that what you learn in these pages also will help you avoid being victimized by white-collar offenders.

Unfortunately, avoiding such offenders is not easy. White-collar criminals lurk in every industry and profession. For example, whenever you engage in a business transaction with any sort of professional, there is the potential for what we will call a "white-collar victimization." We use the term *professional* here in a very loose sense to include anyone who offers to provide a specialized service for a fee. Besides the traditional professions such as law, medicine, and accounting, our definition includes blue-collar and other service "professionals," such as home remodelers, auto mechanics, plumbers, electricians, and real estate agents. Typically, when you hire any sort of professional to do something for you, it is because the professional knows more about it than you do, or can do it better than you can, or simply has more time than you do. In other words, you need the professional to do something that for some reason you can't or don't want to do yourself. However, how do you know that the professional did the *right* thing (i.e., the thing that was necessary and appropriate in your situation) in the *right* way (i.e., the most professional and cost-effective way)? It is always possible that the professional took advantage of your lack of expertise to defraud or cheat you in some way.

Talking about doing the right thing in the right way is obviously vague. So, consider as examples two situations involving professionals that most everyone encounters at some point in time— buying a home and going to the doctor. Buying a home can be a daunting experience, not only because it is for most of us the most expensive thing we will ever buy, but also because it is a very complicated process, involving lots of forms and paperwork (listings, offers, loan applications, titles, insurance, etc.) and lots of different people (realtors, appraisers, surveyors, loan officers, lenders, etc.). Indeed, the process is so complicated that many home buyers simply trust the professionals who work in the home mortgage industry to guide them through it, and they sign papers without reading or understanding them. Unfortunately, between 2005 and 2008, this blind trust in the integrity of the home mortgage industry was often misplaced as literally thousands of Americans fell victim to deceptive and fraudulent lending practices, in which they were tricked by mortgage brokers into taking on loans that were not in their best interests. Besides marketing deceptive loans, the mortgage and banking industries also engaged in a host of other scams and schemes that we will explain more fully in Chapter 5.

Now, consider the health care industry. Suppose you have not been feeling well for a few days and decide to go to a doctor. She looks you over, asks some questions about your symptoms, and then recommends further tests in order to make a definitive diagnosis. You don't really know if you need more tests. Of course, you could go and get a second opinion, but that's going to take more time. Besides, the doctor is supposed to be an expert. You are likely to accept the doctor's advice and agree to get the tests. However, unbeknownst to you, the doctor knows exactly what is wrong with you but, for financial reasons, she wants to order unnecessary tests. Perhaps she is part owner of the testing company and so is interested in directing business that way or has an agreement with the lab to split the fee when she sends business to them.

Both of these examples illustrate different forms of fraud. In both cases, a professional uses his or her superior knowledge and expertise to take advantage of someone. Fraud is not limited to medicine and real estate. It can occur in every profession. It represents one of the most common types of white-collar crime, but there are many other types of white-collar crime that we will discuss in this book. For example, violations of environmental regulations, fraudulent accounting practices, exploitation of workers, securities violations, and antitrust violations are among a host of others that we will consider. Unlike the examples of fraud given here, many of these offenses do not involve a discrete interaction between an offender and a victim. Nevertheless, they are all forms of white-collar crime.

Although there are good reasons to believe that the frauds discussed earlier and other white-collar type of crimes are more common now than they have ever been (Weisburd et al., 1991), it would be a mistake to think that white-collar crime is a new invention of the criminal mind. Unfortunately, criminals have engaged in white-collar type crimes literally for thousands of years.

An Historical Look at White-Collar Crime

What we today would call white-collar crime is not new. It's been around a long time. For example, in the fourth century BC, the Greek philosopher Aristotle wrote about embezzlement of funds by road commissioners and other officials. The theft of public money by government officers was a crime under the Athenian constitution, and a jury could sentence someone convicted of such a crime to pay ten times the amount stolen (von Fritz and Kapp, 1950). The Bible and other ancient religious texts condemn a number of exploitative business activities as harmful and counter to the common good. They may not have been legally defined as crimes, but they were certainly regarded as morally wrong (Geis, 1988). For example, admonitions about the immorality of cheating in the marketplace can be found in Proverbs (11:25): "He that holdeth corn, the people will curse him: But blessing shall be upon the head of him that selleth it." Similarly, Deuteronomy (25:13) declares: "For every one practicing unfairness is abominable to the Lord your God." According to Talmudic scholars, "The Talmud excoriated those who hoarded food in order to resell it at a high price, tampered with weights and measures . . . and raised prices unjustly" (Friedman, 1980).

If we move forward several centuries to the late Middle Ages in England, we find that the common law outlawed three business-related activities: regrating, engrossing, and forestalling (Geis, 1988). Each of these activities represented a different way in which someone could try to control the market on important commodities, especially foodstuffs, in order to charge high prices and make exorbitant profits. For example, engrossing involved buying up the entire stock of some commodity, say corn or wheat, in order to resell it at monopoly prices. These sorts of behaviors foreshadow what today we call antitrust offenses (Geis, 1988). Embezzlement by knights and other officers of the king was also a common offense during the Middle Ages (Pike, 1873).

Continuing our journey through time, in the early twentieth century, the noted American sociologist Edward Alsworth Ross railed against "the criminaloid," that is, powerful business owners and executives who exploit people and manipulate the marketplace out of an uninhibited desire to maximize their profits, all the while pretending to be pious and respectable. As examples of business duplicity combined with the appearance of respectability, Ross noted that

> [t]he director who speculates in the securities of his corporation, the banker who lends his depositors' money to himself under divers corporate aliases, the railroad official who grants a secret rebate for his private graft, the builder who hires walking delegates to harass his rivals with causeless strikes, the labor leader who instigates a strike in order to be paid for calling it off, the publisher who bribes his textbooks into the schools, these reveal in their faces nothing of the wolf or vulture.
>
> (Ross, 1977, p. 31)

Ross accused these individuals of moral insensibility and held them responsible for the deaths of workers and consumers. Thus, long before the term *white-collar crime* was coined, depredations committed by the rich and powerful in the pursuit of profit and wealth have been recognized and denounced.

Many of the themes that run through this book and that permeate the study of white-collar crime can be found in the historical record. For example, the crime of engrossing involves a perversion of legitimate business activities to serve illegitimate ends and to exploit others. As we will see, a defining feature of white-collar crime is its link to legitimate business or economic activities. Another important theme is the observation that supposedly respectable people, who are not thought of by others and certainly do not think of themselves as ordinary criminals, commit these offenses. Aristotle complained about road commissioners and public officials who embezzle public funds, not about ordinary thugs. Also prominent is the idea that these crimes are committed out of greed and a lust for power, not out of desperation or any sort of psychological abnormality. As E.A. Ross argued, the criminaloid's pursuit of profit makes him morally insensitive but not crazy.

But what exactly is white-collar crime?

Defining White-Collar Crime

Throughout his career, Edwin H. Sutherland, who coined the term, used several different definitions of "white-collar crime." In his most famous book, *White-Collar Crime*, he defined it "as a crime committed by a person of respectability and high social status in the course of his occupation" (Sutherland, 1983). He went on to note that this definition "excludes many crimes of the upper class, such as most of their cases of murder, adultery, and intoxication, since these are not customarily a part of their occupational procedures." In a footnote, he added that the term "white-collar is used here to refer principally to business managers and executives." This definition has provoked both admiration and condemnation for more than 50 years. It continues to be a source of debate and controversy, but we will get to those issues a little later.

Sutherland expanded on and further clarified his conception of white-collar crime in a 1949 entry in the *Encyclopedia of Criminology*

(Branham and Kutash, 1949). In the encyclopedia article, he wrote that "the white collar criminal is defined as a person with high socio-economic status who violates the laws designed to regulate his occupational activities." Sutherland continued that the "white collar criminal should be differentiated, on the one hand, from the person of lower socio-economic status who violates the regular penal code or the special trade regulations which apply to him; and, on the other hand, from the person of high socio-economic status who violates the regular penal code in ways not connected with his occupation." Note that according to this definition, some of the people involved in the mortgage fraud we described earlier might not be considered white-collar criminals by Sutherland. We discuss this issue of who is and who is not a white-collar criminal in more detail further, but for now let us return to an examination of Sutherland's definition.

As a way to define a particular type of crime, both of these definitions are unusual in that they refer to characteristics of the actor. Legal commentators addressing other sorts of crimes typically take great pains to establish clear definitions of the acts that must take place and the state of mind that an individual must possess in order for a crime to be committed, but little is said about the characteristics of the actor. Sutherland's approach, however, tells us that only certain types of people can commit white-collar crimes, those with "respectability and high social status." It also specifies that the act must arise out of the course of the actor's occupation. For Sutherland, both the status of the actor and the occupational location of the act determine whether an illegality is a white-collar crime.

The Controversy Surrounding Sutherland's Approach

From the start, Sutherland's approach to white-collar crime provoked criticism and controversy. One issue concerns the legal status of white-collar type of offenses. A distinguishing feature of Sutherland's approach was his willingness to include acts that had been sanctioned through civil or administrative legal proceedings as part of white-collar crime. This decision provoked extensive comment and criticism from legal scholars who contended that only acts that were punished under criminal laws can rightly be called crimes (Tappan, 1947). In Sutherland's view, however, including other types of violations was justified because many civil laws deal with practices that are fundamentally similar to criminal offenses. In addition, many illegal business practices can be sanctioned under either criminal or civil law or both. To exclude offenses that are pursued under civil law arbitrarily limits the range of white-collar offenses. This limitation is especially important in the context of white-collar crime, because the organizations and individuals who commit these offenses often use their political power and economic resources to avoid criminal prosecutions. As many white-collar crime commentators have noted, it is important to investigate how and under what circumstances business activities are criminalized (Cullen et al., 2006).

Another major point of contention that arose out of Sutherland's approach is whether the offender's social status should be a defining characteristic of white-collar crime. Sutherland included respectability and high social status in his definition, because he wanted to draw attention to the criminality of business groups. He argued that the criminological theories of his day were class biased and incomplete because they equated crime with lower-class individuals and ignored crime by upper-class individuals. In addition, he was morally outraged by what he regarded as the lenient and preferential treatment afforded to business offenders in the criminal justice system.

Sutherland undoubtedly was correct about the narrowness of criminological theory and the unfairness of the criminal justice system of his day. Nevertheless, including social status and respectability in the definition of white-collar crime created problems for research and analysis. One problem that arises if social status is a defining element of crime is that it cannot then be used as an explanatory variable because it is not allowed to vary independently of the crime. Thus, by definitional fiat, white-collar crime researchers are prevented from investigating how the social status of individuals influences the types or the seriousness of the white-collar type of offenses they commit. Similar offenses may be committed by corporate executives and by employees at the bottom of the corporate hierarchy, but only the former meet Sutherland's definition of white-collar crime.

Suppose, for example, that a top corporate executive participates in a meeting about his company and learns about a development that will drive the value of the company's stock up in the next few weeks. Hoping to take advantage of this inside information, the executive buys a large share of the company's stock while it is still cheap. Suppose also that a low-level typist who transcribes the minutes from the meeting notices the same information and she also decides to buy company stock just as the executive did. Both the executive and the typist have committed what is called *insider trading*, and it is illegal. In Sutherland's eyes, the executive is clearly a white-collar criminal, but what would he do with the typist? Along with other white-collar crime scholars, we believe it does not make sense to focus only on the corporate executive and to ignore the typist. It is important to investigate how social status is related to white-collar crime, just as we investigate how it is related to ordinary street crime. The issue of how social status is related to white-collar crime should not be decided arbitrarily by definitional fiat. Indeed, a major theme of this book is that social status is important precisely because it influences access to opportunities for white-collar crime. People with high social status may also be able to influence the content of the laws that address their behavior and the way in which law is administered by criminal justice and regulatory agencies.

We need to pay attention to status not only in regard to how it influences access to opportunities but also in regard to who has it and who doesn't. Those who don't have high social status have fewer opportunities to commit white-collar offenses. In the example given earlier, the executive was a man. Although women have made great strides in the corporate world over the past few decades and there are more than a few female top executives, they are still underrepresented in leadership positions in major corporations. According to a survey by Catalyst, a nonprofit research and advisory organization working to expand opportunities for women, in the year 2005, women constituted just 16.4 percent of officers in leading corporations (Catalyst, 2006). Women are even rarer in leading roles in Standard & Poor's 500 companies, where they make up only 4 percent of chief executives and 10 percent of chief financial officers (Davidoff, 2013). As we show later, because of gender stratification in the labor force, women do not commit as many or as serious white-collar crimes as men (Daly, 1989; Steffensmeier, Schwartz, and Roche, 2013). The same is true of African Americans, Hispanics, and other peoples of color. They, too, are underrepresented in leadership positions, and their access to white-collar crime opportunities is equally limited. White-collar crime opportunities are differentially distributed by gender, race, ethnicity, and status.

Including social status in the definition of white-collar crime also rules out the possibility of exploring how variation in the status of offenders influences societal reactions to their offenses. For example, it is important to investigate whether acts of insider trading by corporate executives and by clerical staff are treated the same or differently by authorities. Are small businesses that engage in consumer fraud treated the same in court as are multinational corporations that cheat the public? In order to investigate these issues, white-collar crime must be defined in a status-neutral manner.

Offender-Based Approaches to Defining White-Collar Crime

Sutherland's definition is the most well-known and influential example of what has been called the *offender-based* approach to defining white-collar crime. Offender-based definitions emphasize as an essential characteristic of white-collar crime the high social status, power, and respectability of the actor. Despite its shortcomings, Sutherland's offender-based approach has remained popular. Numerous attempts have been made to define the concept in a manner that is faithful to Sutherland's intentions but that clarify or expand upon his definition. Albert J. Reiss and Albert D. Biderman proposed that "white-collar violations are those violations of law to which penalties are attached that involve the use of a violator's position of significant power, influence, or trust in the legitimate economic or political institutional order for the purpose of illegal gain, or to commit an illegal act for personal or organizational gain" (Reiss and Biderman, 1981). At a 1996 workshop sponsored by the National White-Collar Crime Center's Research and Training Institute, a consortium of white-collar crime scholars proposed an operational definition to which Sutherland probably would not have objected. The group defined white-collar crime as "illegal or unethical acts that violate fiduciary responsibility or public trust, committed by an individual or organization, usually during the course of legitimate occupational activity, by persons of high or respectable social status for personal or organizational gain" (Helmkamp, Ball, and Townsend, 1996). These definitions have several elements in common with Sutherland's approach. They each include the social characteristics of the offender, they locate offenses in the offender's occupation, and they include noncriminal acts.

Another Way of Looking at White-Collar Crime: Offense-Based Definitions

Another approach to defining white-collar crime is called *offense based*, because the definition is based on the nature of the illegal act. In 1970, Herbert Edelhertz, then an official at the U.S. Department of Justice, proposed a highly influential offense-based definition of white-collar crime. He defined white-collar crime as "an illegal act or series of illegal acts committed by non-physical means and by concealment or guile to obtain money or property, to avoid the payment or loss of money or property, or to obtain business or personal advantage" (Edelhertz, 1970). This definition defines white-collar crime according to the means by which the offense is carried out—specifically, nonphysical means that involve concealment or guile. Any illegal act or series of acts committed by any person that meets these formal requirements is considered white-collar crime.

Edelhertz (1970, pp. 19–20) went on to identify four basic types of white-collar crime:

1. Personal crimes: Crimes by persons operating on an individual, *ad hoc* basis, for personal gain in a nonbusiness context—for example, individual income tax violations and credit card frauds
2. Abuses of trust: Crimes in the course of their occupations by those operating within businesses, government, or other establishments, or in a professional capacity, in violation of their duty of loyalty and fidelity to employer or client—for example, embezzlement, commercial bribery, and kickbacks
3. Business crimes: Crimes incidental to and in furtherance of business operations, but not the central purpose of such business operations—for example, antitrust violations and food and drug violations
4. Con games: White-collar crime as a business, or as the central activity of the business—for example, advance fee swindles and home improvement schemes.

Another example of the offense-based school of thought on defining white-collar crime was provided in 1990 by Susan Shapiro (1990). She argued that the essential characteristic of the acts that are commonly called *white-collar crimes* is that they involve the violation or abuse of trust. She proposed that the concept of white-collar crime be liberated by "disentangling the identification of the perpetrators from their misdeeds" (Shapiro, 1990). In Shapiro's view, offender-based definitions create an imprisoning framework. This framework leads scholars to misunderstand the structural sources of white-collar offenses, the problems they create for social control agencies, and the nature of class bias in the justice system. Another prominent white-collar scholar proposes that white-collar crime be defined as "a violation of the law committed by a person or group of persons in the course of an otherwise respected and legitimate occupation or financial activity" (Coleman, 1989). This definition does not refer to the status or respectability of the actor and expands the location of white-collar crime so as to include non-occupational but presumably legitimate financial activities. A similar definition has been proposed by Jay Albanese (1995), who argues for this formulation: white-collar crime is "planned or organized illegal acts of deception or fraud, usually accomplished during the course of legitimate occupational activity, committed by an individual or corporate entity."

Offense-based definitions have proved popular with researchers for several reasons. Because no mention is made of the social status of the actor or the social location of the act, both status and location are free to vary independently of the definition of the offense and can be used as explanatory variables. Researchers who use an offense-based definition have the freedom to explore how variation in the social status of the actor influences characteristics of the white-collar crimes committed and how the status of the actor influences societal reactions to offenses. Researchers can also investigate whether white-collar offenses committed in occupational settings differ from those committed outside occupational settings. Finally, offense-based definitions make it easier for researchers to draw samples of white-collar offenders from official data sources, such as court conviction records. Researchers need only identify a set of statutory offenses that meet certain formal criteria—for example, offenses that are not physical and that are based on deception. Then, it is just a matter of sampling individuals convicted of those offenses. A number of well-regarded studies published in the 1980s and 1990s used this strategy to identify and investigate white-collar offenders in the U.S. federal judicial system (Benson and Walker, 1988; Hagan and Nagel, 1982; Wheeler, Weisburd, and Bode, 1982).

Despite its popularity with some researchers, the offense-based approach to white-collar crime raises troubling issues for many other white-collar crime scholars (Geis, 1996). The very ease with which offense-based definitions can be used to draw samples becomes a trap for investigators, leading them to miss or ignore the most important aspects of the white-collar crime phenomenon. Investigators who use offense-based definitions often end up studying the relatively minor misdeeds of ordinary people of very modest financial means who somehow become caught up in the criminal justice system. Indeed, if you construed Edelhertz's definition loosely, it would permit an unemployed single mother who lied on an application for welfare to claim the status of white-collar criminal. Even more important, with its focus on money and property, Edelhertz's definition turns attention away from the types of white-collar crime that do physical harms to people (Braithwaite, 1985). For example, among the most serious white-collar crimes are illegal discharge of hazardous waste into the environment, manufacture of dangerous products, and the causing of death, injury, or illness of workers via unsafe working conditions. Such crimes rarely appear in studies that follow Edelhertz's approach to defining white-collar crime.

Offense-based samples drawn from the federal judicial system, which supposedly has a larger proportion of white-collar clients than is found in state courts, tend to be composed primarily of middle-class individuals who have committed banal and simplistic offenses (Wheeler et al., 1988a). The powerful corporations and corporate executives that originally provoked Sutherland's interest are largely absent. Offense-based approaches also tend inevitably to draw researchers toward the study of acts that have been officially defined as illegal. As a result, powerful individuals and corporate actors who are able to avoid official labeling in the first place never appear in the resulting samples. Thus, the major criticism of the offense-based approach is that in practice it misses the crimes of the powerful, who simply sidestep the criminalization process. The very people that Sutherland originally sought to bring to the attention of criminologists are ignored. Substituted in their place are small-time con men and cheating welfare moms (Daly, 1989).

Reconsidering the Two Approaches

The critics of Edelhertz's offense-based approach to defining white-collar crime make an important point. In practice, the use of this approach has often (but not always) resulted in studies that do not include the very offenses and offenders that drew Sutherland's attention in the first place. As John Braithwaite (1985) put it, perhaps a bit too strongly, the "practical consequences for empirical research have been that most white-collar criminals end up having blue collars." In addition, those who have used Edelhertz's approach have tended to ignore white-collar crimes that impose physical harm and violence on their victims. Both the manufacture of dangerous products and the maintenance of unsafe working environments are important types of white-collar crime.

We agree that it is important to avoid reducing the study of white-collar crime to small-time frauds by home repairmen and employee theft by retail clerks. But we note that this "practical consequence," as Braithwaite calls it, is just that—a practical consequence. It is not a logical consequence of the offense-based approach. Rather, it is a consequence of how this approach has been used by some researchers (Hagan, Nagel [Bernstein], and Albonetti, 1980; Weisburd et al., 1991; Wheeler et al., 1982).

There is nothing in the offense-based approach to defining white-collar crime that prevents researchers from examining the offenses of people with high social status or respectability or who hold positions of "significant power, influence, or trust." Suitably motivated researchers could use an offense-based approach to focus on the white-collar offenses of high-status individuals who occupy positions of power, influence, and trust. Likewise, suitably motivated researchers could examine how deceit and guile are used to manufacture dangerous products and to maintain unsafe workplaces for business advantage, or to commit civil and regulatory offenses. That this often does not happen reflects a failure on the part of researchers, not a fundamental weakness of the offense-based approach.

The key point to keep in mind is that regardless of the characteristics of the individuals involved, white-collar crimes are committed using particular techniques. That is, they rely upon a certain modus operandi. The characteristics of the individuals who commit these offenses are important insofar as they influence access to the opportunities to use these techniques. As we argue throughout this book, many of the characteristics that are part of offender-based definitions (e.g., high social status, respectability, elite occupational positions) are indeed important precisely because they provide offenders with access to opportunities for white-collar crime.

The idea that white-collar crime involves particular techniques was well known to Sutherland. Throughout his major works on white-collar crime, he describes the techniques for specific misdeeds, as in this passage taken from his presidential address to the American Sociological Society in 1939:

> These varied types of white-collar crimes in business and the professions consist principally of violation of delegated or implied trust, and many of them can be reduced to two categories: (1) misrepresentation of asset values and (2) duplicity in the manipulation of power. The first is approximately the same as fraud or swindling; the second is similar to the double-cross.
>
> (Sutherland, 1940, p. 3;
> see also 1941, p. 112 and 1949, pp. 152–158)

As Sutherland certainly understood, access to these techniques can be greatly facilitated by holding particular occupational positions. In a discussion of financial crime, he noted that "many corporate executives make strenuous efforts to secure positions in which they may have an opportunity to violate the trust for which they are legally responsible" (Sutherland, 1949, pp. 153–154). We would add to Sutherland's observation the caveat that both race and gender influence access to these lucrative positions. All other things being equal, white males are more likely to have access to these positions than women and racial or ethnic minorities.

The offender-based and offense-based approaches to defining white-collar crime are not contradictory or mutually exclusive. Rather, they simply emphasize different aspects of a general empirical regularity involving the characteristics or social positions of individuals and the types of offenses that they tend to commit. The techniques of white-collar offending tend to be used more by people who have high social status and hold certain occupational positions than by people who do not have these characteristics. This is not to say that people of low social status who work in menial jobs or are unemployed cannot use misrepresentation and duplicity to take advantage of others. Of course, they can. But they have much less opportunity to do so than people of high social status who hold positions of significant trust or power. Similarly, members of the middle and upper social classes could commit conventional property crimes, such as burglary and robbery, but they generally do not because they have access to other easier and less risky ways of stealing.

The social and occupational characteristics of white-collar offenders are important in another way as well. These characteristics are related to the seriousness of the offenses that offenders commit. In regard to criminal offenses, seriousness has two primary dimensions: the harmfulness of the offense and the blameworthiness of the offender (Wheeler et al., 1982; Wheeler, Mann, and Sarat, 1988b). The white-collar offenses of high-status individuals who hold positions of power in large organizations tend to be more serious than those of other types of individuals. Consider, for example, an offense such as the illegal disposal of hazardous waste. It is true that many types of small businesses generate hazardous waste and then illegally dispose of it using midnight dumpers (Epstein and Hammett, 1995; Rebovich, 1992). As the name implies, midnight dumping involves the illegal disposal of hazardous waste under the cover of darkness somewhere where it is not supposed to go, such as an abandoned building or a vacant lot. These businesses often are owned by people who do not wear suits and ties and who operate on very thin profit margins. Examples include the electroplating, carpet cleaning, dry cleaning, and furniture-refinishing businesses. The potential harm to the environment posed by the illegal practices of small businesses is a serious problem. Indeed, some evidence from the Environmental Protection Agency suggests that the environmental threat posed by all small businesses taken together may even exceed that posed by large organizations, simply because there are so many small businesses and they are difficult to track—in part because much of the regulatory oversight of small businesses is delegated to the states.

A perfect example is the recent (2013) toxic spill of 10,000 gallons of coal processing compounds into the drinking water of hundreds of thousands of West Virginians from a poorly maintained and rarely inspected storage site along the Elk River owned by Freedom Industries. More than 30 people were hospitalized and hundreds more were treated as a consequence of the spill, and state regulators were left with "egg on their faces" (Barrett, 2014).

Although regulations have lessened industrial point source pollution from larger companies (Vandenbergh, 2001), the danger represented individually by your local dry cleaner pales in comparison to the danger that arises when large organizations illegally dispose of hazardous waste. The examples here are numerous. Consider, for instance, the Hooker Chemical Corporation (Tallmer, 1987), which was responsible for the infamous Love Canal tragedy; or Rockwell International Company, which contaminated Rocky Flats, Colorado with nuclear wastes (Rosoff, Pontell, and Tillman, 2013). The list could go on (for many examples, see Chapter 4 in Rosoff et al., 2013).

The important point to recognize is that environmental offenses (and, obviously, many other types of white-collar offenses) are committed by the high-status executives and managers of powerful multinational corporations and by the economically struggling owners of small businesses (Barlow, 1993). Of course, we should not overlook all the businesses that fall somewhere between these two extremes. They are involved as well. Adopting a research strategy that ends up focusing only on small business owners is a mistake, but it is also a mistake to focus exclusively on multinational corporations. Similar offenses may occur at all levels of business activity.

We must be careful, though, not to overstress the notion of similarity. Just because similar offenses may occur across a broad range of levels of economic organization does not mean that they necessarily have the same causes and consequences. Nor does it mean that they can be controlled in the same way. That sort of one-size-fits-all type of thinking inevitably misses important aspects of the phenomenon of white-collar crime. The causes and consequences of white-collar crime are matters that must be settled through empirical investigation. Likewise, identifying the best response to white-collar crime requires careful analysis of the cost and effectiveness of different types of control strategies.

Measuring White-Collar Crime

Crime can be measured in different ways. For example, one way is to count the number of offenses that occur in a particular time or place. The Uniform Crime Report (UCR), which is published annually, by the Federal Bureau of Investigation does an admirable job of this in regard to ordinary street crimes. Every year it reports extensive information on crimes that have been reported to police agencies across the United States. As an indicator of the size of the crime problem, the UCR is not perfect, of course, because it does not include crimes that are not reported. The problem of underreporting is ameliorated to a certain degree by the National Crime Victimization Survey (NCVS). This survey of the general population in the United States asks people whether they have been victimized by various crimes and if so whether they reported it. By combining information from the UCR and the NCVS, it is possible to obtain a reasonably accurate picture of the extent of crime in the United States and whether the crime rate is going up or down or holding steady. The UCR and NCVS also provide useful information on the characteristics of offenders and victims.

Unfortunately, for the most part, neither the UCR nor the NCVS can be used to study patterns and trends in white-collar crime, because they include only limited data on a small number of white-collar offenses, such as embezzlement and minor frauds. To learn about more serious white-collar offenses and offenders, researchers must seek out data and reports from an assortment of different state and federal agencies. Much of the enforcement of federal white-collar offending statutes, for example, is delegated to agencies such as the Securities and Exchange Commission, the Environmental Protection Agency, the Occupational Health and Safety Administration, the Surface Mining Administration, and the Antitrust Division of the U.S. Department of Justice, as well as a host of other agencies and commissions. In short, there is no single centralized data source for white-collar crime.

Besides the lack of a centralized data source, there are other problems with counting white-collar crime. Obviously, what you count depends on whether you define white-collar crime using an offense-based definition or an offender-based definition. Offense-based definitions result in a much larger number of cases than do offender-based definitions. With an offense-based definition, all offenses based on fraud or deception are counted regardless of who commits them or how trivial they are. As we noted above, someone who lies on a welfare application could be a white-collar offender under Edelhertz's definition. However, if an offender-based definition, such as the one proposed by Sutherland, is used, then the number of offenses is much smaller because only offenses committed by people of high social status are counted. It is also important to recognize that organizations, as well as individuals, can be charged with and convicted of white-collar crimes, and it is not uncommon for both the corporation and individual executives to be charged in regard to a particular offense. When both individuals and organizations are linked in such a manner, determining the number of "offenders" becomes problematic.

There are other problems when it comes to counting white-collar crimes by corporations. Unlike ordinary street crimes, which are handled almost exclusively by the criminal justice system, white-collar crime cases, especially those involving corporations or other business entities, can be subject to different types of control, including the criminal, civil, and administrative justice systems. Should regulatory and civil violations be included, as Sutherland recommended? Or should the domain of corporate crime be limited to violations of the criminal law? In their famous study of corporate crime, Clinard and Yeager (2006, p. 113) reported that approximately 60 percent of the Fortune 500 companies in their sample had had at least one federal action brought against them between 1975 and 1976, which on its face would seem to represent a rather high prevalence rate of offending among corporations. But "federal actions" included civil, regulatory, and criminal actions, and only 30 of these actions involved criminal fines. Indeed, criminal fines accounted for only 3.4 percent of all the federal actions taken against the companies. For a variety of reasons, we agree with those who argue that civil and regulatory violations should be included as part of white-collar and corporate crime, but we note that this makes comparisons between white-collar and street crime difficult if not entirely inappropriate.

Concluding Thoughts on Defining White-Collar Crime

The definition of white-collar crime remains a matter of contention. Though we hope that our proposed reconciliation of the two definitional approaches will be seen as reasonable, we are not foolish enough to think that we have settled the matter once and for all. Criminologists should never forget Sutherland's fundamental insight that the upper social classes are not free from crime. In the course of their occupations, people of respectability and high social status commit serious crimes every day, even though they may never be caught or convicted. To ignore this reality is simply to misunderstand the problem of crime in the modern world. Yet, we believe it is possible to remain true to Sutherland's insight while at the same time adopting a more expansive perspective on the problem of crime in the modern world. In the chapters that follow, we often deal with offenders who do not fit the criteria imposed by Sutherland's offender-based definition. This is not because we think that Sutherland's definition is wrong. Rather, it is because, as we noted earlier, it is simply a fact that people of middle and lower social status can and do use the techniques identified by Sutherland himself—misrepresentation and duplicity—to commit illegal acts just as people of high social status do. Similarly, small businesses can engage in illegal activities just as national and multinational corporations do. What we wish to do is to explore how these variations in social status and organizational size influence the type, seriousness, and patterning of offenses.

2
WHO IS THE WHITE-COLLAR OFFENDER?

In his definition of white-collar crime and in his many writings on the subject, Sutherland described the white-collar offender as a person of respectability and high social status who commits an offense during the course of his or her occupation. If we follow Sutherland's approach, then the question posed in the title of this chapter is already partially answered. The white-collar offender is a respectable person of high social status. Of course, what Sutherland meant by "respectable" and "high social status" is not completely clear, but he did indicate that by white-collar he meant to refer to "business managers and executives" (Sutherland, 1983). If we thought about it for a bit, we could probably come up with definitions for the terms *respectable* and *high social status* that would make sense conceptually. To answer the question, then, of who is the white-collar offender, we would have to identify individuals who fit our definitions and who engage in occupationally related crime. We would want to know what it is that distinguishes respectable high-social-status people who are honest from those who are dishonest. Sutherland had a theory about the answer to this question. Other theories have been put forward by other scholars. We discuss these theories in the next chapter, but for now, we want to consider what happens if we don't use Sutherland's definition.

Suppose that instead of following Sutherland we defined white-collar crime using Edelhertz's approach—that is, as a property crime committed by nonphysical means and by concealment or deception. How would taking Edelhertz's approach affect the answer to the question, who is the white-collar offender? If we follow Edelhertz's approach, our problem boils down to this: What do we know about the people who commit property crimes by nonphysical means and through the use of concealment or deceit?

Thanks to a series of studies that began at Yale University in the late 1970s and continued into the 1990s, we actually know quite a lot about these people. In the mid-1970s, a group of researchers led by Stanton Wheeler of Yale University Law School received funding from the National Institute of Justice (NIJ) to conduct a study on the sentencing of white-collar offenders in the federal judicial system. Although officials at the NIJ were primarily interested in sentencing, they had the foresight to permit the researchers to investigate a broad set of issues and questions that extended far beyond the question of who goes to prison and who does not (Weisburd et al., 1991, p. xiii). From these investigations, an interesting picture of the people who commit crimes of deception has emerged. As we will show, some of these people clearly are white-collar offenders in Sutherland's sense of the term, but many of them are not.

The Yale Studies on White-Collar Crime

The Yale studies on white-collar crime encompassed several different types of projects. In one study, federal judges were interviewed to learn how they thought about the sentencing of white-collar offenders (Wheeler et al., 1988a). In another part of the project, Kenneth Mann (1985) interviewed white-collar defense attorneys about how they went about their work. Another member of the team, Susan Shapiro, delved into securities offenses. She provided a detailed report on how these offenses were committed and how they were discovered, investigated, and sanctioned by the Securities and Exchange Commission (SEC) (Shapiro, 1984, 1985). We will have occasion to look into all of these studies later, but now we want to turn our attention to the studies that focused directly on offenders (Weisburd et al., 1991; Weisburd and Waring, 2001; Wheeler et al., 1988a).

The Yale researchers began by identifying eight offenses in the federal criminal code that most scholars and lay people would agree were white-collar type crimes. For our purposes, what is important is that these are offenses that are committed by concealment and deception rather than brute physical force. The eight offenses were:

- securities violations,
- antitrust violations,
- bribery,
- bank embezzlement,
- mail and wire fraud,
- tax fraud,
- false claims and statements, and
- credit and lending institution fraud.

All of these offenses fit Edelhertz's definition, and we believe that in many cases Sutherland would have no objections, either.

Obviously, the list does not include every white-collar crime in the federal code. Many others could have been used, and this is an issue to which we return later. Nevertheless, we think the researchers are correct in claiming that this set of offenses represents "a broad and heterogeneous view of white-collar criminal activity that is prosecuted in the federal courts" (Weisburd et al., 1991, p. 11).

Having identified a good collection of white-collar crimes, the researchers next turned to finding the white-collar criminals. They found them by reviewing records on convictions in seven federal district courts. The districts and their major cities were Central California (Los Angeles), Northern Georgia (Atlanta), Northern Illinois (Chicago), Maryland (Baltimore), Southern New York (Manhattan and the Bronx), Northern Texas (Dallas), and Western Washington (Seattle).

The researchers identified all of the people who had been convicted of any one of the eight offenses named above. From here on, we will call these the *criterion* offenses. From this pool of individuals, the researchers then selected a sample of offenders from each of the criterion offense categories in each of the seven districts. The total sample included 1,094 offenders.

White-collar crime scholars have always taken it for granted that white-collar offenders are not like ordinary street criminals. We assume that white-collar offenders are better educated and more likely to be employed than common street criminals. We assume that white-collar offenders do not grow up in poverty-stricken families and that when they were children their parents did not beat or abuse them, as is unfortunately the case with many common criminals. Yet, very few studies have actually sought to compare white-collar and common criminals on their demographic and social characteristics. The Yale researchers hoped to do just that. So, in addition to their sample of white-collar offenders, they also selected a sample of 210 individuals who had been convicted of nonviolent financially oriented common crimes. This comparison sample of common criminals included individuals who had been convicted of either postal theft or postal forgery.[1] These federal offenses are similar to the better-known common property crimes of burglary and larceny. Burglary and larceny, however, are crimes that are governed by state rather than federal law, so they could not be used by the researchers for making comparisons.

With their sample in hand, the researchers set out to learn as much as they could about the offenders and their offenses. Most of the information they used came from a document called a presentence investigation report (PSI). A PSI is prepared by a federal probation officer whenever an offender is convicted in federal court. It does not matter whether the conviction is the result of a verdict at trial or a plea by the defendant. Federal judges use PSIs when they make decisions about sentencing. As the majority of cases in the federal system are settled by pleas, judges often do not have an opportunity to learn much about the offender or the offense prior to sentencing. The PSI is designed to help judges overcome this information shortage. It helps the judge learn in detail about the offense and the offender.

Regarding the offense, the PSI informs the judge about the official charges to which the defendant has pled guilty (e.g., one count of violating 18 USC 287, which is a federal statute governing false claims or statements). But in addition to the official charge, the PSI contains a "defendant's version of the offense" and an "official version of the offense." The defendant's version is just that: It is the defendant's version or explanation of what happened. Some defendants write these statements themselves, but many rely upon their lawyers to help them craft a statement that won't be offensive to the judge and that may help them get a more lenient sentence (Rothman and Gandossy, 1982). As a sidelight, we note that compared with the typical street offender, the people who commit white-collar types of crimes often have an advantage at this stage of the process. Because of their wealth and status, they or their companies can afford to hire very skilled attorneys to represent them (Mann, 1985). Thus, status influences not only opportunities to commit white-collar crimes; it may influence official reactions to white-collar lawbreaking. But to return to our discussion of the defendant's version of the offense, defendants not surprisingly often go to great lengths to present themselves in favorable terms. The connection between what really happened and the defendant's *version* of what happened is always questionable.

For our purposes, the official version of the offense is more important and useful. It is supposed to present an unbiased and objective description of the acts that led to the filing of criminal charges against the defendant. The official version is prepared by the probation officer, often with help from the prosecuting attorney or the law enforcement agents who investigated the case. It usually contains a detailed description of the offense, including information on what was done, who was involved, who was harmed, how much money was lost, how complex or simple the offense was, and how long it lasted. This descriptive information about the offense tells us much more about what really happened than does the formal charge. The Yale researchers used the official version of each offense to determine its degree of seriousness. They were then able to compare the characteristics of the offenders to the seriousness of the offenses they committed.

In addition to information on the offense, the PSI contains information about the defendant. Much of this information focuses on the defendant's prior criminal record, including previous arrests, convictions, and sentences. Obviously, these matters are important for judges. They want to know whether they are sentencing a first-time offender or a habitual criminal. However, the PSI also can tell us about the defendant's social, economic, and demographic background. Typically, probation officers will describe the defendant's age, race, gender, family of origin, marital history, educational attainment, employment history, medical and psychological condition, financial status, place of residence, religious preference, alcohol and drug use, and standing in the community. Not all of these topics are covered in detail in every PSI, but most of them receive at least some attention from probation officers. The idea is to give judges an idea of who they are dealing with so that they can render an appropriate sentence.

For our purposes, the PSI is a good source of data. We can use it to find out who commits white-collar types of crimes. We can compare these people to those who commit common street crimes. In short, we can investigate many important questions about white-collar offenders and white-collar crimes. Who commits the most serious crimes—people of high social status or those of low social status? Are the people who commit white-collar crimes really different from those who commit run-of-the-mill common crimes? If so, how are they different?

Now that we have an idea of what the Yale researchers did and how they did it, we are almost ready to turn to their results. However, first we need to make sure that we are aware of what we may be missing.

The federal court system is certainly a good place to find people who have been convicted of white-collar types of crimes, and the PSI is a unique source of data about convicted offenders. However, like all research methodologies, the one used by the Yale researchers is not perfect, as they were well aware (Weisburd et al., 1991, pp. 17–21). The researchers acknowledged four shortcomings in their research design.

First, they studied only eight federal offenses. There are many other federal offenses that could conceivably be called white-collar crimes. It is possible that if the researchers had included a different mix of offenses, their results may have changed. For example, neither environmental violations nor violations of workplace safety laws were included in the study, yet these are exceedingly important forms of white-collar crime.

Second, at the time of the study there were 91 federal district courts. The researchers studied only seven. These seven were selected because they were large and the researchers thought that they would be likely to have a lot of white-collar crime cases. As with the mix of offenses, it is possible that had a different mix of districts been selected, the results might have changed as well. Indeed, one study suggests that sentencing practices may vary by the size and case mix of the district. Judges in smaller districts with fewer white-collar cases apparently handle them differently than their counterparts in the big urban districts (Benson and Walker, 1988).

Taken together, the first two shortcomings raise the possibility that if we were looking at a different sample, we might see a different picture.

For example, it is certainly possible that the people who commit bank embezzlement in New York City are not like those who embezzle in, say, Amarillo, Texas. Whether a sample is representative of all the possible cases from which it is drawn is a common problem in social science research. The best way to address this shortcoming is to look at more than one sample. If the results from different samples and studies converge, then we can have much more confidence in them than we could from a single observation point. Happily for us, at the same time that the Yale researchers were conducting their study, several other investigations of white-collar offenders in the federal system were also under way (Benson and Moore, 1992; Benson and Walker, 1988; Hagan, Nagel [Bernstein], and Albonetti, 1980). We won't describe these studies in detail now, but we will use them later as a check on the results of the Yale project.

The last two shortcomings are potentially more serious. They both involve the types of people and offenses that we end up looking at if our sampling strategy is restricted to convicted offenders. By including only cases that resulted in a defendant's being convicted in federal criminal court, the study missed all of the white-collar cases that were handled in other ways, such as, for example, in civil courts or in regulatory proceedings. In other words, the study missed all of the individuals whose cases could have been handled in criminal court but for some reason were not. This is not an insignificant issue. The picture that we get of the white-collar offender depends entirely on who gets drawn into the criminal justice system. If the process by which people are drawn into the system is biased in some way, then our image of the white-collar offender will be biased in just that way as well.

For example, imagine that at the time of the Yale study two bank employees were caught embezzling by their employers. One of the individuals was an older white man who was a bank vice president, while the other was a young black woman who was a teller. Further suppose that for some reason, the white man's employer decides to fire the man rather than press charges. This apparent generosity on the part of the employer is not as unlikely or outlandish as it may seem at first. The bank owners may wish to avoid the embarrassment of having the bank officer's name in the paper, which would not reflect well on the bank. Who wants to put money in a bank that apparently has crooks in leadership positions? On the other hand, the black woman's employer calls the local U.S. District Attorney, who files charges against the woman in federal court. The woman is eventually convicted of bank embezzlement. You can see the problem. Our two bank embezzlers differ dramatically in their sociodemographic characteristics, but only one can possibly turn up in the Yale study. If something like this happens often, then using conviction records as our data source will give us a distorted view of the characteristics of white-collar offenders.

How often do things like this happen? We don't really know. While there are many studies that inform us about how people are treated once they get into the criminal justice system, far fewer studies have investigated how people get there in the first place. In an ideal world, people would be drawn into the system based on the evidence against them and the seriousness of the offenses that the police think they have committed. But we don't live in an ideal world, especially when it comes to white-collar crime. The few studies that are available on how white-collar offenders get into the criminal justice system suggest that other factors besides evidence and seriousness often play a role. For example, Susan Shapiro (1984) studied how the SEC made enforcement decisions. She found that the accused person's status and organizational position influenced whether the SEC referred suspected securities violators to federal prosecutors for trial or handled them internally through administrative proceedings (Shapiro, 1984). Oddly enough, for reasons that are too complex to go into now, the people who were accused of less serious securities violations were more likely to end up in court than those who were accused of more serious offenses. Of course, Shapiro's is only one study, and the SEC is only one regulatory agency. Nevertheless, her findings should serve as a cautionary warning that we have to be aware of the limitations of court records as data sources.

The final shortcoming of using court convictions to identify white-collar offenders also relates to the issue of who gets into the criminal justice system in the first place. By using convictions as our criterion, we miss all of those offenders who avoided conviction. Obviously, this includes those who are acquitted at trial even though they are really guilty. This is not a big problem, because acquittals of any sort—correct or incorrect—actually do not happen very often. So, we can be pretty safe in ignoring this source of bias. More significantly, however, we will also miss all those offenses that are never detected in the first place. In other words, conviction records give us only offenders who are unlucky or careless enough to get caught. For example, to return again to our two bank embezzlers, suppose that because of his position the bank vice president is able to cover up his offense so that it is never discovered. If bank vice presidents often get away with embezzlement, while bank tellers rarely do, then conviction records will present a biased picture of who commits bank embezzlement. As we will see at many points in this book, detection is a big problem in the study and control of white-collar crime. It is always debatable whether the offenses and offenders whom we detect are the same as the offenses and offenders who escape detection.

On the other hand, we also don't really know whether the offenses that go undetected or that do not result in court convictions really are all that much different from those that do come to light. Some white-collar crime scholars argue that offenders of high social status and economic power use these advantages to avoid prosecution (Coleman, 1989; Reiman, 1979). Opposing this view are studies that suggest that prosecutors actually like to go after the "big cases," so to speak, and are eager to take on cases with high-profile defendants (Benson, Cullen, and Maakestad, 1990; Katz, 1980). For example, when he was attorney general of New York, Elliot Spitzer made a career out of taking on very high profile white-collar cases (Cullen et al., 2006, pp. 329–330). In one of the few studies that looked very closely at which defendants end up in court and which do not, Kenneth Mann found that the underlying criminal conduct of the defendants who went to trial versus those who went free was usually quite similar. What mattered were small variations in the evidence that investigators and prosecutors had to work with (Mann, 1985). As the Yale researchers note, there is no way of knowing for sure whether defendants who are detected are the same as those who avoid detection. Nevertheless, we agree with them that we can learn a lot about white-collar crime by closely examining convicted defendants and their offenses.

Taken together, the four shortcomings of the Yale study add up to this: We can't be entirely positive that the offenders and offenses in this study represent all white-collar crimes. The reasons for our uncertainty are that: (1) a different mix of offenses might produce different results, (2) a different mix of districts might produce different results, (3) some offenders who could have been included in the study were not because their cases were handled in other ways, and (4) offenders who are convicted may not be the same as those who avoid detection in the first place. These are not trivial shortcomings, but we shouldn't overstate their importance. We can address the first two by looking at other studies of federal offenders that use different offenses and different districts. Regarding the last two short-comings, probably the best we can do is to acknowledge that what we see may not be all there is. Nevertheless, the Yale studies on white-collar crime at least can show us what convicted white-collar offenders look like. We will have to leave it to others to find out whether those who somehow avoid conviction really are all that much different.

The Social and Demographic Characteristics of White-Collar Offenders

Andrew Fastow, Kenneth Lay, Bernard Ebbers, Dennis Kozlowski, Martha Stewart, Bernard Madoff—if you've been following the news the past few years, these names and most likely the faces are familiar to you. These are high-profile people who have been accused and in some cases convicted of white-collar crimes. Andy Fastow was the former chief financial officer for Enron. He pled guilty to accounting fraud in 2004 and was sentenced to federal prison. His former boss, Ken Lay, was convicted of fraud in 2006 but died before he was sentenced. Bernard Ebbers was the former head of World Com; he has been convicted of accounting fraud. Dennis Kozlowski was the former head of Tyco International, a large conglomerate; he was convicted of stealing billions of dollars from his company. Martha Stewart was convicted of lying to federal authorities concerning a stock transaction and was sentenced to serve 5 months in a federal correctional institution. And, finally, there is Bernie Madoff, mastermind of the largest Ponzi scheme in history, who was convicted of stealing literally billions of dollars from his clients (Henriques, 2011). These individuals represent the archetype of the white-collar offender. They are rich, white, and well-educated adults. At the time that they committed their offenses, they held powerful leadership positions in major corporations. Although they were not all born wealthy, none of them came from what could be called a disadvantaged or troubled family background.

It would be hard to find a group that more closely fits the common conception or stereotype of the white-collar offender than these people. You would never mistake them for common criminals. Is this what most of the people who are convicted for white-collar crimes are like? The answer is partly yes and partly no.

The "yes" part of the answer relates to the age, race, and sex characteristics of white-collar offenders and to their employment status and level of education. The data in Table 2.1 are taken from the Yale study (Wheeler et al., 1988a). It compares the white-collar criminals in the sample to the common criminals and to the general population of the seven districts in which the study was conducted.

Let's look first at the gender, race, and age characteristics of the people who were convicted of white-collar crimes and compare them with the general public. The most striking and obvious fact is that the white-collar offenders are overwhelmingly male. About half of the general public is male, but nearly nine of ten white-collar offenders are male. The white-collar offenders also are more likely to be white (81.7%) than are members of the general public (76.8%), but the over representation of whites in the sample is only little more than we would expect by chance. Finally, the

Table 2.1 Demographic, education, and employment characteristics of white-collar offenders, common criminals, and the general public (adapted from Tables III and IV in Wheeler et al., 1988a)

	Common Criminals	White-Collar Criminals	General Public
Sex (male)	68.6%	85.5%	48.6%
Race (white)	34.3%	81.7%	76.8%
Age (mean)	30	40	30
Education			
High school graduates	45.5%	79.3%	69.0%
College graduates	3.9%	27.1%	19.0%
Employment			
Unemployed	56.7%	5.7%	5.9%
Steadily employed	12.7%	58.4%	Not available

average age of the persons convicted of white-collar crimes is 40, a good bit older than the average age of 30 of the general public in these districts. Compared with the general public, then, the people who are convicted of white-collar crimes are older, a bit more likely to be white, and much more likely to be male.

How do the white-collar criminals compare with the people who commit nonviolent common crimes? Here there are substantial differences, especially in regard to race. While 81.7 percent of white-collar criminals are white, only about one of three common criminals is white (34.3%). To look at the data from the nonwhite perspective, we can say that about two-thirds of the common criminals are nonwhite (65.7%). Social scientists would put it this way: Nonwhites are grossly overrepresented among common criminals and underrepresented among white-collar criminals. In contrast, whites are grossly underrepresented among common criminals and overrepresented among white-collar criminals.

There are other differences as well. The persons convicted of nonviolent common crimes are on average 10 years younger than the white-collar criminals. It is also clear that common crime is more of an equal opportunity employer than is white-collar crime. More than 30 percent of the common criminals are female compared with less than 15 percent of the white-collar criminals. Overall, though, women are much less likely than men to commit any sort of crime.

Now we turn to the "no" part of the answer to our question regarding how well the people described earlier represent white-collar offenders in general. Advanced education and steady employment are two of the standard markers of success in our society, and they are two characteristics that are commonly associated with white-collar criminals. The data presented in Table 2.1 on education and employment need to be examined closely. In some ways, it suggests that we may need to rethink the status part of the image of the white-collar offender. As should come as no surprise, white-collar offenders are indeed much more likely to be well educated than are common criminals. Almost 80 percent of white-collar offenders have at least graduated from high school versus less than half of common criminals. More than one-fourth of white-collar criminals are college graduates (27.1%) compared with less than 5 percent of the common criminals (3.9%).

In one sense, these results are exactly what we would expect. The white-collar offenders are more highly educated than the common criminals. However, in another sense, these results do not fit the standard view of the white-collar offender. Most of the white-collar offenders are *not* highly educated. More than 70 percent of them are *not* college graduates. It is true that white-collar offenders are more likely to have graduated from college than members of the general public (27.3% versus 19.0%, respectively), but the difference is not huge. In regard to education, then, the white-collar offenders are better off than the public in general, but it would not be correct to say that they are always highly educated.

With respect to the standard view of white-collar offenders, the finding that most of them do not have college degrees is important. Advanced education is an indicator of high social status. Offenders who have not completed a college education lack one of the badges of high social status that Sutherland and those who adopt his approach often identify with white-collar criminals.

The results on employment status also call into question the standard image of the white-collar offender. As was the case with education, white-collar and common criminals differ dramatically in employment status. More than half (56.7%) of the common criminals were unemployed at the time that they committed the criterion offense that brought them into federal court. In contrast, only 5.7 percent of the white-collar offenders were unemployed at the time of their offenses. This percentage corresponds almost exactly with the unemployment rate for the general public (5.9%). So far, so good. Again, this is what we would expect. It is not surprising to find that most common criminals are unemployed. We expect them to live in disadvantaged circumstances. But the picture gets more puzzling when we look at the rate of "steady employment" for the white-collar offenders. In the Yale study, steady employment meant that the individual had had uninterrupted employment during the 5-year period preceding the conviction. Fewer than 60 percent of the white-collar offenders had been steadily employed (58.7%) prior to their convictions. Granted, that looks pretty good compared with the common criminals, who had a steady employment rate of only 12.7 percent. But it also means that *more than* 40 percent of the white-collar offenders were *not* steadily employed prior to their convictions.

It is easy to get lost in numbers and tables and, as the old saying goes, to miss the forest for the trees. So, let's step back and try to summarize the main conclusions that we can draw from Table 2.1. First, as expected, the typical white-collar offender is a middle-aged white male. Second, as expected, on average white-collar offenders are better educated and more likely to be employed than common criminals. Third, however, and *not* as expected, most white-collar offenders have only a high school diploma, and a substantial proportion of them could not count on steady employment prior to their offenses. Thus, the people convicted of white-collar crimes in federal courts are indeed different from common criminals, but on average they do not appear to be social elites. They do not appear to have high social status.

The data presented in Table 2.1 apply to all of the white-collar offenders in the Yale study considered as a group. But recall that the Yale researchers selected individuals who had been convicted of eight different types of white-collar crimes, ranging from antitrust violators to bank embezzlers. It takes only a moment's thought to realize that the people who commit antitrust violations may not be the same as the people who commit bank embezzlement. Although we know that on average white-collar offenders are not like common criminals in terms of age, race, employment, and education, this doesn't mean that therefore all white-collar offenders are alike. There may be substantial variations in the social characteristics of white-collar offenders, and these variations may be linked to the types of offenses they commit.

In Table 2.2, we again explore the social and demographic characteristics of white-collar offenders. However, this time, instead of looking at the group as a whole, we categorize offenders by the type of offense they committed. This cross-categorization results in a complex table that may look daunting. Indeed, it does contain lots of information, but if we proceed systematically, we should be able to make sense of it. And, as we will see, our efforts will be rewarded as some intriguing findings about white-collar offenders emerge.

Let's begin by considering the standard demographic characteristics, beginning with race, which is in the first row of the table. It would not be an exaggeration to say that in the decade of the 1970s your chances of finding a nonwhite antitrust or securities violator were slim to none. More

Table 2.2 Social and demographic characteristics of white-collar offenders by statutory offense (adapted from Table VII in Wheeler et al., 1988a)

	Antitrust	Securities Fraud	Tax	Bribery	Credit Fraud	False Claims	Mail Fraud	Bank Embezzlement
Race (white)	99.1%	99.6%	87.1%	83.3%	71.5%	61.8%	76.8%	74.1%
Sex (male)	99.1%	97.8%	94.1%	95.2%	84.8%	84.7%	82.1%	54.8%
Age	53	44	47	45	38	39	38	31
Financial Standing								
Median assets	$650,000	$59,000	$49,500	$45,000	$7,000	$4,000	$2,000	$2,000
Median liabilities	$81,000	$55,000	$23,500	$19,000	$7,000	$5,000	$3,500	$3,000
Education								
College graduates	40.0%	43.0%	27.0%	27.0%	18.0%	29.0%	23.0%	13.0%
Homeowners	87.8%	62.1%	57.7%	57.0%	44.8%	42.1%	33.5%	31.0%

than 99 percent of both antitrust and securities violators were white. There were 117 antitrust violators in the Yale sample, and 116 of them were white; astonishingly, of the 225 securities violators, 224 were white. On the other end of the spectrum, only 61.8 percent of the false-claims violators were white, which obviously means that almost 40 percent of them were nonwhite, and only 71.5 percent of those who committed lending and credit fraud were white. The percent white in the other four offense categories falls between these two end points. Thus, at the time of the Yale study, antitrust and securities violations were committed virtually exclusively by whites. It is a striking finding that there are such large variations in the racial composition of the different offense types.

The story is similar when we look at gender. As with race, we find notable variations across the offense types by gender. With only very few exceptions, antitrust, securities, tax, and bribery violations are committed by males. In contrast, almost half of the bank embezzlers are females. Again, we observe large variations across offenses on a major demographic characteristic.

Finally, there is age. Two numbers stand out. The average age of the antitrust violators is 53, while the average age of the bank embezzlers is 31. Relatively young people commit bank embezzlement, while people who are almost eligible for early retirement engage in antitrust conspiracies. We apologize for the repetition, but as you have no doubt already noted, there are large variations across offenses in age.

Systematic variations, such as the ones we found here for race, gender, and age, are important. They are clues to how the world works. By definition, systematic variations do not arise randomly. They are the result of some sort of systematic causal process. If we can identify and understand these variations, then we are well on our way to understanding the underlying causal processes that produced them. In our case, this means understanding how and why particular types of people tend to commit particular types of white-collar crimes. By particular types of people, we mean only people who have certain demographic characteristics. As you should know, we have an idea or hypothesis about what is going on with white-collar crime, which we introduced in Chapter 1 and will be developing throughout this book. In brief, our hypothesis is that access to white-collar crime opportunities varies by race, gender, and age as well as other variables, and it is access to opportunities that explains patterns in the social and demographic characteristics of white-collar offenders. In Table 2.2, we see the first preliminary evidence in favor of that hypothesis.

It may be helpful if we explain our reasoning in more detail and with an example. In order to commit certain types of white-collar offenses, it is virtually required that you have access to particular occupational positions. In other words, you have to work in a particular type of industry or have a particular type of job to get the opportunity to commit the offense. For example, it is much easier to commit a securities offense if you work in the securities industry as, say, a stockbroker or a stock analyst. Since most of the people who work in the securities industry are white males, we should not be surprised to find that most securities offenders are white males. Neither should we be surprised that most antitrust violators are white males. To commit an antitrust violation, you have to have an executive-level position in a fairly large company. As we document later in Chapter 8, these positions are held disproportionately by white males.

There are other indications in Table 2.2 that social characteristics influence access to white-collar crime opportunities. The bottom half of the table shows information on the financial standing, education, and homeownership of the white-collar offenders in each of the offense categories. Financial status is assessed by the median assets and liabilities of the offenders in each offense category. Comparing the antitrust offenders with the bank embezzlers is instructive. The median assets for the antitrust offenders are a whopping $650,000. For the bank embezzlers, the median assets are a puny $2,000, which means that by definition half of them have less than $2,000 in assets. Since their median liabilities are $3,000, many of them are actually in the hole. The financial standing of the antitrust offenders looks rock solid, while the bank embezzlers look like they are just scraping by from paycheck to paycheck.

We see similar extreme differences between antitrust offenders and bank embezzlers in education and homeownership. Four of ten of the antitrust offenders (40%) were college graduates versus about one of ten of the bank embezzlers (13%). Close to 90 percent of the antitrust offenders (87.8%) owned their homes, whereas fewer than a third of the bank embezzlers did. The rest of the offense categories are arrayed between these two extremes. The securities offenders did not appear to be quite as well off as the antitrust offenders in financial standing or homeowner-ship. Nevertheless, they were definitely better off in these regards than the people convicted of mail fraud, who more closely resembled the bank embezzlers. Less than one-fourth of the mail fraud offenders had a col-lege degree; only one-third owned their own homes; and their average liabilities exceeded their average assets. Indeed, the only notable differ-ence between those who committed bank embezzlement and those who committed mail fraud was gender. Almost half of the bank embezzlers were women, while eight of ten mail fraud offenders were male. Like others, we found race-and gender-linked differences in offending (Daly, 1989), which we interpret to mean that there are race-and gender-linked differences in opportunities to offend.

A Validity Check

Up to this point, what we have learned about white-collar offenders has come entirely from the Yale study. As we noted at the outset, the Yale study is only one study, and it is always possible that the sample of offend-ers used in the Yale study is in some way unusual or not representative of white-collar offenders generally. Luckily for us, at approximately the same time as the Yale study was going on, another federally funded investiga-tion of white-collar sentencing was also underway. This study, conducted by Brian Forst and William Rhodes, used a similar methodology and sampled 2,643 individuals convicted of six ostensibly white-collar crimes from eight federal district courts.[2] The white-collar offenses were bank embezzlement, bribery, false claims, mail fraud, income tax violations, and postal embezzlement. The researchers also included individuals convicted of non–white-collar or common crimes in their sample. The non–white-collar crimes included bank robbery, narcotics trafficking, homicide, and postal forgery. Then, as in the Yale study, data on the offenders and their offenses were abstracted from PSIs.

For our purposes, the important thing about the Forst and Rhodes study is that the offenders come from different federal districts, and the set of offenses is similar although not exactly the same. For example, postal embezzlement, which is in the Forst and Rhodes sample, was not included in the Yale study, and the Forst and Rhodes study lacks anti-trust and securities offenders. The four common crimes in the Forst and

Rhodes study generally are more serious than the two nonviolent common property crimes (postal theft and postal forgery) in the Yale study. With the Forst and Rhodes data, we can check on the importance of at least one of the potential shortcomings of the Yale study. We can see how the social and demographic characteristics of white-collar offenders convicted of similar offenses but in different federal districts compare. Are they similar or different?

The answer to this question is that they are remarkably similar. Table 2.3 presents information on the social and demographic characteristics of the offenders in each offense category for both the Yale and the Forst and Rhodes studies. However, to keep things simple, we will discuss only the results for tax violators and bank embezzlers. The results for the other offenses parallel these closely. With respect to age, race, and gender, the tax violators in the Yale study are virtually identical to those in the Forst and Rhodes study, and the same is true of the bank embezzlers from both studies. The average age of a tax violator in the Yale study was 47 compared with 48 in the Forst and Rhodes study, while the average age of a bank embezzler in the Yale study was 31 versus 30 in the Forst and Rhodes study. The differences in race and gender are equally small. What is most striking is the similarity in the overall pattern of characteristics. In both studies, tax violators overwhelmingly were white males in their late 40s. This result probably stems from the predominance of males as heads of households and, by default, as chief tax preparers in the 1970s. In both studies, we also find that bank embezzlement involved individuals who were younger and more likely to be female or nonwhite than were tax violators. These similarities in patterns extend to other characteristics such as graduating from college and owning a home. In both studies, we find that tax violators were more likely than bank embezzlers to have attained these two markers of social success. Although we won't discuss them here, if you look at the other offense categories in Table 2.3, you will see that the offenders in one study match up well with their counterparts in the other study.

The similarity between the offenders in the two studies means that we can be reasonably sure that they generally represent the type of people who are convicted of these particular white-collar type of crimes in federal courts. In other words, we can have some confidence in the validity

Table 2.3 Descriptive statistics on two samples of white-collar offenders

Postal Sample	Tax		Bribery		False Claims		Mail Fraud		Bank Embezzlement		Embezzlement[a]
	Y	F&R	Y	F&R	Y	F&R	Y	F&R	Y	F&R	F&R
Demographic characteristics	47	48	45	47	39	38	38	37	31	30	34
mean age											
% White	87.1	89.3	83.3	77.5	61.8	56.9	76.8	78.7	74.1	75.5	65.0
% Male	94.3	91.8	95.2	89.4	84.7	72.8	82.1	85.5	55.2	52.6	89.5
Personal History											
% College degree	27.4	23.5	28.9	24.3	29.2	18.4	21.7	13.1	12.9	9.3	1.4
% Home owners	57.7	70.6	57.0	63.2	42.1	40.0	33.5	31.3	28.4	41.8	49.3

Notes
Y = Yale study sample data from table 3.1 in Weisburd et al. (1991); F&R = Forst and Rhodes sample differences greater than 10 percentage points are bolded.
[a]Postal embezzlement was not included in the Yale study sample.

and generalizability of what we have learned thus far about white-collar offenders, at least those who were convicted in federal district courts in the 1970s.

What can we conclude from all these numbers and comparisons? Two points stand out. First, as a group, white-collar offenders are not like common criminals. The two groups come from different sectors of the population. Second, not all white-collar offenders are alike. They are not all highly educated or wealthy. Indeed, there is substantial variation in the social and demographic characteristics of the people who commit white-collar types of crimes. Some indeed do fit the stereotype of the white-collar offender as an educated, wealthy, employed, white male, but others do not share these attributes. Thus, white-collar criminals turn out to be more socially and demographically variegated than the standard view would have us believe.

Contemporary White-Collar Offenders

The Yale study and the Forst and Rhodes study represented important contributions to our understanding of the social and demographic characteristics of white-collar offenders. Both studies, however, relied on data from offenders who had been convicted for crimes committed in the mid-1970s. In the almost four decades that have intervened since then, the United States has changed in many ways. Consider, for example, the role of women in the workplace. In 1970, women's labor force participation rate was just over 40 percent. By the year 2000, after three decades of steady increases, the female labor force participation rate had reached 60 percent, a level it has held relatively steadily since then (U.S. Bureau of Labor Statistics, 2013a). There were other changes involving working women as well. In 1970, about 11 percent of the women aged 25 to 64 in the labor force held college degrees, but in 2011 the proportion of women in the labor force holding college degrees had more than tripled to 37 percent. Indeed, among high school graduates in 2011, women were more likely to be in college than men (U.S. Bureau of Labor Statistics, 2013b). Obviously, it was not only women who experienced changes in work and education in the late 20th and early 21st centuries. These changes cut across both sexes and all races and ethnicities. The percentage of young men who went on to college increased between the mid-1970s and 2011, as did the percentages of African Americans and Hispanics (Ingels et al., 2012). Thus, compared with the decade of the 1970s, when the Yale study was conducted, more women are working now and are more likely to have college degrees, equipping them for different kinds of work than they did in the past. Likewise, nonwhites are also more highly educated now and presumably have access to more white-collar type of jobs now than they did in the past. In short, the educational and occupational makeup of the U.S. population has evolved since the 1970s.

Since access to white-collar types of jobs is a prerequisite for many white-collar crimes, it is possible that changes in the occupational and educational characteristics of the U.S. population over the past four decades have been reflected in the social and demographic characteristics of those who commit white-collar crimes. In other words, it is an open question whether older white males dominate white-collar crime as much now as they did in the past. Although no studies like the Yale study have been conducted since it was finished, data are available from the U.S. Sentencing Commission (USSC) that permit us to make a few comparisons between the people convicted for white-collar crimes today versus those in the 1970s. Although it is always tricky to make comparisons over time involving broad offense categories because there may be other important factors that also explain changes, the Sentencing Commission collects data on the age, race, sex, and educational characteristics of individuals convicted of several white-collar offenses that are similar to those included in the Yale study, including antitrust, tax, bribery, and embezzlement (see Table 2.4). For comparison purposes, Table 2.4 also includes three other white-collar offense categories—fraud, environmental offenses, and food and drug offenses.

As Table 2.4 shows, there have been changes in the race and ethnicity characteristics of white-collar offenders, and in some cases age and gender characteristics are also different. For example, whites no longer dominate antitrust to the same degree. In the 1970s, 99.1 percent of antitrust offenders were white, but only 75 percent of contemporary offenders are white. The race composition of tax and bribery offenders has also changed dramatically. Whereas whites constituted over 80 percent of tax and bribery offenders earlier, they now make up less than half (48.5%) of tax offenders and just two-thirds (67%) of bribery offenders. However, there has

Table 2.4 Descriptive statistics on contemporary white-collar offenders

	Antitrust	Tax	Bribery	Embezzlement	Fraud	Environmental	Food and Drug
Demographic Characteristic							
Mean age	52	50	46	43	40	46	47
% White	75	67	48.5	60.7	46.9	75.7	68.6
% Male	99.1	78.8	83	44.8	60.4	94.3	79.6
% College Graduates	52.2	35.1	30.9	14.5	20.3	15.7	41.8
Convictions 2006–2012	92	4,320	1,453	2,978	48,299	991	433

Note: Although the Yale study includes "fraud" as one of its categories of white-collar crime, we believe it is not appropriate to compare the Yale fraud data to the Sentencing Commission's fraud data. The Sentencing Commission's definition of "fraud" includes a much broader array of statutes and behaviors than was used in the Yale study.

Source: U.S. Sentencing Commission, Interactive Sourcebook of Statistics, 2006–2012.

been little change in regard to the mean age or gender for white-collar offenders. In the Yale study the average age was 53 compared with 52 for contemporary antitrust offenders. The gender composition of antitrust has also remained virtually unchanged, with 99.1 percent of offenders being male. For tax and bribery offenders, the mean age for contemporary offenders is nearly the same as it was in the 1970s, with the average offender being somewhere between 47 and 50. Finally, for embezzlement, the proportion of whites (74% in the Yale study) and males (55% in the Yale study) has fallen noticeably to 61 and 45 percent, respectively, in the Sentencing Commission's data. For all four offenses, the proportion of offenders who are college graduates has risen, though not markedly. That there has been an increase in the proportion of white-collar offenders with college degrees is not unexpected in light of the growth in college attendance rates throughout the American population.

Taken together, the results for Tables 2.3 and 2.4 suggest that over the past 40 years white-collar crime has become more of an equal opportunity employer and is no longer the exclusive preserve of middle-aged white males as it was in the past. Both women and nonwhites are more involved now, reflecting perhaps some of the social advances that these groups have made in American society toward the end of the 20th century. However, we do not want to suggest that race and sex no longer matter in regard to white-collar crime. White males still predominate in most offense categories, and it is telling that for antitrust violations, the highest level offense in our analysis, the demographic makeup of the offending population has changed very little.

White-Collar Criminal Careers

The phrase *white-collar criminal career* seems like an oxymoron. Part of the standard view of white-collar offenders is that they are mainstream, law-abiding individuals. They are assumed to be one-shot offenders, not people who engage in crime on a regular basis. Unlike the run-of-the-mill common street criminal who usually has had repeated contacts with the criminal justice system, white-collar offenders are thought not to have prior criminal records. Think of the white-collar offenders mentioned earlier in this chapter and others who have recently been in the news. Martha Stewart and Bernard Madoff, for example, certainly do not have long arrest records. When they appeared before their sentencing judges, they could correctly claim to be first-time offenders. But, as we have already learned, Martha Stewart and Bernard Madoff are not typical of the people who are convicted of white-collar types of crimes. Most of the people convicted of white-collar offenses are not like them. Most white-collar offenders who appear in the federal justice system are not as wealthy, highly educated, or socially connected as they are. So, perhaps most white-collar offenders are not like these elite individuals in terms of their involvement in criminal activity either.

Until recently, we really did not know much about the criminal careers of white-collar offenders. However, thanks to the Yale study and the Forst and Rhodes project, the situation has improved. In both of these studies, the researchers abstracted detailed information from the PSIs on the criminal records of the offenders. In addition, David Weisburd, Elin Waring, and Ellen Chayet collected more data on the offenders in the Yale study 10 years after their convictions for the original criterion offenses (Weisburd and Waring, 2001). Analysis of these data has revealed some surprising discoveries about the criminal activities of white-collar offenders. It turns out that, as a group, white-collar offenders are not quite as upstanding and law-abiding as we had thought. Yet, neither are they as entrenched in criminal lifestyles as common street criminals. So, as we will see, our image of the white-collar offender will have to be modified again but not completely abandoned.

One of the more remarkable findings to emerge out of the Yale study and that is replicated in the Forst and Rhodes study concerns the prior criminal records of white-collar criminals. Contrary to what we would expect, in both studies we find that at the time of their convictions for the criterion offenses, a surprisingly large proportion of white-collar criminals already had prior criminal records.

Table 2.5 presents information on the prior arrests for all of the white-collar offense categories and for the common offense categories in both studies. First, note that it is not at all unusual for a white-collar offender to have a prior arrest. In both studies, we find that about 40 percent of the white-collar offenders hade prior arrest. So, a substantial proportion of white-collar offenders have some familiarity with the business end of police work. But they probably do not know their way around a police

Table 2.5 Percent with prior arrests among white-collar and common offenders

Offense	Yale Study*	Forst and Rhodes Study**
White-collar	43	39
Antitrust	3	n.a.
Securities	32	n.a.
Income tax	47	42
Bribery	23	24
Lending and credit fraud	55	n.a.
False claims	56	49
Mail fraud	54	66
Bank embezzlement	29	18
Common	90	83

n.a. = not available.
*Adapted from table 2, Weisburd et al. (1991).
**Adapted from Benson and Moore (1992).

station as well as the common criminals. As Table 2.5 shows, a much larger percentage of common criminals have prior arrests. Clearly, the white-collar criminals are not as experienced with the criminal justice system as the common criminals.

It may be surprising that four of ten white-collar criminals have had prior contact with the justice system, but are they really that unusual? Perhaps this is about average for the general public. It is hard to say for sure, because there are few studies on the criminal histories of the general population, and estimates of the overall prevalence of arrest vary between 10 and 25 percent (Singh and Adams, 1979; Tillman, 1987), although one study estimated that fully half of all males in the United States will be arrested at some point in their lifetimes (Christensen, 1967).

Although it is not uncommon for white-collar offenders in general to have a prior arrest, this is not true of those who commit some particular types of white-collar crime. Just as we found when we investigated the social and demographic characteristics of white-collar offenders, we also find considerable variation in their criminal histories. In the Yale study, for example, only 3% of the antitrust offenders had a prior arrest. This figure is considerably below the norm for the general population. But more than half of the people convicted for lending and credit fraud, false claims, or

Table 2.6 Mean number of prior arrests for white-collar and common offenders

Offense	Mean	At Least One Arrest, %
White-collar	1.79	39.0
Embezzlement	0.52	18.4
Bribery	0.65	23.6
Income tax	1.91	42.1
False claims	2.29	49.0
Mail fraud	3.90	65.9
Common	5.63	81.1
Narcotics	3.55	72.2
Forgery	6.49	82.6
Bank robbery	6.85	88.4
All offenders	3.41	57.8

mail fraud had a prior arrest, which is considerably above the population norm. Persons convicted of income tax violations, securities fraud, bribery, or bank embezzlement fell between these two extremes. A very similar pattern is found in the Forst and Rhodes study, with those convicted of bribery and bank embezzlement on the low end of the scale compared with those convicted of making false claims or mail fraud.

It appears, then, that bribers and bank embezzlers have less extensive criminal histories than the people who make false claims or commit mail fraud. There is evidence that in this case appearances are not misleading. Table 2.6 shows the average number of prior arrests for each of the white-collar offense categories in the Forst and Rhodes study. On average, bribers and bank embezzlers have far fewer prior arrests than false claims and mail fraud offenders.

As we did when we looked at social and demographic characteristics, we need to ask what general conclusions can be drawn from these numbers. Two conclusions that mirror those we reached earlier on social and demographic characteristics stand out. First, many white-collar offenders do not fit the standard view of this type of offender. In the standard view, the white-collar offender is portrayed as an essentially law-abiding, upstanding person. However, it appears that not all of those who are arrested for white-collar crimes are first-time offenders. A nontrivial proportion of white-collar offenders are repeat offenders. Many have been in the courthouse more than once. Second, the people who commit some types of white-collar crime are much more criminally experienced than the people who commit other types of white-collar crime. Specifically, antitrust offenders, bank embezzlers, and bribers appear to be much less caught up in a life of crime than people who make false claims, commit lending and credit fraud, or use the U.S. postal system to commit fraud. Thus, as we found with age, gender, and race, it appears that different types of people who have different criminal backgrounds commit different types of white-collar crime.

As Tables 2.5 and 2.6 show, it is not uncommon for white-collar offenders to have multiple arrests, which indicates that at least some white-collar offenders engage in a longitudinal sequence of offending as they age. That is, they have what can be called criminal careers. But what do these careers look like? When do they typically start? What types and how many offenses are committed during an active career? When do careers end? We know from the study of ordinary street criminals that most offenders start committing crimes sometime between the ages of 15 and 17 and they typically end their careers in their early 20s (Blumstein et al. 1986; Piquero, 2008). In other words, most criminal careers are relatively short, lasting around five to eight years. We also know that most offenders are generalists and commit different types of crime rather than specializing in one particular form of offending such as burglary or auto theft (Piquero and Weisburd, 2009; Tracy, Wolfgang, and Figlio, 1990). There are only a few studies that have attempted to examine the criminal careers of white-collar offenders (see Benson and Moore, 1992; Piquero and Weisburd, 2009; Weisburd and Waring, 2001), but although they are few in number, these studies clearly suggest that more "differences than similarities exist between the criminal careers of white-collar offenders and those of common offenders" (Piquero and Weisburd, 2009, p. 156).

In their careful analysis of the Yale data, David Weisburd and Elin Waring (2001) found that white-collar offenders typically start much later in life than common offenders. The average age of onset for white-collar offenders was 35 and their careers tended to last longer, with an average career length of 14 years (Weisburd and Waring, 2001). However, even though white-collar offenders tend to have long criminal careers, for the most part they commit relatively few offenses during them, at least as offenses are indicated by official arrests. It is always possible, of course, that active white-collar offenders commit many offenses that go undetected.

In addition to examining career length and rate of offending, Weisburd and Waring (2001) looked at the general shape of the trajectories followed by white-collar offenders. Their analyses indicated that there were three prominent trajectories or offending patterns in the data: low rate, medium rate, and high rate. As the name implies, the low rate offenders, who were about 70 percent of the Yale sample, committed very few offenses, in what can be called an episodic manner, that is, they offended very infrequently and only under certain conditions (Piquero and Weisburd, 2009). Weisburd and Waring suggested that these people were either "crisis responders" or "opportunity takers." Crisis responders are those who commit white-collar crime out of a sense of desperation. Opportunity takers, on the other hand, are those who more or less accidentally find themselves in a position to take advantage of their occupations to enrich themselves.

The medium rate group were about 25 percent of the sample (Piquero and Weisburd, 2009). This group also offended relatively infrequently but nevertheless more persistently than the low rate group. The medium rate group appeared to be made up of "opportunity seekers," that is, people who would actively look for opportunities and situations in which they could take advantage of others to make a buck.

Finally, the high rate group was small, only about 5 percent of the sample (Piquero and Weisburd, 2009), but they offended more often and more consistently overtime than the other two groups. The people in the high rate group also committed a broader array of offenses. Their crimes involved a mix of white-collar and non–white-collar offenses, which raises an important point about the difficulty of identifying white-collar offenders. Recall that the Yale researchers selected their original sample by identifying individuals who had been convicted of eight selected white-collar crimes (called the criterion offenses) between 1974 and 1976. Yet, an analysis of the criminal histories of the individuals both before and after their criterion offenses indicates that a nontrivial number of them (5%–30%) had arrests for non–white-collar crimes. In other words, these individuals do not necessarily specialize in white-collar crime. Rather, they appear to be stereotypical criminals who occasionally commit white-collar offenses. The lesson to be learned from this is that a single arrest may not be the best way to identify white-collar offenders.

What about Sutherland and High-Status Offenders?

Up to this point, we have learned a lot about the social, demographic, and criminal characteristics of the people convicted of white-collar crimes in the federal judicial system. But in our investigation thus far we have taken an offense-based approach to white-collar crime, and as we saw above, this can sometimes lead to a mixed bag of offenders. How would things change if instead we followed Sutherland and others who focus on individuals who score high on respectability and social status and who hold positions of significant influence or power in legitimate public or private organizations? What determines who of this group becomes a white-collar offender? For two reasons, this is a particularly difficult question to answer.

First, there are very few quantitative studies to guide us. Most of what we know about high-status white-collar offenders comes from case studies of particularly egregious offenders or offenses. Although case studies can be enormously informative, it is always risky to generalize from them. That there are so few quantitative studies is not surprising. It is hard to study high-status individuals using standard research methodologies such as surveys or interviews. They often are unwilling to cooperate in studies, and it is even harder to get them to cooperate when the focus of the study is crime or wrongdoing.

The second reason is more complex. A large proportion of the really egregious white-collar offenses, the ones that make the evening news and the newspaper headlines, are committed in organizations, often large complex organizations. This complicates our task of describing the white-collar offender enormously. In complex organizations, people often—if not always—work in groups to accomplish complex tasks and goals. Because many people can be involved, it often is difficult to determine who should be held accountable when an organizational project or goal involves criminal activities. The job becomes even harder if the criminal activities persist over a long period of time. Throughout the duration of the offense, different people may be involved. Individuals may participate for a while but then move on to different positions in the organization or out of it altogether.

For example, in an organization such as the Ford Motor Company, literally hundreds of thousands of people work at producing automobiles. In the late 1970s and early 1980s, Ford was alleged to have produced an unsafe vehicle—the Ford Pinto. Because of a poorly designed and badly located gas tank, the Pinto had a disturbing tendency to explode if it was rear-ended by another car. It is estimated that hundreds of people died as a result of exploding Pintos (Dowie, 1987). As a result of one horrific accident, a local prosecutor in Elkhart, Indiana charged the Ford Company with negligent homicide when three teenage girls were burned to death after the Pinto they were riding in was struck from behind and exploded (Cullen et al., 2006). Ford was eventually acquitted at trial, but the case raises an interesting question. Suppose Ford had been convicted. In that case, who should we say were the responsible individuals—that is, who were the white-collar offenders? Many people were involved at different points in time, and many people made decisions that contributed to the final design of the Pinto. Indeed, Michael Cosentino, the prosecutor who tried the Pinto case, found this to be such a vexing question that he decided to charge the Ford Motor Company rather than individual executives at Ford (Cullen et al., 2006).

The problem here is a general one that criminologists and prosecutors have long recognized when it comes to understanding and controlling crimes committed in organizational settings. In large complex organizations, responsibility for projects often is diffused or spread out over a number of people. The diffusion of responsibility makes it difficult to single out a particular individual or group of individuals who ought to be held responsible when things go wrong. In these cases, it may make more sense to focus on the organization itself rather than the individuals involved in it at any particular point in time. Indeed, there is a long and respectable tradition in white-collar crime research that focuses on organizational behavior as opposed to the behavior of individuals (Clinard and Quinney, 1973; Clinard and Yeager, 1980). In Chapters 3 and 7, we explore the issue of how organizations may shape individual behavior in more detail. However, in this chapter, our focus is on individuals.

Accordingly, we return to the question, what if anything distinguishes the high-status individuals who engage in white-collar crime from other high-status individuals who do not? Since by definition the individuals of concern here are of similar social status, we have to look elsewhere for factors that may separate the offenders from the non-offenders. Two possibilities suggest themselves. First, something external to the offenders, something in their social situation or experience besides their social status may distinguish them from other individuals. For example, they may be under some type of strain that drives them to offend. One of the theories that we examine in the next chapter makes this argument. Other theories suggest other events or conditions that promote offending. We cover these as well in Chapter 3. For now, however, we consider a second possibility, one more directly related to offenders' personal characteristics, and that is their psychological makeup. Perhaps certain psychological traits facilitate or are associated with elite white-collar offending.

Historically, the psychology of white-collar offenders is not a subject on which researchers have invested an enormous amount of time and effort (Meier and Geis, 1982). However, recently the number of studies focused on the psychology of white-collar offending has started to grow, and some intriguing findings have begun to emerge (for a review, see Benson and Manchak, 2014). We review these new findings below. However, before we do that, we note that even though there has not been a lot of research attention focused on the individual characteristics of white-collar offenders, the idea that elite white-collar offenders are somehow psychologically distinctive has been around for a long time. Nearly a century ago, the sociologist Edward Alsworth Ross, writing about what he called "criminaloids," argued that the distinctive characteristic of the business leaders of his day, whom today we would call white-collar criminals, was *moral insensitivity*. In the pursuit of profit, criminaloids are not bothered by the harm that they inflict on others or on society in general. However, and this is an important qualification, criminaloids (i.e., white-collar offenders) are not the victims of any sort of serious psychological disturbance or abnormality (Ross, 1977). White-collar offenders may be unusual, but they are not crazy. Ross (p. 31) described them this way,

> The key to the criminaloid is not evil impulse but moral insensibility. . . . Nature has not foredoomed them to evil by a double dose of lust, cruelty, malice, greed, or jealousy. They are not degenerates

tormented by monstrous cravings. They want nothing more than we all want—money, power, and consideration—in a word, success; but they are in a hurry and they are not particular as to the means.

Sutherland held a similar view of white-collar offenders as more or less psychologically normal. Indeed, he used the apparent psychological normalcy of white-collar offenders to ridicule the criminological theories of his day. These theories typically presented the criminal as a person who grew up in poverty and who was psychologically damaged by all of the social pathologies that go along with poverty. Poverty and the psychopathic conditions associated with it were seen as the root causes of crime. In a famous passage, Sutherland argued that this approach cannot be correct. Poverty and psychopathology cannot be general explanations of crime, because with respect to white-collar offenders, "With a small number of exceptions, they are not in poverty, were not reared in slums or badly deteriorated families, and are not feebleminded or psychopathic" (Sutherland, 1940).

We examine Sutherland's theory of crime and its application to white-collar crime in greater detail in the next chapter. For now, though, we note that Sutherland believed that white-collar offenders interpret or define their business-related activities in terms that favor or justify lawbreaking. For him, what distinguishes white-collar offenders is a particular value system or view of the world in which illegal behavior in the conduct of business is seen as acceptable and justified. Hence, white-collar offenders do not acknowledge the criminality of their actions, and they certainly do not think of themselves as criminals.

A good deal of anecdotal evidence indicates that Sutherland's understanding of the psychology of white-collar offenders has considerable merit. One of the authors (Benson) interviewed a small sample of individuals who had been convicted of white-collar crimes. With only a few exceptions, these individuals denied that they had ever intended to commit a crime. They described their crimes as normal business practices or at worst as honest mistakes. For example, two men who ran a public construction firm and had been convicted of bid rigging and other violations of antitrust law presented this interpretation of their activities: "It was a way of doing business. Like, you know, why do you brush your teeth in the morning? It was the way things were done long before we got into the business" (Benson, 1985).

This way of looking at illegal antitrust activities apparently is quite common among business executives. In his famous case study of the heavy electrical equipment antitrust case of 1961, Geis reports the comments of an executive involved in the case. Testifying before the Senate Subcommittee on Antitrust and Monopoly, the executive responded to a question from the committee's attorney:

Committee attorney: Did you know that these meetings with competitors were illegal?

Witness: Illegal? Yes, but not criminal. I didn't find that out until I read the indictment. . . . I assumed that criminal actions meant damaging someone, and we did not do that. . . . I thought that we were more or less working on a survival basis in order to try to make enough to keep our plant and our employees.

This theme often is repeated by white-collar offenders, particularly by high-status executives who commit offenses in the furtherance of legitimate businesses. They deny that their actions were intended to harm anyone directly, and they deny that anyone was directly harmed. They do not define their actions as morally wrong. Rather, they define them as economically necessary in order for their businesses to survive. If we take their words at face value, it appears that these executives view violating the law to protect their businesses as the lesser of two evils. Because their actions are not in their view harmful or morally wrong, it is acceptable for them to break the law in order to protect their companies. Indeed, for businessmen, whether a practice is defined as ethical depends in large measure on whether it is a standard practice. If something is normal practice, then it is ethical. It may not be legal exactly but it is ethical in the eyes of business executives (Chibnall and Saunders, 1977). Thus, two characteristics of high-status offenders appear to be a willful blindness to the criminality of their behavior and a belief that the economic survival of the firm is more important than obedience to the law.

Business executives are not alone in denying the guilty mind. Medical and legal professionals of all sorts routinely commit fraud and, when caught, vigorously deny that they knowingly broke the law. For example, a dentist who was convicted of fraud against the Medicaid system explained his offense by blaming others in the practice:

> Inwardly, I personally felt that the only crime I committed was not telling on these guys. Not that I deliberately, intentionally committed a crime against the system. My only crime was that I should have had the guts to tell on these guys, what they were doing, rather than putting up with it and then trying gradually to get out of the system without hurting them or without them thinking that I was going to snitch on them.
>
>   (Benson, 1985, pp. 597–598)

Physicians who have been caught violating the laws governing their profession are especially unwilling to acknowledge that their actions are motivated by greed. Instead, they see themselves as "sacrificial lambs" who have fallen victim to idiotic rules and regulations or mendacious employees (Jesilow, Geis, and Pontell, 1991). Like business executives, medical professionals often profess allegiance to a different set of priorities. As they put it, focusing on patient care is far more important than obeying some silly law or regulation. Consider this example from a physician convicted of fraud against Medicaid (Jesilow et al., 1991, p. 3321):

> They [the Medicaid officials] are the ones who eventually look over all this and say: "No, that was wrong." Now their idea of right and wrong is very different from what is considered right and wrong by normal people, or by physicians who are not necessarily normal, but at least [have their own] ideas about what is right and wrong. And to us, right and wrong have to do with things like patient care, whether we give them the right treatments. It doesn't have anything to do with some Medicaid regulation.

Case studies of well-known and egregious white-collar offenses suggest several additional psychological factors that may be involved in high-status white-collar crimes. One of these traits is the offender's relish of a *sense of superiority over the victim* (Stotland, 1977). For example, in the

1970s a man named Robert Vesco orchestrated a series of elaborate investment frauds to steal millions of dollars from other businessmen. Vesco was openly contemptuous of his victims, whom he described as fools. Another case involved an insurance company called Equity Funding. In the Equity Funding case, a group of conspirators defrauded hundreds of millions of dollars from legitimate insurance companies by creating fraudulent policies on fictitious persons (Seidler, Andrews, and Empstein, 1977). As the fraud progressed, the conspirators seemed to take delight in fooling the auditors, the SEC, and other insurance companies. More recently, in the Enron case, a telephone call between two California energy traders was taped as they discussed how they had illegally manipulated the price of energy that Californians had to pay. The exchange begins with the traders talking about California's demand that Enron refund $8 million in overcharges for energy:

Trader 1: They're [expletive] taking all the money back from you guys, all the money you guys stole from those poor grandmothers in California?

Trader 2: Yeah, Grandma Millie, man.

Trader 1: Yeah, Grandma Millie, man. But she's the one who couldn't figure out how to [expletive] vote on the butterfly ballot.

Trader 2: Yeah, now she wants her [expletive] money back for all the power you've charged right up, jammed right up her [expletive] for [expletive] $250 a megawatt hour.

As this conversation indicates, the traders appeared to take a perverse delight in manipulating and making fools of their victims. The feeling of power and superiority that arises out of the offense is psychologically rewarding to the offender and may become a source of motivation for continued offending (Shover, 2007; Stotland, 1977).

The white-collar offender's sense of superiority is often accompanied by arrogance (Shover and Hochstetler, 2006, pp. 66–67). Elite white-collar offenders seem to believe "they don't have to follow the rules because they made them" (Swartz, 2003, p. 302). As Shover and Hochstetler (2006, p. 67) note, the arrogant are accustomed to being in charge and to doing things their own way. Convinced of their own superiority, they assume that whatever they want to do must be right. They do not have to be bothered with the minor technicalities of the law, because in their view their personal integrity is beyond question. Like old-time Calvinists, they seem to believe that their personal success in reaching the top of the corporate hierarchy indicates that they have been chosen by a higher power. Thus, they are entitled to do as they please and to take what they want (Shover and Hochstetler, 2006).

Related to arrogance and a sense of superiority is the gratification that comes from mastering a complex situation. Stotland (1977) calls this source of motivation "ego challenge." It may be a particularly important and prevalent aspect of long-term frauds that are carried out in large organizations and that require highly specialized skills. For example, many of the offenses that were committed during the Enron scandal involved highly complex schemes designed to manipulate and misuse the standard rules and practices of accounting and the reporting requirements of the SEC (McLean and Elkind, 2003). The schemes had to make Enron appear to be more profitable than it really was. Further, the schemes had to be constructed so that they did not raise the suspicions of regulators at the SEC or Wall Street investors or industry analysts. In short, the executives at Enron had to fool a lot of very smart people, at least for a period of time. On the other hand, it is possible that the people who were supposed to be watching the barn door, the so-called gatekeepers, fell down on the job (Coffee, 2002). Nevertheless, it took smart people with a good deal of skill to come up with the accounting schemes used at Enron. The executives who carried it off clearly were proud of their skills and enjoyed exercising them (McLean and Elkind, 2003).

As we discuss in greater detail in the next chapter, some scholars believe that large organizations, especially large for-profit private corporations, are inherently criminogenic. Further, they tend to be led by individuals with particular personality traits conducive to crime (Gross, 1978, 1980). According to Edward Gross (1978), the people who end up as leaders in large organizations tend to be "organizational strainers." They are ambitious, shrewd, and morally flexible. They are ambitious in the sense that they have a strong desire to get to the top, to be seen as persons of importance, power, and status. Ambition alone is not enough, however. It must be coupled with shrewdness, the ability to spot organizational opportunities for advancement. They understand that success is not based on talent alone. It also involves the ability to fraternize with and to make a good impression on people with power, people who can help your career advance in the political infighting that characterizes large organizations. Finally, organizational strainers tend to be morally flexible. They are not troubled putting organizational goals ahead of ethical principles and legal mandates.

There is some intriguing evidence in support of the idea that white-collar criminals are socially adept and that their sociality may indirectly facilitate their involvement in white-collar crime. In one of the few quantitative studies of the psychology of white-collar offenders, researchers compared a sample of persons who had been convicted of various white-collar crimes with a matched control sample of noncriminal white-collar employees on several personality scales (Collins and Schmidt, 1993). Offenders scored differently from non-offenders in two areas: social conscientiousness and social extraversion. First, offenders scored lower on four scales—performance, socialization, responsibility, and tolerance—that tap a broad personality construct called *social conscientiousness*. Individuals who display social conscientiousness are dependable, responsible, rule-abiding, honest, motivated to high job performance, and committed to social and civic values. The white-collar offenders were less likely to display these traits than their law-abiding counterparts. On the other hand, the white-collar offenders scored higher than the non-offenders on two other scales: social extraversion and extracurricular activities. The social extraversion scale measures how individuals have in the past had friendships, been popular, and been effective in social situations. The researchers speculate that socially extraverted people are more likely to get involved in extracurricular activities. The experiences gained in these activities, coupled with their outgoing personalities, aid potential white-collar offenders in the competition for higher level jobs. These jobs, in turn, provide access to white-collar crime opportunities, which persons who lack social conscientiousness may well take advantage of (Collins and Schmidt, 1993). In a replication of the work of Collins and Schmidt (1993), a study of "high level" white-collar offenders in Germany found that the white-collar offenders were more narcissistic and hedonistic and exhibited less behavioral control than a comparison sample of non-offenders (Blickle et al. 2006). Others have also noted a connection between narcissism and elite white-collar offending (Perri, 2013).

Narcissism and arrogance are not exactly attractive traits in people, but they may not be the most disturbing or threatening psychological characteristics of high level white-collar offenders. Surpassing them in potential harmfulness is psychopathy. Psychopathy is a psychological construct that incorporates many of the traits and characteristics that white-collar offenders seem to possess, such as narcissism, arrogance, and extraversion, but in addition psychopaths are characterized by a paucity of affective experiences and an inability to feel empathy (Benson and Manchak, 2014). Psychopaths are intelligent and they can be very charming and engaging, but at bottom they lack a sense of morality and do not care about others (Hare, 1993). Some scholars have suggested that this combination of characteristics allows psychopaths to gain access to and take advantage of vulnerable people and corporations (Babiak and Hare, 2006; Babiak, Newmann, and Hare, 2010). As Hare famously put it, "not all psychopaths are in prison, some are in the boardroom."

Babiak and Hare (2006) argue that many psychopaths have excellent communication skills and are good at reading other people and situations. Their verbal fluency and lack of social inhibitions enable them to speak up freely in meetings, which helps them to appear to be capable of leadership. In theory, they can use their charm and psychological insight to manipulate others so as to advance their own interests and rise in corporate hierarchies.

It is difficult to know, of course, exactly how prevalent psychopathy is among business leaders. One small study, however, suggests that the rate is higher in corporations than in the general public, though less high than you would find in prison (Babiak et al., 2010). The researchers studied 203 individuals involved in management development programs in several different companies. They administered a standard psychopathy checklist and found that approximately 3 percent of the management trainees scored high on the checklist. Three percent is significantly above the estimated 1 percent rate of psychopathy in the general population, though far less than the 15 percent psychopathy rate found in prisons. Thus, Hare may have been correct that some psychopaths are in boardrooms.

All in all, several potentially important characteristics of the psychology of white-collar offenders appear to stand out. They include the offenders' unwillingness to define their behavior as crime, belief that economic survival is more important than obeying the law, sense of superiority over victims, need for ego challenge, a lack of social conscientiousness, arrogance, narcissism, and perhaps most disturbingly psychopathic characteristics, such as superficial charm and lack of empathy. Although plenty of anecdotal evidence suggests that some or all of these characteristics play a role in many white-collar crimes, we must be careful how we interpret this evidence. It is important not to overstate the causal importance of these psychological factors. Just because people who commit white-collar crime appear to have a sense of superiority over others, it does not follow that people who think that they are better than everyone else are white-collar criminals. Similarly, even though some white-collar offenders appear to find intrinsic gratification in orchestrating a complex illegal scheme, we cannot conclude that people who like solving complex problems will resort to white-collar crime when they are bored. These cautionary remarks hold even for full-blown psychological constructs, such as psychopathy. People can be insensitive and manipulative without necessarily doing anything criminal. In addition, we must remember that almost all of the research on the psychology of white-collar offenders involves case studies or very small samples of offenders. These studies have been based almost exclusively on high-status offenders. How strongly we can generalize from this empirical base is not at all clear. Whether they would apply, for instance, to low-status offenders is an open question. Nevertheless, it would seem not too much of a stretch to speculate in one way. If individuals with the characteristics identified earlier find themselves in situations that offer opportunities for white-collar offending, then we should not be particularly surprised when they take advantage of those opportunities. It may also be the case that these very same traits may under certain conditions help people advance in the world of business. This is not to say that all corporate leaders are crooks, but on the other hand being a crook may not necessarily disqualify one from getting ahead in the corporate world.

People or Organizations

On June 15, 2002, Arthur Andersen LLP, at the time one of the "big five" accounting firms in the world, with tens of thousands of employees, was convicted in federal court of criminal charges relating to its handling of

Enron's auditing and became a convicted felon. A little over 2 months later, on August 31, 2002, the company voluntarily surrendered its CPA license and effectively collapsed. The case of Arthur Andersen illustrates an important point about white-collar crime. The offender is not always a person. Rather, at times, an entire organization can be thought of as the offender. The idea that organizations should be considered criminal actors dates back to Sutherland (1983). Even though Sutherland defined white-collar crime in terms of the characteristics of individual offenders, his analyses were based on "decisions of courts and administrative agencies against the 70 largest mining, manufacturing, and mercantile corporations" of his day (Sutherland, 1983, p. 13).

Expanding on Sutherland's lead, Clinard and Quinney (1973) proposed that a distinction be made between organizational crime and occupational crime. Organizational crime refers to offenses committed by an organization or its agents acting on its behalf for the benefit of the organization. Occupational crime, on the other hand, refers to offenses committed by an individual using his or her occupational position for personal advantage. This typology is now widely accepted among white-collar crime scholars.

The Characteristics of Organizational Offenders and Offenses

Assuming that companies can commit crime (a supposition, as we discuss below, that is challenged by some scholars), what do we know about organizational offenders and the types of crimes they commit? The USSC tracks case and offender information for organizations sentenced in federal courts. These data can offer insight into some of the attributes of sentenced offenders. For instance, the USSC data reveal that the majority of sentenced organizations are small. In fiscal year (FY) 2012, we can see from Figure 2.1 that nearly 70 percent have fewer than 50 employees, while only 12.4 percent have more than 1,000 employees.

Using FY 2011 USSC data, the following image of the corporate offender emerges:

1. Most cases involve fraud and environmental offenses (this is a broad category), followed by import-export offenses, food and drug violations, and public corruption.

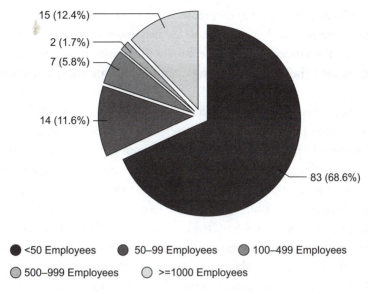

Figure 2.1 Number of employees of organizational offenders
Source: USSC Interactive Sourcebook (isb.ussc.gov) for FY 2012 Datafile, USSCFY2012.

2. Almost all organizational defendants (over 98%) had no previous criminal or administrative record, i.e., they are not—officially at least—recidivists.
3. A notable number of the convicted organizations appear not to have substantial financial assets. Indeed, nearly 30 percent of the organizations were deemed unable to pay and were therefore granted a reduced fine.
4. Self-reporting is infrequent. A central component of the sentencing guidelines encourages a cooperative relationship between business and legal authorities (this is considered a mitigating circumstance); yet, only three sentenced organizations self-reported the offense to authorities.[3]
5. With only 160 cases sentenced under Chapter 8 during the fiscal year (compared with 86,201 total cases handled across all U.S. circuit and districts courts), criminal behavior by corporations would appear to be relatively rare (U.S. Sentencing Commission, 2011 Datafile, USSCFY11).

How does this picture of corporate crime and the typical organizational offender comport with what we have learned from other research, and how useful are the guidelines data to estimate the scope and character of corporate crime? The early Sentencing Commission data are problematic due to case-specific missing data and entire cases omitted from the database (Alexander, Arlen, and Cohen, 2001). After 2005, the case information, however, became more consistent and reliable. Most corporate offenses are litigated civilly or administratively and are not referred for criminal prosecution. Because the USSC data comprise criminal cases, extrapolating about the dark figure of corporate crime or offender characteristics from this source says nothing about the likely characteristics of corporate crime cases and offenders handled outside of the criminal justice system. Arlen (2012, p. 353) suggests that the guidelines' self-reporting provisions perversely reward, through mitigation points, the types of offenders that would be the easiest for authorities to discover and who are also the least troublesome. The self-reporting provision therefore is apt to attract less sophisticated offenders who are likely involved in less serious or less consequential crimes. It is unclear what the true distribution of serious versus minor cases of corporate crime would be in the general population, but Arlen's argument implies that using these data to project a dark figure of corporate crime will underestimate them. The guidelines data also capture offenders at the end of the criminal justice process, measuring convictions and not charges or crimes known to authorities. We know little about what happens to cases that are discovered but not investigated, or about which cases move from an "arrest" to some kind of diversion. Studies of traditional offenders suggest that those who begin the justice process are quite different from those who make it all the way through to the conviction and sentencing stages. It is likely that in the case of corporate crime, the organizations that travel all the way through the criminal justice funnel differ from those that are diverted or shunted out of the system along the way. However, at this point in time we know little about offender similarities and differences from one stage of the process to the next and how that may vary by justice system (criminal, administrative, or civil).

The USSC data would appear to offer some sense of the dark figure of crimes by small businesses, but only for certain types of offenses. And given how difficult it is to police and prosecute corporate crimes in the criminal justice system, the recidivism data are highly suspect (Simpson, 2013).

Can Organizations Offend?

Treating organizations or corporations as criminal actors raises tricky ontological questions on which scholars disagree. For example, Donald Cressey (1989) argues against treating corporations as criminal actors for the purposes of criminological theory. Cressey recognizes that as far as the law is concerned, corporations can be treated as fictitious persons, but in his view, criminological analysis is different than legal analysis. Criminology should focus on real people, not ones that are legal fictions. Corporations do not act, people do. Treating a corporation as though it were a person is misplaced anthropomorphism, and trying to explain corporate as opposed to individual behavior leads to conceptual confusion. Thus, according to Cressey, the distinction between corporate and occupational crime is unnecessary. Other scholars disagree. They contend that corporations do act and that corporate actions are more than the sum of the acts of individual organizational members. John Braithwaite and Brent Fisse (1990) provide an illustration. They note that in a corporation, each member of a board of directors can vote to declare a dividend, but only the board as a collectivity has the power to actually declare a dividend. The collective action of the board is qualitatively different from the actions of the individuals who make up the board. In addition, the board's collective decision may result from processes such as "groupthink" or the group risky shift phenomenon that do not apply when individuals make decisions in isolation from one another. Hence, for Braithwaite and Fisse, it makes sense to treat corporations as distinct objects of explanation.

Regardless which side of this philosophical debate is correct, a large body of research has focused on exploring the characteristics of organizations and industries that are related to corporate crime (for examples, see Clinard and Yeager, 2006; Ermann and Lundman, 1978; Gross 1978, 1980; Simpson, 1986, 2002; Simpson, Garner, and Gibbs, 2007). We discuss this research in more detail in later chapters, but for now we note it is important to keep in mind that many white-collar crimes have an organizational dimension and cannot be reduced to individual-level propensities or characteristics. To understand why these offenses occur and how they can be prevented, we must recognize the dynamics of organizational behavior and develop theories that integrate and combine both individual and organizational levels of analysis (Vaughan, 2007). So, the term "white-collar offender" should be used with caution because at times it may make more sense to focus not on individual wrongdoers but rather on organizations as a whole.

Summary

The main objective of this chapter has been to describe what is known about the white-collar offender or, to put it more accurately, about the people who commit white-collar types of crimes. Two large empirical studies of offenders agree that the people who are convicted of white-collar types of crimes in the federal judicial system are not like the people who are convicted there of ordinary street crimes (Benson and Kerley, 2000; Weisburd et al., 1991). Those convicted of white-collar types of offenses come from a different social and demographic background than common offenders. Compared with common street-crime offenders, white-collar offenders are older, more likely to be male, and more likely to be white. They also are more likely to be married, to own their own homes, to be financially secure, and to be employed at the time of their offenses. Although data from the U.S. Sentencing Commission suggests that the social and demographic profile of white-collar offenders has changed since the 1970s, the people who commit white-collar crimes today do not "look" like ordinary street offenders. These findings should not come as a major surprise to anyone. But it is surprising how many of the white-collar offenders in these studies do not appear to conform to Sutherland's definition of the white-collar offender as a person of respectability and high social status. As David Weisburd and his colleagues (1991) put it, these are primarily middle-class offenders. However, this picture of the white-collar offender is necessarily limited by the data on which it is based. Samples drawn from the federal judicial system miss all of those offenders who for whatever reason avoid being drawn into the system in the first place. It seems likely that if anyone is going to avoid the system, it will be Sutherland's type of high-social-status offender.

Regarding the psychology of white-collar offenders, it is probably safe to say that the vast majority of them do not view themselves as criminal or their activities as crimes. With very few exceptions, they go to great lengths to deny having any intent to commit a crime against anyone (Benson, 1985). It also seems clear that the perpetrators of really big-time white-collar crimes possess an exaggerated sense of self-confidence and entitlement, and they may share some personality traits that are found among psychopaths. Indeed, recent research makes E.A. Ross seem particularly prescient. Recall that nearly a century ago, he asserted that the key characteristic of white-collar criminaloids was insensitivity to the moral implications of their actions. They may also have other characteristics, such as shrewdness and extraverted personalities, that enable them to fare well in the competition for high-level jobs where opportunities for white-collar crime are plentiful.

Finally, unlike ordinary street crime, white-collar crime often has an organizational dimension, that is, it is situated in an organizational context and involves people who are engaged in organizational roles or activities. Thus, both individuals and organizations can be thought of as white-collar offenders.

Notes

1 The crime of postal forgery may seem similar to white-collar crime in that it would appear to involve deception. However, most of the time, postal forgery is simply straightforward theft. Typically, the offender steals a government issued check for a welfare or social security benefit from a mailbox and is caught when trying to cash the check by forging the recipient's endorsement. Whether the offender is charged with postal theft or postal forgery depends mainly on whether he or she is caught at the time of the theft or when trying to pass the check (Weisburd et al., 1991:17).

2 The districts were New Jersey, Eastern New York, Connecticut, Northern Ohio, Middle Florida, Western Oklahoma, Northern New Mexico, and Northern California.

3 Arlen (2012, p. 349) shows that larger companies, where offenses are significantly less apt to be discovered by the government, have little to gain and much to lose by self-reporting. Further, deferred prosecution agreements—an increasingly common tool utilized by the Department of Justice for "dealing with large corporations that employ thousands and have a significant influence on the health of industries and the markets" (Lydon, 2012, p. 1) as long as firms admit wrongdoing, cooperate with an investigation, pay a fine, and improve internal compliance—reinforce the argument that the USSC data are biased toward smaller and likely less powerful firms.

PART II
CRIMINOLOGICAL THEORY AND THE OPPORTUNITY PERSPECTIVE

Like scientists in other fields of study, many criminologists would like their subject matter—crime—to be predicted and explained by one inclusive general theory. That is, they desire a theory that can be applied to all forms of criminal offending at all times and in all places. Indeed, Sutherland himself was one such criminologist. Whenever a theory is put forth as a candidate for being *the* general theory of crime, one of the first questions asked is "What about white-collar crime?" Indeed, sometimes this question is raised first and then answered by the general theorists themselves as a way of mounting an anticipatory defense against this very attack (see Hirschi and Gottfredson, 1987a, 1987b). The reason why white-collar crime is always raised as a counterfactual to so-called general theories of crime is obvious. Neither the offenders nor the offenses fit common stereotypes of crime and criminals. Hence, it reasonable to ask whether a theory of apples can also be a theory of oranges.

In Part II, we review the efforts that have been made by various theorists to bring white-collar crime under the umbrella of mainstream criminological theory. While there are, of course, important differences among these theoretical efforts, they all share one thing in common. They all focus on the offender and attempt to explicate the factors that cause offenders to do what they do. In essence, they are theories of criminality, not theories of crime. However, as we explain in Chapter 4, crime and criminality are not the same things. They are conceptually distinct, and it is possible to think theoretically about white-collar crimes as objects of study separate from white-collar criminals. Thus, in Chapter 4 we develop our opportunity perspective as it applies to white-collar crime.

3

EXPLAINING WHITE-COLLAR CRIME
Traditional Criminological Theories

One of Sutherland's professed goals in writing about white-collar crime was to reform criminological theory. In the 1930s, when Sutherland began working in this area, criminological theory was dominated by the view that crime was concentrated in the lower social classes and was caused by the personal and social pathologies that accompany poverty. Sutherland contended that this approach was wrong on two counts. First, it failed to "fit the data on criminal behavior." As he correctly pointed out, many—indeed most—poverty-stricken people are not criminal. Therefore, poverty and the pathologies associated with it cannot be general or sufficient causes of criminal behavior. Second, theories that use data taken from the poverty-stricken classes are based on "a biased sample of all criminal acts." Specifically, they ignore the many serious crimes committed by individuals in the upper social classes in the course of their occupations—in other words, white-collar crime. A truly adequate criminological theory should account for or explain crime in all its different forms (Sutherland, 1940). Accordingly, Sutherland proposed a theory of white-collar crime based on his famous differential association theory.

Sutherland has not been the only one to attempt to develop a theory of white-collar crime. Just as with conventional crime, many theoretical approaches have been tried in the search for a better understanding of white-collar crime. The process of applying standard criminological theories to white-collar crime often involves what Simpson (2013a) calls "conceptual acrobatics." Theorists have to take ideas and concepts that were originally developed to apply to traditional forms of crime and tweak them to account for the special features of white-collar crime and the distinguishing characteristics of white-collar offenders. Despite these conceptual challenges, variants of differential association, anomie, control, rational choice, and integrated theories have been proposed to explain white-collar crime.

Yet, for a variety of reasons, none of these efforts has achieved widespread acceptance, and there is little consensus on how best to explain white-collar crime. Empirical work in this area is difficult to conduct. Researchers rarely have access to the financial resources that are made available to those who study traditional forms of street crime. There are few solid facts to work with, and none of the theories of white-collar crime have been subjected to extensive empirical scrutiny. In addition, some theories of white-collar crime are constructed in such a way that it is difficult to design tests for them. For example, some theories use variables that apply at different levels of analysis. Individual-, organizational-, structural-, and cultural-level variables may all be cited as necessary parts of the overall explanation of white-collar crime (Coleman, 1987). Though this kind of approach is comprehensive and provocative, it is also very difficult to test. It is almost impossible to measure or control for all of the factors that are cited in the explanation. Thus, the empirical validity of the theories of white-collar crime remains unknown.

In this chapter, we review the theories that have been proposed for white-collar crime. Because we are not yet at the stage where we can identify the theoretical approach that provides the best or the most promising explanation, it is important to get an overview of the various approaches that have been tried. This review serves another purpose as well. It helps to show how criminology has continued to be influenced by and make progress toward one of Sutherland's original objectives. He wanted to reform criminological theory so that it would take into account all forms of criminal behavior, not just juvenile delinquency and common street crimes. Although criminologists have not made a great deal of progress in testing theories of white-collar crime, they have continued to pursue the objective that Sutherland established. They have explored how standard criminological theories can be applied to white-collar crime.

Differential Association

In keeping with his objective of reforming criminological theory, Sutherland theorized that the same general processes that cause other sorts of crime also cause white-collar crime. He argued that individual involvement in white-collar crime comes about as a result of a process called *differential association*. The theory of differential association postulates that "criminal behavior is learned in association with those who define such criminal behavior favorably and in isolation from those who define it unfavorably and that a person in an appropriate situation will engage in white-collar crime if, and only if, the "weight of definitions favorable exceeds the weight of the unfavorable definitions." Sutherland thought that attitudes and cultural orientations that define illegal business behavior in favorable terms are pervasive throughout the business world. Newcomers to the world of business are socialized to accept these attitudes and orientations. They learn how to commit certain types of offenses and how to rationalize these offenses so that, in the offender's mind, they are seen as acceptable, ordinary, and necessary business practices. Thus, a white-collar criminal culture permeates the world of business and is passed from one generation of executives and employees to the next.

Sutherland had many examples of how young people new to the world of business were socialized into the self-serving morality of the marketplace by their bosses. For example, a manager of a shoe store explained the rules of the game to a new employee this way (Sutherland, 1983, p. 243):

> My job is to move out shoes and I hire you to assist in this. I am perfectly glad to fit a person with a pair of shoes if we have his size, but I am willing to mis-fit him if it is necessary in order to sell him a pair of shoes. I expect you to do the same. If you do not like this, someone else can have your job. While you are working for me, I expect you to have no scruples about how you sell shoes.

Retail sales may be a cutthroat business, but it is not the only profession in which dishonesty prevails. Consider another example from Sutherland

(1983, pp. 244–245) regarding a certified public accountant who worked for a respected firm of public accountants. After the accountant had been on the job for several years, he had this to say about the morality of his profession (Sutherland 1983, p. 244).

> While I was a student in the school of business I learned the principles of accounting. After I had worked for a time for an accounting firm I found that I had failed to learn many important things about accounting. An accounting firm gets its work from business firms and, within limits, must make the reports which those business firms desire. The accounting firm for which I work is respected and there is none better in the city. On my first assignment I discovered some irregularities in the books of the firm and these would lead anyone to question the financial policies of that firm. When I showed my report to the manager of our accounting firm, he said that was not a part of my assignment and I should leave it out. Although I was confident that the business firm was dishonest, I had to conceal this information. Again and again I have been compelled to do the same thing in other assignments. I get so disgusted with things of this sort that I wish I could leave the profession. I guess I must stick to it, for it is the only occupation for which I have training.

The attitudes and practices that Sutherland found during his research have persisted. In the early 1980s, Benson conducted a series of interviews with businessmen convicted of white-collar offenses. These offenders expressed sentiments very similar to those reported by Sutherland. For example, recall the owner of a public construction firm whom we introduced in Chapter 2, who was convicted of antitrust violations for bid rigging. He had this to say about how business was conducted in his industry: "It was a way of doing business before we ever got into the business. So, it was like why do you brush your teeth in the morning or something . . . It was part of the everyday . . . It was a method of survival" (Benson, 1985, p. 591).

Recall as well the attitudes of the Enron traders quoted in Chapter 2. What these and many, many other examples that could be found suggest is that Sutherland was right. The culture of business does not promote morality or obedience to the law. Rather, it provides to those who come in contact with it definitions of the world that are favorable to violation of law (Hochstetler and Copes, 2001).

But the mere presence of definitions favorable to the violation of law is not enough by itself to cause white-collar crime. Definitions favorable to violation of the law must be of sufficient magnitude or "weight" so as to overwhelm competing definitions unfavorable to violations of law. According to Sutherland, in the world of business, this condition is satisfied because of isolation and social disorganization. Members of the business community are isolated from definitions unfavorable to their law violations because the government, entertainment industry, and news media have traditionally equated crime with the lower socioeconomic classes. Hence, businesspersons rarely are confronted with unfavorable definitions of their behavior, and they are unlikely to experience criminal labeling.

An often overlooked dimension of Sutherland's theory of white-collar crime is his argument that white-collar crime flourishes because society is not socially well organized against it. He identified two types of social disorganization: *Anomie* refers to a lack of standards regarding behavior in specific areas of social action; *conflict of standards* refers to conflict between social groups with reference to specific practices. Sutherland thought that anomie regarding harmful and illegal business practices was widespread for a couple of reasons. First, business behavior is complex, technical, and difficult to observe. Second, because America was founded on the ideals of competition and free enterprise, the public is ambivalent about government control of business activity. Taken together, these factors have prevented the development of a strong public consensus on the wrongfulness and harmfulness of shady business practices. Lacking clear signals of concern from the public, law enforcers are not vigorous in their pursuit of business misconduct.

Also mitigating against control of business misconduct is an enduring conflict of standards between the business community and other interests in society. According to Sutherland, the business community is tightly organized against regulatory control of business practices. It always vigorously contests any effort by government, consumer groups, labor unions, and environmental organizations to expand regulatory controls and to criminalize harmful business practices. The continual conflict between the business community and those who would control it undermines the development of a strong public moral consensus against misconduct. The idea that regulations are "bad for business and the economy" has been a catchphrase for business leaders and their defenders throughout American history. It is summed up neatly in the title of an article in *Capitalism Magazine*: "Paralyzing America's Producers: The Government's Crackdown on American Businessmen Is Devastating Our Economy." According to the authors, Yaron Brook and Alex Epstein, "America's economy is staggering because America's businesses are staggering. The cause—and the factor that must be removed to revive the economy—is the government's ongoing regulatory crackdown on business." The article was written shortly after the multibillion dollar scandals at Enron and WorldCom broke (Brook and Epstein, 2002).

Anomie Theory

The concept of anomie has a long history in sociology and criminology. It was famously proposed by Emile Durkheim (1951) as an important factor in suicide. For Durkheim, *anomie* referred to a sense of normlessness or lack of regulation in society. With respect to criminology, anomie theory was originally developed by Robert Merton. For Merton (1938), *anomie* referred not only to a sense of normlessness, as Durkheim proposed, but to a distinctive feature of American society. According to Merton, American society strongly emphasizes the desirability of material success and individual achievement. These goals are promoted as worthwhile—indeed, essential—objectives that everyone should pursue. At the same time, however, access to legitimate opportunities to achieve these goals is not equally available to everyone, and less emphasis is placed on achieving these objectives through legitimate means. The strong emphasis placed on the goals of individual material success, coupled with the limited access to and emphasis on legitimate means of achievement, means that goal-seeking behavior is not well regulated or channeled in American society. Hence, people look for other ways to get ahead and sometimes resort to criminal means. Merton used anomie to explain why some societies have higher crime rates than others and why crime is concentrated in the lower social classes (Merton, 1938).

Merton's theory has sometimes been criticized as being class biased because as it was originally formulated it ignored the crimes of the rich and powerful. However, the idea that the particular configuration of cultural values and structural opportunities found in American society influences our crime problem is not necessarily restricted to street crime. And even Merton (1964) acknowledged that anomie and strain could be features of upper-class life with his observation that "[l]ess often than one might believe is there room for repose at the top" (p. 221). This idea can be extended to white-collar and corporate crime as well (Messner and Rosenfeld, 2013; Vaughan, 1983). Indeed, in a thoughtful effort to extend Merton's anomie theory to corporate deviance, Nikos Passas (1990) argues that societies based on capitalistic economic principles have cultural and structural contradictions that promote widespread corporate deviance. Passas argues that a cultural emphasis on wealth and material success permeates all levels of the class structure and shapes both individual and corporate behavior. Although business corporations can have multiple goals, in capitalist economies the dominant goal is always profit maximization (Vaughan, 1983). Corporations compete with one another to maximize profits in a game that is never ending. There is no obvious stopping point at which enough is enough. Weak competitors may fall by the wayside, but new ones emerge to take their place. So, even companies that are leaders in their industries must always worry about potential competition. Hence, because of the competitive structure of capitalist economies, corporations are continually under pressure to do better.

Coupled with the cultural themes of success and endless striving are a cultural uncertainty and confusion about where the line between acceptable and unacceptable business behavior should be drawn. In this anomic environment, there is strong and constant pressure to engage in corporate deviance to achieve profit goals, and corporations often succumb to this pressure. In Passas's view, corporate crime and deviance are the unavoidable by-products of capitalistic economies. Other commentators agree (Messner and Rosenfeld, 2013).

Edward Gross takes a similar view of corporate deviance, but he focuses more on the culture and structure of organizations than on those of society as a whole (Gross, 1978). Gross argues that organizations are inherently criminogenic, because they are goal-directed entities, and their performance is evaluated according to their effectiveness in achieving their goals. Hence, they are continually under pressure to achieve. Further, organizations always confront competition and uncertainty in working toward their goals. The emphasis on performance combined with competition and uncertainty creates pressure to break rules and to achieve goals at all costs.

Gross hypothesizes that variation in organizational crime results from several sources. First, the degree of accountability of an organization or an organizational subunit is directly related to the likelihood of rule breaking. Organizations that are held accountable to specific criteria by which success in goal attainment can be judged are under greater pressure to perform than organizations whose success in goal attainment is not as strictly judged.

Second, pressure to engage in organizational crime is directly related to the objectivity of performance measures. Business corporations can be judged and compared against one another in terms of their profitability. Hence, their relative level of success in meeting this goal can be easily determined by others. For example, one very simple and objective measure of the relative success of a corporation is its "earnings per share." As the term implies, earnings per share can be roughly defined as the total earnings that a company has in a particular reporting period, which is usually a quarter of the year, divided by the total number of shares outstanding in the company. If a company earned a million dollars and there were ten million shares outstanding, then the company would have earned ten cents per share. In general, the higher a company's earnings per share, the better it is doing for shareholders. Hence, this number is important to investors and Wall Street analysts. Not surprisingly, companies try very hard to reach their expected earnings per share numbers every quarter. Failure to generate significant earnings per share may cause investors to move their money elsewhere, which from the perspective of the company is not good. This possibility puts company executives under a great deal of pressure to do whatever is necessary, including, as we have seen recently, engaging in fraudulent accounting practices, to meet Wall Street's expectations regarding earnings per share.

In contrast to for-profit corporations, many other types of organizations, such as hospitals, universities, and government bureaucracies, are not subject to such a brutally simple and objective measure of their success. Like all organizations, they are goal driven. It is more difficult to tell, however, exactly how well they are doing relative to their goals and to one another. Hence, we expect the leaders of these organizations to experience less pressure to break the law to achieve organizational goals than business executives.

Third, within corporations, the more a subunit interacts with the organizational environment, the more likely it is to deviate to achieve goals because of the uncertainty generated by the environment. The environment of an organization includes competitors, suppliers, government regulators, and customers. Thus, among manufacturers, we should expect to find more illegal or fraudulent activity in sales departments than in engineering departments. People in sales must interact regularly with competitors, suppliers, customers, and regulators. These environmental entities are a source of uncertainty. They can impede goal attainment and must, therefore, be controlled. Engineers, on the other hand, are relatively isolated from environmental contingencies and hence have less need to resort to fraudulent or criminal means to reduce environmental uncertainty.

Fourth and finally, pressure to engage in organizational crime is inversely related to goal displacement. If an organization that is threatened by lack of success in achieving its manifest goals can shift to other more attainable goals, then the pressure to deviate is lessened. The ability to displace goals is probably less available to private for-profit organizations than it is to nonprofit and governmental organizations. Consider, for example, the March of Dimes, an organization that was formed in 1938 to combat polio, a disease that had crippled thousands of young children. The organization funded research on polio and eventually, in 1952, Dr. Jonas Salk developed a vaccine that proved effective. By 1958, hundreds of millions of children had been vaccinated, and the disease was essentially defeated. So, what happened to the March of Dimes? Did the organization disband now that its goal had been accomplished? No. Rather, it began to focus on other childhood diseases and continues to do so today. This sort of goal displacement is more difficult if not impossible for profit-making business organizations. They either must make money or go out of business. The option of just doing something else is not open to them.

Altogether, accountability, objectivity of performance measures, environmental uncertainty, and flexibility in goal displacement influence the degree of pressure that organizations are under to deviate. And this pressure, while it may rise and fall, never disappears entirely. It is always there, always demanding that the organization surpass its performance goals.

As we noted in the preceding chapter, according to Gross, the individuals who are most likely to rise to the top of the organizational hierarchy are "organizational strainers." Strainers are ambitious, shrewd, and morally flexible. They are characterized by a strong desire for occupational achievement, the ability to spot patterns of organizational opportunity, and a willingness to treat organizational goals as their own and to change their moral stance as the situation demands. Organizations, thus, tend to be led by individuals for whom personal success is closely tied to the organization's success in meeting performance goals. Hence, they are especially susceptible to the emphasis on successful performance and to pressures to deviate in pursuit of success.

Control Theory

Another avenue of approach toward explaining white-collar crime takes control theory as its starting point (Hirschi, 1969). There are several variants of control theory, but all share in common the idea that deviance is natural and must be controlled by external social forces or internal predispositions. Travis Hirschi's social bond theory is the most well-known version of control theory. Social bond theory starts with the premise that delinquent acts are more likely to occur when an individual's bond to society is weak or broken. The social bond is composed of four interrelated elements: attachment to others, commitment to conventional lines of action, involvement in conventional activities, and belief in society's common value system. To the extent that these elements are strong, they restrain individuals from involvement in criminal behavior. But if they are weak, then the individual is free to engage in crime.

Although control theory is most often applied in the context of juvenile delinquency or ordinary street offending, it can also be used to explain white-collar crime by corporate executives (Lasley, 1988). To do so requires that the elements of the social bond be reconceptualized within the context of the corporation and its executives. It is the strength of the executive's bond to the corporation, as opposed to society in general, that regulates involvement in executive white-collar crime. James R. Lasley proposes four theorems regarding executive white-collar crime, which are straightforward translations of Hirschi's basic propositions regarding juvenile delinquency and the social bond (Lasley, 1988). First, the more strongly an executive is attached to other executives, coworkers, and the corporation, the less likely the executive is to commit white-collar crime. Second, the more strongly an executive is committed to corporate lines of action, the lower the frequency of executive white-collar crime. Third, the more strongly an executive is involved in corporate activity, the lower the frequency of white-collar offending. Fourth, the more strongly an executive believes in the rules of the corporation, the lower the frequency of white-collar offending. Lasley tested his theory with data drawn from a survey of 521 executives employed by a multinational automobile company. He found support for all of his theorems.

In the late 1980s and early 1990s, Travis Hirschi and Michael Gottfredson developed a new version of control theory that has been called self-control theory (Hirschi and Gottfredson, 1987a, 1987b). The basic premise of self-control theory is that crime and other forms of deviance result from the combination of low self-control and criminal opportunities. Low self-control is conceived to be a behavioral predisposition that inclines individuals to pursue their short-term self-interest with little regard for the long-term consequences of their actions or for the rights and feelings of other people. One's level of self-control is assumed to be established early in life and to remain relatively constant thereafter. Persons with low self-control are more likely to take advantage of criminal opportunities than persons with higher levels of self-control.

Hirschi and Gottfredson argue that self-control theory is a general theory of crime and that it applies to white-collar crime. Indeed, they argue that the pursuit of special theories of white-collar crime is misguided. Based on their theory of self-control, they contend that white-collar crime should be relatively rare compared with street crimes because persons with low self-control are unlikely to succeed in white-collar types of occupations. Hence, people with low self-control have limited opportunities to commit white-collar offenses. Conversely, people who are likely to succeed in white-collar occupations have high levels of self-control and hence are not likely to take advantage of the criminal opportunities that their occupations provide them. The few white-collar persons who do engage in white-collar crime are assumed to have less self-control than their similarly situated counterparts, though they may have more self-control than ordinary street criminals.

The ideas that white-collar crime is rare and that it can be explained by the same control-based factors as other crimes have been vigorously contested by many white-collar crime scholars (Benson and Moore,1992; Geis, 1996; Reed and Yeager, 1996; Steffensmeier, 1989; Yeager and Reed, 1998). There are three problems with self-control theory as applied to white-collar crime.

First, whether white-collar crime is rare is debatable for both empirical and theoretical reasons. Sutherland himself documented extensive lawbreaking among America's leading corporations. Decades after Sutherland's pioneering work, Clinard and Yeager (1980) also found evidence of widespread lawbreaking in corporate America. Finally, as the past decade has demonstrated, scandals involving business organizations, both big and small, and their executives continue to be uncovered. In short, there is considerable empirical evidence that lawbreaking in business is not uncommon. As one indicator of the extent of corporate deviance, consider the spate of restatements of corporate earnings in the late 1990s and early 2000s. Restatements soared after the exposure and criminal prosecution of the executives involved in accounting fraud at Enron, WorldCom, and a host of other major corporations. According to a report by the U.S. General Accounting Office (GAO) between January 1997 and June 2002, the annual rate of earnings restatements grew by 145 percent. During this 5-year period, about 10 percent of the companies listed on the NYSX, Amex, and Nasdaq stock exchanges filed earnings restatements because of accounting irregularities (U.S. General Accounting Office, 2002). While the GAO does not directly say that all of these restatements involved criminal activity, the strong implication from the report is that a notable proportion of the leaders of corporate America are not above breaking the rules to their advantage—at least until they think they might get caught. If we consider that accounting fraud is only one type of white-collar offense that companies can engage in, then the figure of 10 percent becomes even more notable.

Other research suggests that the GAO may not be far off in estimating that one out of ten corporations engaged in accounting fraud between 1997 and 2002. Economists Dyck, Morse, and Zingales (2013) took advantage of the natural experiment that arose after the collapse of Arthur Andersen in 2002. Recall that Arthur Andersen handled the auditing for Enron and was convicted of accounting fraud for its role in Enron's schemes. As one of the big five accounting firms in the world, Andersen had many large corporate clients. When Andersen collapsed, these companies had to find new auditors. Dyck, Morse, and Zingales theorized that the new auditors would be especially vigilant in looking for signs of corporate fraud and would want to clean house to avoid the fate that befell Arthur Andersen. Using sophisticated statistical techniques that looked at the rate of fraud detection both before and after the new auditors took over, Dyck and colleagues estimate that the "probability of a company engaging in fraud in any given year is 14.5%." The researchers arrived at this estimate by comparing the rate at which fraud was detected by Arthur Andersen before it collapsed with the rate that fraud was detected among former Andersen clients by the new more vigilant auditors. The researchers assumed that the new auditors detected all the fraud that was occurring among former Andersen clients. The new higher detection rate can be used to estimate the overall rate of fraud among all public companies. Again, as with the GAO, this estimate of the pervasiveness of corporate fraud and wrongdoing applies only to accounting fraud. There is no telling how high the percentage would rise if we could somehow count all of the various offenses available to corporations. Clearly, however, it would not be in the range that we would ordinarily call *rare*.

In addition, there are theoretical reasons for believing that as extensive as the empirical record is, it may nevertheless greatly understate the amount of white-collar lawbreaking. This is because there are fundamental differences between white-collar crime and other forms of crime that affect the rate of detection. We will develop this theme more fully in the next chapter, but we briefly introduce it here. When an ordinary street crime is committed, such as, for example, a robbery, burglary, auto theft, or assault, it is obvious that an offense has occurred. The offender may not be known, but the fact that there has been an offense is plain to see. Some sort of physical evidence is present. However, many white-collar crimes are not obvious in this way. They leave no obvious physical evidence such as a missing car, broken window, or bloodied body. White-collar offenders use deception to commit their offenses. If they are successful, then the fact that an offense has occurred may never be known, not even by the victim. For example, think back to the doctor whom we discussed in the first chapter. If the victim in this case simply accepts the doctor's recommendations regarding further tests, then who will ever discover that the doctor committed fraud by knowingly ordering tests that were medically unnecessary? The fundamental problem here is that for crimes that are non-self-revealing, it is very difficult, if not impossible, ever to figure out the true number of offenses.

A second problem with self-control theory involves the concept of self-control. The theory assumes that self-control is always exercised for conforming or socially accepted ends. In other words, the theory assumes that people with high self-control always do the right thing. Yet, there is no logical reason why self-control and the abilities associated with it (intelligence, foresight, and persistence) could not be used to plan and execute a complicated criminal scheme (Tittle, 1991). Why assume that people who have self-discipline are always nice people?

Finally, there is a problem with how criminal opportunities are conceptualized in the theory. Criminal opportunities are conceived as simple obvious things, such as an unguarded purse in an office or a car in a parking lot with the keys in it. The basic idea is that criminal opportunities arise whenever a criminally inclined person has access to some sort of object that he or she would like to have. In technical terms, a criminal opportunity consists of a suitable target and a lack of capable guardianship (Cohen and Felson, 1979). In self-control theory, it is assumed that targets such as the purse or the car are intrinsically attractive or desirable, and the only thing holding us back from trying to get them is our level of self-control. But is this really true? We would suggest that the attractiveness of a target depends at least in part on the potential offender's situation (i.e., on factors in his or her life that are independent of his or her level of self-control). For example, suppose a person with low self-control sees a car with keys in it in a parking lot. Further suppose that the offender doesn't have his own car and he really needs to get across town quickly because he is late for a date with his girlfriend. Will he steal the car? It seems pretty likely. But what happens if we change one fact? Suppose that the offender has a car. Even though he is still saddled with low self-control and late for his date, will he steal the one with the keys in it? Now, it seems less likely than before. An offender with a car simply has less motivation to commit auto theft than an offender without a car, regardless of level of self-control. Whether a criminal opportunity is viewed as more or less attractive, then, depends in part on the external situation of the offender. Recognizing this feature of criminal opportunities is particularly important for white-collar crime, because, as we will demonstrate later, situational factors can be important sources of motivation for white-collar crime. For example, would the executives at Enron have bothered to run the risk of accounting fraud if the company really was making a lot of money?

Rational Choice Theory

Another theoretical perspective that has been applied to white-collar crime is rational choice theory (Paternoster and Simpson, 1993; Shover and Hochstetler, 2006). Rational choice theory assumes that all actors are self-interested and make decisions about whether to engage in criminal or conventional behavior according to an assessment of costs and benefits associated with each line of behavior. In simplified terms, the theory posits that rational actors will choose to engage in crime rather than noncrime when the perceived net benefits of crime (i.e., benefits minus costs) are larger than the perceived net benefits of noncrime. Both benefits and costs have subjective and objective dimensions. A subjective cost of crime might be feelings of guilt or fear of apprehension, while a subjective benefit of crime would be the thrill and excitement of getting away with something illegal. An objective cost of crime would be formal punishment by the criminal justice system, while an objective benefit would be the gains made from the illegal act.

Like other traditional criminological theories, the rational choice perspective has been applied most often to ordinary street offenders. Paternoster and Simpson (1993), however, have explicated a rational choice theory of the decision to commit corporate crime (see also Shover and Hochstetler, 2006). They call their approach a *subjective utility theory of offending*. It focuses on individual and organizational benefits and costs as they are subjectively perceived by individuals. Hence, their rational choice theory is aimed at individual decision makers rather than the corporation as a whole. According to their theory, the individual's decision to commit a corporate crime or violate a regulatory rule involves a series of factors. To calculate the potential costs of corporate crime, actors subjectively estimate the certainty and severity of formal legal sanctions, the certainty and severity of informal sanctions (for example, discovery and subsequent rejection or ostracism by friends, business associates, or family members), and the certainty and importance of loss of self-respect. Actors also consider the benefits of corporate crime, which include the perceived benefits of noncompliance (i.e., higher profits, greater market share, or some other organizationally relevant goal) and the perceived cost of rule compliance (i.e., expenses that follow from complying with regulatory standards). Paternoster and Simpson argue that in addition to these standard rational choice variables, the strength of the actor's moral beliefs, whether he or she perceives rule enforcers as legitimate and fair, the characteristics of the potential criminal event, and prior offending by the person also influence the likelihood of offending.

Another attempt at applying the choice perspective to white-collar crime has been made by Neal Shover and Andrew Hochstetler (2006). The theory developed by Shover and Hochstetler, however, focuses less on the individual decision maker and more on the economic and political conditions that influence opportunities for white-collar and corporate crime. They argue that in order to understand why white-collar crime flourishes, we need to pay attention to the supply of "lure" and the lack of "credible oversight." We discuss each of these provocative concepts in turn.

The concept of "lure" is not formally defined by Shover and Hochstetler. They describe it simply as "arrangements or situations that turn heads" (Shover and Hochstetler, 2006, p. 27) and note that it is not the same as "criminal opportunity" (p. 68). However, their discussion of lure suggests that it should be thought of as any situation in which people can enrich themselves by (1) gaining privileged and unjustified access directly to financial resources or (2) gaining access to some means by which to enhance their own financial interests through the exploitation of others. As an example of the first form of lure, consider federal health care initiatives, such as Medicare and Medicaid. As we discuss in detail in Chapter 5, these programs handle literally billions of dollars, and these dollars can be powerfully alluring to people. By virtue of their positions in the health care industry, physicians and many others associated with the health care profession have opportunities to obtain money through fraud. In short, because of the tremendous amounts of money spent on healthcare via these government programs, they lure or attract criminal entrepreneurs. The second type of lure can be illustrated by the corporate exploitation of illegal immigrants who come to America in search of a better life. Because undocumented immigrants cannot go to authorities to complain about horrendously unsafe working conditions or scandalously low pay, they can be very attractive as potential employees in some industries. Employers can exploit them with little fear of legal consequences.

As another example of lure, consider the opportunities to make an easy dollar that arise after every natural disaster, such as Hurricane Katrina, Hurricane Sandy, or the Haitian earthquake. In their efforts to help those who are afflicted, government agencies and nongovernmental organizations often pour millions of dollars into disaster relief programs. Because of the urgency of the need, these programs focus on getting help to people quickly without asking a lot of questions or checking carefully into the legitimacy of relief claims. For the unscrupulous, this is an ideal situation. Money is being handed out with few questions asked. Disaster relief fraud is now a well-known and perennial form of white-collar crime (National White-Collar Crime Center, 2009).

According to Shover and Hochstetler (2006, p. 76), "Lure becomes criminal opportunity in the absence of credible oversight." Oversight refers to the attention that others (such as customers, law enforcement officials, or regulators) pay to a person's or an organization's activity and to the ability of those others to impose some sort of negative consequence when they observe misconduct. Oversight can be generated either by private sources or through the state. Private oversight arises through such mechanisms as civil lawsuits or whistleblowers. Private parties, such as customers, for example, can file class action lawsuits against companies that harm them in some fashion. The threat of a lawsuit serves as a check on the misbehavior of private enterprises. Similarly, a whistleblower can expose illegal or unethical conduct and thus bring unwanted attention to corporate wrongdoers. Although private oversight can play an important role in the control of white-collar crime and in the calculus of white-collar offenders, it has limitations and is by no means perfect. Hence, in modern industrial and post-industrial societies, the state is called upon to provide additional oversight. State oversight occurs through criminalization, lawsuits brought by the government, and regulation. As we discuss more fully in Chapter 9, the state attempts to assert oversight and control over white-collar crime by criminalizing, regulating, or filing civil lawsuits over activities that it deems harmful, but it does so with only limited and often only temporary success.

Taken together, both private and state oversight expose potential white-collar offenders to the possibility that their illegal activities will come to light and be sanctioned. According to the rational choice perspective, if this possibility is perceived by potential offenders to be low, then the credibility of oversight is low and the choice to engage in white-collar crime becomes correspondingly more attractive. Like many white-collar crime scholars, Shover and Hochstetler (2006) argue that there is a lack of credible oversight in the United States and indeed throughout the modern world, creating conditions in which white-collar crime can flourish.

Of the theories presented here, rational choice, or simply "choice theory," as it is sometimes called, is the one most compatible with our opportunity perspective. It explicitly recognizes opportunity as an important cause and necessary ingredient of crime. It suggests that in order to understand patterns in white-collar crime, we need to pay attention to how changes in the organization and functioning of the legitimate business world can affect opportunities for white-collar crime (Shover and Hochstetler, 2006). Indeed, as Neal Shover and Andrew Hochstetler have argued, new opportunities for fraud and embezzlement have emerged over the past few decades because of the expansion of government programs, the revolution in financial services, the growth of communications technology, and the rise of the global economy.

Integrated Theory

Criminologists have begun to explore ways to integrate standard criminological theories, such as differential association, anomie, and control theories, in hopes of providing more comprehensive explanations of street crime. John Braithwaite (1989) has extended this line of thought to white-collar crime and organizational crime. He argues that to understand the causes of organizational crime, we need to integrate the insights of strain, labeling, subculture, and control theories. From strain theory, he draws the premise that failure to achieve highly valued goals, such as material success, creates pressure or strain to deviate. To relieve strain, actors, including corporate actors, may resort to crime as an alternate means of achieving success. Whether actors do resort to crime depends in part on the availability of illegitimate means for achieving the blocked goal. Illegitimate means are made available through deviant subcultures. With respect to corporate crime, business subcultures can transmit knowledge of how organizations and their leaders may successfully violate the law. In addition, deviant subcultures may attempt to force members to conform to the subculture's values and expectations. Thus, strain, the availability of subculturally endorsed illegitimate means and enforced conformity to deviant subcultural values are criminogenic forces that foster corporate crime.

Opposition to these criminogenic forces comes from social controls within the organization and from shaming imposed on offenders by the larger society. Drawing from control theory, Braithwaite argues that corporations can reduce the likelihood that their members will violate the law by strengthening internal controls against illegal behavior. This can be accomplished when organizational leaders promote pro-social values, socialize all corporate members to these values, and create strong internal control units to monitor corporate compliance with the law.

Braithwaite introduces the idea of differential shaming to explain how shaming by society may either promote or retard corporate crime. Shaming, which in the case of business corporations is carried out primarily by regulatory agencies, may be either stigmatizing or reintegrative. When actors are stigmatized, they are treated as outcasts, and their involvement in deviance is treated as an indication of a true deviant inner character. Reintegrative shaming, on the other hand, is focused on the evil of the deed rather than the evil of the actor. Those who administer the shame attempt to maintain bonds of respect with the offender, and they try to reintegrate the offender back into the social whole after shaming is terminated. Braithwaite argues that stigmatizing shaming tends to create resistance to change in actors and to push them ever more deeply into their deviant subculture. Hence, stigmatizing shaming is counterproductive. It

actually promotes rather than deters corporate crime. Reintegrative shaming deters crime because it clearly announces the wrongfulness of the act
but then attempts to make the actor feel like a respected member of society, a member who has a vested interest in conforming to society's rules.

Another integrated theory has been proposed by Coleman who argues
that white-collar crime results from "a coincidence of appropriate motivation and opportunity" (Coleman, 1987). Motivation refers to symbolic
constructions that define certain goals and activities as desirable. In the
case of white-collar crime, it is especially important that the offender be
able to define his or her behavior so that it is socially acceptable. Hence,
white-collar offenders use neutralizations and rationalizations to justify
or excuse behavior that is illegal. For example, business executives will
complain that laws and regulations are unfair or unnecessary and that they
interfere too much in the operation of the free market. Breaking a law
that is unfair, unnecessary, and counterproductive is more acceptable than
violating a standard that everyone agrees is just and necessary for society's
survival. According to Coleman, the neutralizations that offenders use to
justify their crimes are rooted in what he calls "the culture of competition."

The culture of competition refers to a complex of beliefs common in
capitalistic societies that hold that the pursuit of wealth and success are
the central goals of human endeavor. The idea here is that striving to make
a profit, to get ahead, to be successful, to be the best is the most appropriate and meaningful way to approach life. As autonomous individuals,
we are each responsible for our own success, and it is appropriate to try
to get ahead by whatever means are available. In other words, chasing
the American dream is what we are supposed to do, and our success in
doing so is a measure of our intrinsic worth as human beings (Messner
and Rosenfeld, 2013). In Coleman's view, then, the culture of competition
provides a source of rationalizations and neutralizations that white-collar
offenders use as motivations for illegal behavior.

The other pillar in Coleman's theoretical framework is opportunity. An
opportunity is a potential course of action that is made available by a
particular set of social conditions and that the actor recognizes as being
available to him or her. Opportunities vary in their attractiveness according to four factors: (1) the size of the gain to be obtained by the illegal
act, (2) the risk of detection and punishment, (3) the compatibility of the

act with the offender's own beliefs and values, and (4) the availability of other opportunities. In short, a white-collar crime opportunity will be considered attractive from the offender's point of view when it promises a worthwhile gain, involves little chance of being caught, does not violate the offender's own personal standards of behavior, and appears more likely to accomplish the offender's objectives than any other course of action.

Exactly how white-collar crime opportunities are distributed is difficult to say with certainty. Coleman identifies four factors that influence the distribution of opportunity: law and enforcement, industries, organizations, and occupations. The law obviously determines what is criminalized, and the level of resources allocated to enforcing the law determines the relative risk of detection and punishment. As Coleman and others have noted, business organizations go to great lengths to try to prevent the criminalization of their activities, and if that fails, they try hard to limit the size and resources of enforcement agencies.

A second factor that shapes opportunities is the structure of an industry. For example, antitrust violations should be more common in industries that are heavily concentrated, that is, in which there are a few large producers, than in industries where there are many small producers. It is harder to organize and control a conspiracy involving many participants than one involving only a few. The research, however, on market structure and the prevalence of antitrust violations is mixed (Coleman, 1987, p. 428). There are other characteristics of industries that influence the types of opportunities for white-collar crime found in them. We discuss some of these further in Chapters 5 and 6, which treat specific types of white-collar crime.

Organizations themselves shape or provide opportunities. Whether an organization is highly profitable or not so highly profitable can influence how organizational members view potential illegal acts. The types of controls that an organization has in place to deter illegal activities by its members influence opportunities, as may the structure of the organization, in particular whether it is multidivisional.

Finally, occupations present different types of opportunities. For example, attorneys, physicians, financial advisers, and other independent professionals all have opportunities to take advantage of their clients that are built into their professions. The work of professionals often occurs without the direct supervision of the client (Shapiro, 1990). This situation gives unethical professionals the freedom to pursue their own interests at the expense of their clients. Occupational opportunities also vary according to one's position or status in an organization. For example, consider bribery of government officials. Many people work for the government, but most do not work in positions where they are likely to be offered bribes or be able to solicit bribes. Whether a government worker is likely to be offered bribes depends on the economic value of the services that the person controls (Coleman, 1987, p. 433). People in high positions in government, such as Congressional Representatives, exert control over enormous sums of money in the form of valuable government contracts. Hence, it should not be surprising that they are lobbied and cajoled by corporations for preferential treatment and are regularly caught selling their services to the highest bidder (Rosoff, Pontell, and Tillman, 2013, pp. 427–435).

To summarize, Coleman's theory works on multiple levels—individual, occupational, organizational, industrial, societal, and cultural. White-collar crime occurs when actors with suitable motivations confront attractive opportunities. Motivations for white-collar crime are rooted in the culture of competition and are disseminated via organizational and occupational subcultures. The attractiveness of opportunities depends on their monetary value as compared to other courses of action, level of risk, and compatibility with the potential offender's beliefs and values. Opportunities are distributed differently across industries, organizations, and occupations.

Greed or Fear?

Most theories of white-collar crime implicitly or explicitly assume that the pursuit of individual material success or some kind of business advancement is the core motivation behind white-collar crime. White-collar offenders are assumed to be greedy and egocentric. But recent research suggests another motivational route to white-collar crime (Benson and Kerley, 2000; Benson and Moore, 1992; Weisburd and Waring, 2001; Wheeler, 1992). White-collar crime may result not only from the drive for material success but out of a fear of losing what one already has. Some individuals may become involved in white-collar offenses because they fear that if they do not, they are at risk of losing their station in life. For people accustomed to high social status and the material comforts of a middle-class lifestyle, the prospect of losing it all because of a downturn in the economy or a miscalculation in a business transaction may provoke strong pressure to deviate in defense. For example, someone who runs a small business may be quite willing to abide by the law in return for a comfortable but not extravagant standard of living. However, if the business is threatened by competition or a downturn in the economy, the same individual may feel that the only option is to break the law in order to survive. For example, a businessman who ran a small construction firm got involved in a check-kiting scheme because he was afraid of losing his business. He argued that his offense was motivated by his fear of losing what he had worked so hard to get (Benson, 1985, p. 598):

> I was faced with the choice of all of a sudden, and I mean now, closing the doors or doing something else to keep that business open. . . . I'm not going to tell you that this wouldn't have happened if I'd had time to think it over, because I think it probably would have. You're sitting there with a dying patient. You are going to try to keep him alive.

Thus, fear of failure as well as the drive for success may impel individuals to engage in white-collar crime. Indeed, the fear of failure may be a unique motivational cause of white-collar crime.

Summary

Despite their differences, the theories reviewed above share one thing in common. They all focus in some way on the offender's motivation for committing white-collar crime or some aspect of his or her personal situation or psychological makeup. Sutherland stressed the cultural norms and attitudes that prevail in the business world. Business executives are indoctrinated to these norms and attitudes and come to see illegal behavior as somehow an acceptable and necessary part of doing business. Anomie theory focuses on the widespread cultural emphases on competition and material success. These cultural emphases drive individual business executives and their organizations to constantly seek out innovative, often illegal, ways to get ahead and stay ahead. Rational choice theory directs attention to the offender's calculus regarding the costs and benefits of illegal versus legal behavior. It is assumed that everyone, including white-collar offenders, is motivated to act in accordance with what they perceive to be their own best interests. Although control theories do not posit that any sort of special motivation is involved in white-collar crime, they do nevertheless draw attention to the offender's personal situation or his or her psychological makeup. It is the offender's weak social bond or lack of self-control that leads to offending. Integrated theories combine features from different theories but with the same overall objective of explaining why people break the law. Thus, in all of these theories, the focus is strongly on offenders and the factors that push or pull them toward offending.

Focusing on offenders is, of course, perfectly appropriate. Indeed, it has been standard practice throughout the history of criminology. We need to understand what causes some people to violate the law while others conform to its demands. However, motivations or personal characteristics by themselves do not explain why offenders violate the law at one time but not another, or in one place but not another. In other words, the motivations and personal characteristics of offenders cannot explain why they commit particular crimes at particular times and places. There is another factor that comes into play, and that factor is the presence or absence of a criminal opportunity.

Without some kind of criminal opportunity, even the most habitual career criminal cannot commit a crime. Bank robbers cannot rob banks if there are no banks available, and bank embezzlers cannot embezzle if they do not have a job in a bank. Banks provide opportunities for both bank robbers and bank embezzlers. Thus, to understand crime requires an analysis of both offenders and their opportunities. In the next chapter, we take up the topic of white-collar criminal opportunities.

Of course, we are not the first to recognize that opportunity plays a role in white-collar offending. All of the theoretical approaches that we have discussed in this chapter have something to say about opportunity, but the approach toward opportunity is more broad-based and less focused than the one advocated here. For example, Coleman explicitly incorporates opportunity into his theory, but, for him, opportunity is found in the very structure of capitalism and not so much in the detailed characteristics of industries and occupations.

4
EXPLAINING WHITE-COLLAR CRIME
The Opportunity Perspective

Criminologists spend an enormous amount of time and energy investigating criminals. They ask all sorts of questions about them. What kind of person is likely to become a criminal? Why do they do it? When do they start? When do they stop? How many crimes do they commit? What kind of crimes do they commit? What are their families like? Where do they live? What kind of friends do they have? The list could go on. Of course, all of these are important questions. We hope that by answering them we will eventually understand why individual involvement in crime seems to vary so much. For a lot of reasons, we need to know as much as possible about the factors that affect involvement in crime. Indeed, throughout this book, we ask and try to answer many of these questions in regard to the people who commit white-collar crimes. Nevertheless, it is important to keep in mind that knowing about criminals is not the same as knowing about crime. People often confuse the problem of explaining crime with the problem of explaining criminals, but the two should be kept separate (Gottfredson and Hirschi, 1990). Crime is an event, something that happens. A criminal, on the other hand, is an individual who behaves in a certain way, a way that society has defined as unacceptable. Explaining why people behave one way or another is not the same as explaining why a particular event happens at a particular time and in a particular place.

To understand why a particular crime occurs at a particular time and place, it is necessary to pay attention not only to the person who commits the crime but to the situation in which the person is located. Obviously, it is important to know about an offender's motives or reasons for committing an offense. But suppose that we know that an offender has a strong motive to, say, steal money. The desire for money, however, does not explain why he robs a liquor store as opposed to a bank that sits next door to the liquor store. Both places have the money that the offender needs. Why choose one instead of the other? Of course, there are any number of reasons why an offender might choose a liquor store over a bank. Banks often have security guards who have guns. Banks have video cameras that take pictures. If it happens to be after business hours and the bank is closed, the chances of breaking in and stealing anything are nil. Nowadays, bank vaults are virtually impregnable. Liquor stores, on the other hand, are open for longer hours than banks. They may be staffed by only one person. They may not have security cameras, and best of all, the money is right there in the cash register. So, if you look at the situation from the offender's point of view, the liquor store presents a better *criminal opportunity* than the bank, especially if the criminal is working alone and in a hurry.

Understanding Criminal Opportunities

Criminal opportunities are now recognized as an important cause of all crime (Felson, 2002). Without an opportunity, there cannot be a crime. In the past few decades, the study of crime has increasingly focused on the situational and ecological factors that create or facilitate opportunities for street crime (Clarke, 1983; Cohen and Felson, 1979; Felson, 2002). Opportunities also are important causes of white-collar crime. However, as we will show, the opportunity structures of many white-collar crimes are dramatically different from those for ordinary street crimes. These differences create special difficulties for control, but they also provide new openings for control.

What exactly is a criminal opportunity? According to routine activity theory, a criminal opportunity comprises two elements: a *suitable target* and a *lack of capable guardianship*. A target can be a person or some kind of property. What makes a person or a piece of property suitable as a target for crime? That depends on a lot of factors. Without exploring all of them, we can identify some of the main considerations. From the offender's point of view, the attractiveness or suitability of a person as a target depends on that person's vulnerability and in some cases on the person's symbolic or emotional value to the offender. All other things being equal, we assume that violent offenders would rather attack someone who is not well equipped to fight back (i.e., someone who is vulnerable). As one researcher puts it, big people hit little people (Felson, 1996). In addition, we assume that violent offenders would rather go after someone they have a grudge against as opposed to just any random person. In other words, it seems likely that it is more fun and rewarding to beat up someone you are mad at than someone whom you don't have strong feelings about one way or the other. Thus, the main factors that determine the suitability of people as targets are vulnerability and emotional value.

There are also many factors that can make one piece of property more suitable than another. Property becomes attractive to an offender if it is portable, valuable, and fungible. The importance of value for property offenders is obvious. So, we won't dwell on it. Portability is important because if you are going to steal something, then by definition you have to move it from one place to another. That being the case, a DVD player is a lot easier to steal than a refrigerator. Lastly, there is fungibility. Something is fungible when it can be exchanged for something else. Money is very fungible. You can exchange it for just about anything. Property offenders look for things that are fungible, because ordinarily they are not interested in using the things they steal. Rather, they want to sell them for money. Thus, smart thieves try to steal things that are easy to exchange for money (i.e., easy to sell). For example, suppose you need some cash and you break into a house to steal something. Inside, you have your choice of a valuable painting or a brand new DVD player. The painting may actually be worth more than the DVD player, but which is going to be easier to sell to someone else? To sum up, all other things being equal, thieves look for property that is valuable, easy to carry, and easy to sell for money or exchange for something else such as drugs or alcohol.

The other component of a criminal opportunity is capable guardianship, or rather the lack of capable guardianship. You may think of capable guardianship as a big strong person who can defend you or your property, but the term *guardianship* is meant to be interpreted in a much broader way. It is just a convenient figure of speech. By capable guardianship, we mean anything that can either physically prevent the offender from getting to the target or that can make the offender decide it is too risky to go after the target. Guardianship takes two main forms: blocking access and surveillance.

Techniques of guardianship that can physically prevent an offender from getting to a target include walls, locks, and bars on windows as well as anything else that has the effect of blocking the offender's access to the target. It makes sense to think that violent offenders look for victims who are easy to get at—that is, people who are out in the open or near the offender rather than people who are hiding behind closed and locked doors. Similarly, property offenders can be prevented from carrying out their intentions if their access to their desired target is blocked by a wall of concrete or a barred window. Of course, offenders can always try to break through whatever it is that is blocking their access. But the general point remains: Blocking access makes it more difficult for an offender to carry out his or her intentions, and this makes the criminal opportunity less attractive to the offender.

Besides having their access to a target blocked, offenders can also be put off if they feel that it is too risky to attack a particular target. By risky we mean the risk to the offender of being observed or otherwise detected either while committing the crime or afterward. So, if a target, be it a person or a piece of property, is under surveillance by a police officer, a neighbor, a security camera, an alarm system, or anything else, potential offenders have to take this into account. Surveillance increases the likelihood that the offender's actions will be noticed, and accordingly, the offender faces an increased risk of being caught. Thus, surveillance reduces the attractiveness of criminal opportunities. This is why, of course, security cameras are now ubiquitous in retail establishments, other buildings, and increasingly, public streets.

As ways of thinking about criminal opportunities, the concepts "suitable target" and "lack of guardianship" have obvious similarities to the concepts "lure" and "lack of credible oversight" articulated by Shover and Hochstetler (2006), but they are not identical. For street crime, a suitable target is usually a concrete physical object such as a piece of jewelry, or cash in a register, or a person. In contrast, lure refers less to physical objects and more to particular types of situations in which a person can take advantage of certain categories of economic transactions in such a way as to enrich himself or herself without any kind of physical object being involved and without necessarily stealing from or interacting with another person. Likewise, guardianship and credible oversight are related but not identical concepts. Guardianship usually involves some effort to directly block access to a target or some way of putting the target under direct and constant surveillance. As we will discuss later in Chapters 9, 10, and 11, when we explicate the problem of controlling white-collar crime in detail, oversight usually does not involve blocking access to or directly watching some potential target. Rather, it involves developing mechanisms to review the activities of business men and women in order to ascertain whether their behavior complies with legal or ethical standards. For example, to prevent burglary we lock our doors and install alarm systems. To prevent insider trading we review the stock trading activities of corporate executives to determine whether they were or were not based on inside information. In regard to white-collar crime, lure and the credibility of oversight may be the most appropriate ways to conceptualize criminal opportunities, because white-collar crimes almost always represent perversions of legitimate economic activities.

The Nature and Techniques of White-Collar Crime

Criminal opportunities are exploited through the use of particular techniques. That is, in order to take advantage of a criminal opportunity, the offender often has to know how to use a particular technique. Indeed, sometimes it is the availability of a technique that determines whether a situation presents a criminal opportunity or not. For example, an auto thief who knows how to hot-wire a car has many more opportunities to steal cars than does a thief who does not know the technique of hot-wiring. The unskilled thief must spend time looking for cars with the keys in them, while the skilled thief can go after any car that is unguarded. Thus, in order to understand criminal opportunities, we have to learn about the techniques that offenders use to commit particular types of crimes. This is especially true in regard to white-collar types of crimes. The techniques of white-collar crime are distinctly different from the techniques of other sorts of offenses. Thus, it is time now to explore the matter of techniques in a more systematic fashion.

First, exactly what is a "technique"? The dictionary definition of technique that is most appropriate for our purposes here is "a method for accomplishing some desired aim." Thus, a technique is a way to get something done. Obviously, depending on what you want to get done, there may be different techniques that you can use. For example, a burglar's technique for breaking into a house might involve carefully drilling a hole in a door, then using a needlepoint saw to enlarge the hole, then reaching inside to unlock the door, and then sneaking in to steal silver or jewelry. Most burglars don't do this. They use a simpler technique: Kick the door hard until the doorframe or the lock breaks, then dash in and grab whatever is out in the open, looks valuable, and is small enough to carry.

There are several important points to notice about this example. First, regardless which technique was used, the burglar employed physical means (drilling a hole or kicking in the door) to accomplish the goal. Second, the burglar was somewhere he or she was not supposed to be and doing something that is obviously and clearly illegal. Third, the burglar was in direct contact with the victim or target of the offense, which in this case would be the homeowner's property. Fourth, the victim is a specific identifiable individual—in this case, the homeowner. Finally, the illegal activities that made up this offense (kicking in the door, grabbing the stuff, running away from the house) took place at a discrete point in time and space. We can specify exactly where and when the event happened: 6990 Bramble Hill Drive on Tuesday, May 18, 2014, at 2:30 PM.

Many conventional street crimes are like this. They involve physical actions. There is direct contact between the offender and a specific target or victim of the illegal activities. They are obviously illegal while they are occurring, and they occur at particular places and times.

White-collar offenses, on the other hand, often are not like this. They do not involve physical actions except in the most trivial sense that we move our bodies or parts of our bodies whenever we do anything. The physical activities of white-collar crime are very simple common-place activities such as writing, or talking on the phone, or entering information into a computer. Unlike our burglar, white-collar offenders do things differently. They often have a perfect right to be where they are and where the offense occurs. The offense itself may not involve any direct physical contact between the offender and the victim or the target of the offense. Finally, the offense typically will not be obviously illegal while it is occurring. In short, many white-collar offenses manifest the following three properties: (1) The offender has *legitimate access* to the location in which the crime is committed, (2) the offender is *spatially separated* from the victim, and (3) the offender's actions have a *superficial appearance of legitimacy*.

To illustrate how these properties come together in a particular example of white-collar crime, consider the recent and famous case of Bernie Madoff, who orchestrated a Ponzi scheme that resulted in losses of billions of dollars to thousands of individuals (Henriques, 2011). Madoff was the founder of Bernard L. Madoff Investment Securities, a company that received money from individuals, pension funds, and other types of organizations for purposes of investment. Like all investment advisors, Madoff promised to invest money for his clients. He claimed to have a secret and highly sophisticated strategy that would produce consistent returns over long periods of time. If you were accepted by Madoff as a client (and he did not accept everyone), you were going to see your money grow more reliably than anywhere else. For many years, this was exactly what his clients experienced. They invested money and received periodic statements reflecting how much their money had grown during good times and bad times in the market. To his clients and to Wall Street, Madoff seemed to be a financial wizard. Unfortunately for his clients, however, Madoff was not a wizard but a fraud. He was running a very sophisticated Ponzi scheme, and the "profits" that clients thought they were making existed only on paper. Madoff would take funds from one investor to pay off other investors. The scheme worked for years, until 2008, when too many of his clients demanded their money back at the same time and he did not have the funds available to cover all of the redemptions. His scheme collapsed and billions were lost. Madoff was arrested and eventually convicted of investment fraud. Madoff's scheme illustrates the properties of white-collar crime. First, he had legitimate access to other people's money.

Indeed, they willingly gave it to him to invest on their behalf. They did so because he had a superficial appearance of legitimacy, as a famous investor on Wall Street. Finally, as for spatial separation, most of Madoff's clients never actually saw or met him, as they were spread across the country and around the globe.

Of course, not all white-collar crimes manifest all of these characteristics. Some, for example, do involve direct contact between the offender and the victim. White-collar crimes come in a bewilderingly large variety. Nevertheless, it is important to try to identify the key characteristics that appear in many white-collar offenses. They are important because they affect how white-collar offenses are carried out as well as our ability to develop effective prevention strategies.

So, how do white-collar offenders carry out their crimes? They use three main techniques. In order of importance, the techniques are: (1) *deception*, (2) the *abuse of trust*, and (3) *concealment and conspiracy*. For analytical purposes, we consider each of these techniques separately but, in the real world, more than one of them may be involved in any particular white-collar offense.

The primary technique used by white-collar offenders is deception. It is the master modus operandi of white-collar offenders. Indeed, the other two techniques that we will be discussing—abuse of trust and concealment—are in a sense simply very important ways in which deception may be accomplished or situations in which it is particularly easy to deceive others.

Deception is a commonplace word, and we do not need to make it too complicated. However, because it is such a familiar word, it is easy to gloss over some of the conceptual subtleties that are involved in deception. For the study of white-collar crime, it is important to think carefully about exactly what deception is and how it is accomplished. Deception occurs when one person misleads another by making things appear other than as they really are. Or, more formally, we could say that deception occurs whenever one person or organization causes another to experience a discrepancy between appearance and reality (Rue, 1994, p. 84). From the point of view of the person who is doing the deceiving, deception is "the advantageous distortion of perceived reality" (Bowyer, 1982). On the other hand, for the person on the receiving end, the distortion of reality definitely is not advantageous.

Deception is always a relational phenomenon. That is, it is a characteristic that describes the nature of the interaction between two entities—the deceiver and the deceived (Rue, 1994). The relational nature of deception complicates its analysis. In order to be sure that deception has occurred, we have to know something about the intentions of the person or organization that is creating the deception. We also have to know something about the perceptions of the person or organization that we think is the object of the other's attempt at deception. Deception occurs only when two conditions are met. First, one person must deliberately intend to mislead another about the nature of reality, and second, the other person must be misled about reality, must misperceive it, that is. As we will see later, the relational nature of deception makes it difficult to control the offenses which use this technique.

Deception requires a deliberate attempt by one person to mislead another into doing something that the person would not do if he or she had all the facts (i.e., if he or she hadn't been deceived). We say deception requires one person's misleading another only for rhetorical convenience. Obviously, deceptions can be carried out by groups of people working together to take advantage of individuals or groups of other people. But to continue with an example, suppose the owner of a business applies for a loan from a bank and, on the loan application, the owner deliberately overstates her financial assets and understates her financial liabilities. She does this in order to make her financial status appear better than it really is in the hope that the bank loan officer will approve her loan application. Obviously, she is engaging or attempting to engage in deception. She is also committing the crime of making false statements on a loan application.

Deception by virtue of false or misleading statements is a common technique of white-collar crime. It underlies all consumer fraud-type cases, not to mention a good bit of most advertising. There is no shortage of examples of false and misleading advertising by major manufacturers in which the goal is to convince consumers that a particular product is a better value than its competitors. Although examples of false and misleading advertising can probably be found in almost every industry and trade, many of the most well known and publicized cases involve the major corporations that manufacture or process food items, pharmaceuticals, and automobiles. For instance, the pharmaceutical giant Johnson & Johnson recently had to pay $2.2 billion in fines in regard to the false marketing of two antipsychotic drugs and a heart medication (Kmietowicz, 2013). In 2010, the yogurt maker Dannon was accused of false and misleading advertising in regard to its Activa and DanActive yogurt products. The company claimed that both products were "clinically" and "scientifically" proven to improve immunity and regulate digestion, but a judge in a class action lawsuit disagreed and ordered Dannon to pay $45 million in damages (McMullen, 2010). Another famous case involved a television commercial for Rise shaving cream in which a man was shown applying "ordinary" lather to his face. The lather dried out almost immediately as the man tried to shave. Then, the man applied Rise shaving cream and it stayed "moist and creamy" throughout his shave. What the manufacturers of Rise neglected to mention in their commercial was that the "ordinary" lather was not shaving cream at all. Rather, it was a special aerosol substance that was designed to come out in a big puff and then fade away almost immediately (Preston, 1975). The Campbell's Soup Company once promoted its "chunky style" soup by putting marbles in the bottom of the bowl so that the soup would appear absolutely filled with meat and vegetables—in other words, "chunkier." There is no shortage of other examples, ranging from large multinational corporations to small retail stores.

Exactly what counts as being deceptive can be complicated to determine. Deceptiveness is subjective. What fools one person might not fool another. Deception can be complex or simple. It can involve an orchestrated advertising campaign by a large company or a simple misstatement of fact by an individual applying for a bank loan or a government benefit. It can involve the actions of individuals against large organizations, or the actions of large organizations against individuals, or individuals against individuals, or large organizations against other large organizations. These variations in the nature of the relationship between the person or organization being deceived and the person or organization doing the deceiving will be important to consider when we come to the topic of preventing white-collar crime. However, for our purposes now, the important point to note is that the use of deception is one of the standard techniques of white-collar crime. As we review different types of white-collar crime in subsequent chapters, we will want to identify how they are based on deception, to think about how this form of deception, whatever it may be, is possible, and to explore how we can reduce the likelihood that the deception will be successful.

Deception is closely related to the next technique—the abuse of trust. Abuses or violations of trust occur in what are called "agent-client relationships" or simply "agency relationships." An agency relationship arises whenever an individual or an organization is authorized to "act for" or "on behalf of" another individual or organization (Shapiro, 1990). We call the person or organization that acts for someone else the *agent*. The other party to the relationship is called the *principal*. Typically, agents provide principals with some sort of specialized service based on the agents' expertise or training. They do things that we don't have the ability, expertise, time, or willingness to do for ourselves. As principals, we place our trust in agents and hope that they will act in our best interests. But agents sometimes abuse the trust that we place in them through the use of some form of deception. For example, suppose you have some money you want to invest in the stock market but you do not feel confident about picking stocks yourself. So, you contact a stockbroker and ask her for some advice in picking stocks and help in buying them. The stockbroker agrees to take you on as a client. You give her your money with the understanding that she will invest it in the market for you. You are now in an agency relationship based on trust. You hope that the stockbroker, your agent, will take good care of your money and invest it wisely. It is her duty to use her professional skills to invest your money so as to help you achieve your financial goals. However, she may not do this at all. She may simply take your money and run off with it. She may foolishly gamble with it in high-risk stocks and lose it all. She may advise you to buy stock in a company that has promised to pay her a kickback for every new client she brings in. In short, she could do a lot of things that would violate the trust you placed in her when you asked her to be your broker.

Agency relationships can vary in many ways (Shapiro, 1990). In some relationships, the principal exerts a great deal of control over the agent, which reduces the chances that the agent can take advantage of the principal. Some agency relationships involve a one-to-one interaction between the agent and the principal, as in our example above with you and the stockbroker. Other relationships involve an agent who acts on behalf of a large number of principals. For example, if you work for a company that has a retirement plan for its employees, the people who manage the pension fund are agents for all of the employees who participate in the retirement savings program. These variations in how agency relationships are structured influence opportunities for fraud and abuse by agents.

The main trouble with agency relationships is that they are unbalanced (Shapiro, 1990). Agents typically have access to much more information than principals do. Thus, the agent's actions may be based on factors that you as the principal have no way of knowing about. In the stockbroker example given above, the broker obviously has access to a lot more information than you do about the stock market. That's why you went to her in the first place. In addition, what the agent does for you is hidden in the sense that you usually don't actually observe the agent as he or she works. You assume that your broker is taking your money and investing it for you, but you probably don't sit in her office and look over her shoulder as she makes transactions. Next, agents often may have control over your property, which they can use to their advantage. Finally, there is a built-in ambivalence in agency relationships. This ambivalence arises out of the potential conflict between the principal's interests and the agent's self-interests. The people who act as your agents—stockbrokers, accountants, financial advisors, doctors, pension fund managers, and so on—all have to make a living themselves. Thus, in addition to looking out for you, they are also looking out for themselves. They're trying to make a living, and sometimes what is good for their interests may not be good for yours and vice versa. As Susan Shapiro notes, in the modern world, agency relationships are problematic but unavoidable. Hence, we are all potential victims of the abuse of trust.

The degree to which agency relationships are unbalanced and to which the agent's actions are hidden from the principal can vary. Large private corporations, for example, are usually run by professional managers who in effect act as agents for the owners of the company. Some owners take a very active role in their company's day-to-day operations. They may know as much about what is going on as the professional managers. In this type of situation, the managers, as agents, may not have an information advantage over the principals, the owners. Active, participatory owners make it difficult for managers to hide what they are doing. This type of agency relationship is not as unbalanced as one in which the principal has less power over the agent and is more likely to be disadvantaged in information.

Concealment and conspiracy are the final techniques of white-collar offenders and are important ways in which deception is achieved. Concealment and conspiracy are also used by ordinary street offenders but for a different purpose than that of white-collar offenders. For ordinary street offenders, concealment may be used to hide the offender's identity. In the case of white-collar crime, it is used to hide the crime. For example, a couple of robbers might work together to rob a liquor store. Perhaps one would hang around outside the store and observe traffic patterns, while the other would go inside and check out the layout of the store: where the cash register is located, how many people are working, whether there are any security cameras, and whether there is any sign that whoever works in the store has a firearm. Then, the robbers might meet and compare notes to decide the best time for their attack, presumably when the store is relatively empty and the cash register relatively full. They might also decide to wear masks to hide their identities. They try to do whatever they can to ensure that when they initiate the robbery, it will go as quickly and efficiently as possible. They want to get in and out fast, and they hope that no one will recognize them in the process. In this case, the would-be robbers are conspiring to hide the true nature of their activities until the time of the robbery, and then they hope to hide their identities from the victims and the police. Once the robbery gets started, however, it becomes blazingly obvious that a crime is underway. It is easy to imagine other sorts of offenses in which offenders engage in similar clandestine activities before the offense occurs.

White-collar offenders also conspire to hide the true nature of their activities but in a way different from that of conventional offenders. In the case of many white-collar crimes, the conspiratorial activities of the offenders are designed to hide the crime itself. The object of the conspiracy is to conceal and coordinate activities so as to illegally benefit the members of the conspiracy without ever revealing that anything illegal has taken place. Price fixing is a good example. In his famous study of price fixing in the heavy electrical equipment industry, Gilbert Geis (1977) describes how executives from the major manufacturers of electrical equipment would meet and communicate with one another in secret to coordinate the bids that they gave to the purchasers of heavy electrical equipment. Rather than competing against one another by submitting their bids in isolation from one another, these executives would decide among themselves in advance who was going to win each contract. The chosen company would then be allowed to submit the "low" bid on the contract, while all of the other companies submitted slightly higher or otherwise less competitive bids.

Although this case eventually came to light and the executives were charged and convicted, it went on for several years before the price-fixing conspiracy was uncovered. Only after detection did it become apparent that laws had been broken and crimes committed. Indeed, the conspiracy came to light only because the executives apparently made the mistake of submitting identical bids in sealed envelopes in response to a contract solicitation from the Tennessee Valley Authority (Geis, 1977). To the Tennessee Valley Authority officials, it seemed highly unlikely that they would receive identical bids for the highly technical electrical equipment that they wanted to purchase. The officials complained to the federal government, which then initiated a grand jury probe that eventually uncovered the facts of these antitrust violations. If the conspirators had been more clever and submitted bids that were not identical but just similar, there is no telling how long the price fixing would have gone undetected.

Concealment and conspiracy also were instrumental to the longevity of the accounting scandals that rocked corporate America in the late 1990s and early 2000s. The most famous case, of course, concerned Enron, the giant energy trading company that was forced into bankruptcy after its accounting frauds were revealed. The story of Enron is bewilderingly complex and included many different types of fraud, but one of the most clever schemes involved creating and then misusing what are called "special purpose entities" (SPEs). SPEs are set up by companies who want to hedge risk or for other purposes. By law, SPEs are required to have a certain degree of independence from the company that established them. In other words, an SPE is not supposed to be wholly owned or controlled by the company that sets it up. However, the SPEs set up by Enron were not independent and were used illegally as a way of hiding some of the company's debt. By conspiring to conceal the true level of the company's debt, executives at Enron could make the company appear to be much more profitable than it really was (McLean and Elkind, 2003, pp. 157–158).

Stock manipulation is another example of a white-collar offense that is based on concealment and conspiracy. As described by Shapiro (1984, pp. 14–15), stock manipulation typically involves a group of individuals who secretly work together to orchestrate the buying and selling of a particular stock in a manner designed to drive up its price. Misleading publicity and gossip about the stock are used to reinforce the appearance that the stock is becoming a hot item that will continue to rise in value. At some point, when the price has risen high enough, the conspirators sell all of the stock that they had previously bought at a low price and take their profits.

In these cases and in others that rely on concealment and conspiracy, the perpetrators of the offense try to take advantage of how our economic system works by mimicking legitimate activities. In a capitalistic free-market economy, such as ours, we assume that the costs of goods and services are set through competition between producers and the principles of supply and demand. We assume that stock prices reflect objective evaluations made by honest buyers and sellers of the value of particular stocks. And we assume that when a company, such as Enron, reports its assets and liabilities, the figures are accurate. Based on these assumptions, we make decisions to buy products, or sell stocks, or invest in a company, or in some other way part with our money. Through the use of concealment and conspiracy, white-collar offenders can take advantage of our reliance on these assumptions to enrich themselves or their organizations illegally.

Reconsidering Sutherland: Techniques and Power

Sutherland urged criminologists to acknowledge and to investigate the crimes of the powerful. For this, he is rightly remembered and venerated. Regardless of whether you agree or disagree with his approach to white-collar crime, there is no doubt that without his fundamental insights, criminology would have been impoverished, and our society would be even more vulnerable to the abuses of the rich and powerful than it already is. Thus, it is important to remember Sutherland's basic point that wealthy and powerful individuals commit occupationally related crimes that cause great social harm.

However, we believe that Sutherland's analysis can be extended by investigating not only who the white-collar offender is but also how white-collar offenses are committed—that is, we must pay attention to the techniques used by white-collar offenders. We believe that this focus on techniques will permit us to develop a firmer understanding of how and why these crimes occur. We also believe it will shed new light on the problem of control by directing our attention toward the strategy of fighting white-collar crime by manipulating situational conditions that affect the attractiveness of crime opportunities.

Even though we intend to concentrate on techniques and opportunity structures, we will not ignore Sutherland's concern with power. Indeed, the economic and political power of white-collar offenders is important precisely because it provides them with access to white-collar crime opportunities and facilitates their ability to deceive, to conceal, and to abuse trust. White-collar offenders also use their economic and political power to shape the legal environment—both criminal and regulatory—within which they operate. Their ability to shape the legal environment directly affects opportunity structures for white-collar crime by reducing the credibility of oversight. Thus, social and economic power plays a central role in the rest of our analysis.

Summary

White-collar crimes are different than ordinary street crimes in regard to their opportunity structures and the techniques that are used to commit them. In this chapter, we have identified three important features of white-collar crime: specialized access, the superficial appearance of legitimacy, and spatial separation from victims. Of these features, specialized access is probably the most important (Felson, 2002). It is the offenders' access to a particular occupational or organizational role that provides the access to the crime target. Specialized access helps offenders to paint their actions with a superficial appearance of legitimacy and often allows them to separate themselves from any direct contact with individual victims.

This chapter makes the argument that white-collar crimes are based on deception, which, following Bowyer (1982), we have defined as the "advantageous distortion of reality." The trick for the offender is to hide the crime, to make what is illegitimate appear legitimate. Offenders who are in trust relationships with their victims often are in particularly good positions to accomplish this task. Deception can be achieved in different ways. As we show in the next chapter, some offenders try to make their illegal activities blend in with legal activities, while others simply try to conceal what they are doing.

Part III

Applying the Opportunity Perspective to White-Collar Crime

The literature on white-collar crime has been criticized by some for its overreliance on typologies. And it is true that those who teach and write on the subject often organize their material in typological fashion, devoting attention to different types of crime. In the *Encyclopedia of White-Collar and Corporate Crime*, for example, entries have been penned on no less than 68 different types of white-collar and corporate crime (Salinger, 2005), ranging from accounting fraud to wire fraud. The underlying criteria that govern these typologies are rarely the same and rarely internally consistent. For example, an examination of two popular texts—*Profit Without Honor* (Rosoff, Pontell, and Tillman, 2013) and *Trusted Criminals* (Friedrichs, 2010)—reveals crimes categorized according to their victims as in "crimes against consumers" and according to their perpetrators as in "crimes by professionals" or "crimes by employees." Sometimes the industry in which the crime occurs is the determining factor, as in "securities fraud," while at other times, it appears to be the specific type of offense itself, as in "antitrust offenses" or "bribery." The *Encyclopedia* pays particularly close attention to preciseness, including entries on such highly specific and esoteric forms of white-collar crime as "debt restructuring fraud" and "nonprofit organization fraud."

The main complaints against typologies are that they imply that white-collar crime is somehow special or distinct from other sorts of crime and that it, therefore, requires a different type of explanation or explanations. Thus, the typological approach is seen as not well suited to developing general theories of crime (Hirschi and Gottfredson, 1987a). Although we have argued throughout this book that white-collar offenses have unique characteristics, we appreciate that typological approaches make general theorizing difficult. Nevertheless, in this chapter, we follow tradition and present our material in typological fashion. Our main reason for doing so is that the opportunity perspective advocated here requires it. The opportunity perspective assumes that particular crimes have particular opportunity structures (i.e., conditions that make a white-collar crime possible or attractive to a potential offender). The necessary conditions may vary substantially from one white-collar offense to another. Thus, the opportunity perspective prompts us to focus on highly specific forms of crime.

Here, we apply the opportunity perspective to specific forms of white-collar crime. Obviously, as noted above, there are many different ways of looking at white-collar crime and many different forms. We cannot cover all of them here. Instead, we take a representative sample of well-known and important types of white-collar crime and use them to illustrate how our approach would work. Our goal is to focus on how the different offenses are committed. We hope that understanding how an offense is committed will suggest ways in which to prevent or reduce similar offenses in the future.

Because we are focusing on "how" particular white-collar offenses are committed, we leave aside for the time being the issue of "why" they are committed. That is, at this point, we assume that a motivated offender is present without attempting to understand exactly what his or her motivations are or what causes him or her to engage in the offense. However, in many cases, it is safe to assume that the underlying motivation for white-collar crime is financially based. Indeed, white-collar offenders often are motivated by one or more of four objectives: to benefit themselves financially, to benefit the financial standing or competitive position of a company or an employer, to stay in business, or to avoid losing financial assets.

The white-collar offenses that we cover in Chapter 5 include health care fraud, mortgage fraud, securities violations, and antitrust violations.

We group these offenses together because their effects are primarily financial and not physical. In the following chapter, we cover three types of offenses that often do have physical effects and that raise more complicated issues with respect to their opportunity structures—environmental offenses, workplace safety offenses, and manufacturing offenses. For each offense, we first present some background material that explains the structure of the industry or business activity out of which the offense arises. Then, we examine the opportunity structure for each offense. In all cases, there are a variety of different types or subtypes of each offense within each of our general categories. For the sake of brevity, we concentrate on only a few of the subtypes.

5

FINANCIAL CRIMES IN HEALTH CARE, MORTGAGES, SECURITIES, AND MARKETS

Health Care Fraud

The health care industry is the largest single industry in the U.S. economy. In 2011, it accounted for roughly 17.9 percent of the United States gross domestic product (Fuchs, 2013). Considering that the United States has a trillion-dollar-plus economy, it's certain that big numbers are involved. What does the health care industry comprise? Obviously, doctors and all of the medical services that they provide are a part of the industry, but only part. The health care industry also includes hospitals, treatment centers, nursing homes, outpatient clinics, testing laboratories, and a host of other health-related facilities and programs. Any sort of organization that provides any kind of medical service is part of the health care industry. It also includes all of the companies that provide medical equipment and supplies, which can range from Band-Aids to advanced magnetic resonance imaging machines. As we will see, there are also companies that provide record keeping, accounting, and billing services for health care providers and organizations. Finally, of course, there are the pharmaceutical companies. So, it's a big industry, involving a lot of money. Unfortunately, a lot of the money that goes into the health care industry is lost to fraud and abuse.

Just how much is lost? Nobody knows for sure, and estimates vary widely from $80 billion to over $250 billion (Sharp, 2011). In the late 1990s, Sparrow (1998) estimated that as much as 10 percent was lost annually to fraud and abuse. Other estimates put the figure at 3 percent. Considering that currently around $2.7 trillion is spent annually on health care, the amount lost to fraud may exceed $270 billion per year if the 10 percent figure is accurate. This works out to about $740 million per day or $31 million per hour.

Anyone who is involved in the health care industry can be an offender. This includes not only physicians but pharmacists, physical therapists, health care organizations, testing laboratories, medical suppliers, and companies that manage billing and records for health care organizations. When most people think of health care organizations, they think primarily of hospitals. However, there are many other types of health care organizations, such as home health care providers, nursing homes, psychiatric clinics, substance abuse programs, and mental health facilities. All of these organizations potentially can be sites for fraud. Finally, in recent years, there is evidence that organized criminals and con artists have gotten into the lucrative business of fraud in health care (U.S. Federal Bureau of Investigation, 2010).

In order to understand why fraud is such a huge problem in the health care industry, we must first understand how the industry works. The most important thing to know is that most of the money spent on health care is not spent by individual consumers. This is unlike most other industries that provide services and products to consumers. If you go to a restaurant and order a meal, you pay for it. If you buy a car, you pay for it. If your car needs to be fixed, you go to a mechanic and you pay for it. In all of these transactions, you have a vested interest in making sure that you get your money's worth. But for most of us, health care doesn't work like this. Most health care costs are covered by insurance. The costs are paid, at least in part, either by a private insurance company or by one of the two big government insurance programs—Medicare and Medicaid. What this means is that the people who pay are not the people who receive the medical service, whatever it might be. This difference in the structure of the industry is crucial to understanding the opportunity structure for different forms of health care fraud.

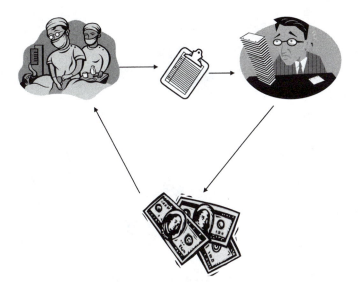

Figure 5.1 The ideal medical insurance system

To demonstrate the significance of the structure of the health care industry, let's consider a few diagrams. The first diagram is an idealized illustration of how the health care system is supposed to work.

In Figure 5.1, here's what happens. An elderly patient goes to a doctor and receives some sort of medical service. Let's say it is a minor surgical procedure performed in the office. The doctor's office submits a claim for reimbursement to Medicare. (Note: Keep in mind that any of a number of health care providers and health care organizations could take the place of the physician and submit the claim. Our example uses a physician only to keep things simple.) The claim is reviewed by an agent at Medicare. After the agent has determined that the claim form is acceptable, a check is sent to the doctor's office.

You may have noticed that the agent in Figure 5.1 does not look very happy. That's because he's got a lot of work to do. On average, the Medicare system receives literally millions of claims per year, far too many to be checked individually by real people. As a result, the Medicare system really operates as depicted in Figure 5.2, where the agent has been replaced by a computer. The computer reviews the claims and, based on certain decision rules, decides whether it should be paid.

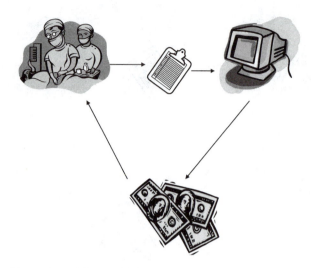

Figure 5.2 The reality of the medical insurance system

Considering how the health care industry is organized, where are the opportunities for fraud? The key point in the cycle presented in Figure 5.2 occurs when the health care provider submits the claim to Medicare. That is the point at which fraud can occur. Figure 5.3 shows a simple example of how an ill-intentioned physician could take advantage of this system. In Figure 5.3, the physician simply sits in his office and submits a claim form even though he or she did not actually treat a patient. However, the form submitted in Figure 5.3 looks just like the form submitted in Figure 5.2. That is, it looks legitimate, and the computer authorizes payment to the doctor. There are many variations on this theme and many ways of subtly changing the fraudulent information that is submitted as well as how it is submitted (Moffat, 1993). However, in a nutshell, that is how many health care frauds work. A claim is filed with Medicare, Medicaid, or a private health insurance company that does not accurately reflect what actually happened in the field.

For example, a more systematic variation on the physician's scam and one that can produce a lot of money in a short period of time is called the "rent-a-patient" scheme (Hast, 2000). The scheme involves a network of individuals, often including legitimate physicians. It works as depicted

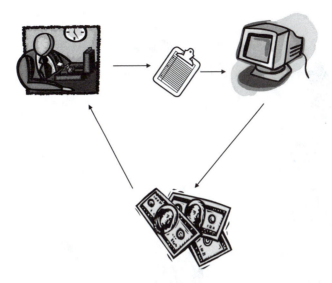

Figure 5.3 Ripping off the medical insurance system

in Figure 5.4. "Recruiters" solicit patients, called beneficiaries, usually from low-income housing projects and retirement communities, and take them to a local clinic. Recruiters are paid a commission for the patients they round up, and they pay the patients a fee out of their commission. The patients understand that if they really need a doctor, they should go someplace else. At the clinic, a cooperating physician or medical student performs a very cursory exam and then writes referrals for further tests, treatment, or medical equipment. The physicians sign charts for the services that they don't really provide or for equipment that patients don't really need. Medicare or Medicaid is then billed for these fictitious services and equipment.

You shouldn't think, however, that only physicians are defrauding the health care system. In recent years, the FBI has investigated a number of high-profile cases of massive fraud by large organizations. For example, in 2011, the owners of a company called American Therapeutic Corporation (ATC) located in Miami, Florida, were convicted of filing approximately $205 million of fraudulent claims with Medicare. ATC operated the largest community mental health centers in Florida. In a ruse that is a variation on collection of the rent-a-patient scheme, they were alleged to have paid kickbacks to assisted living facilities in order to recruit patients for group therapy

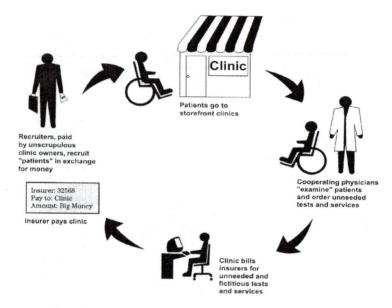

Figure 5.4 Rent-a-patient scheme
Source: Hast (2000)

programs that the patients didn't really need. In 2010, GlaxoSmithKline, one of the largest pharmaceutical companies in the world, pled guilty and paid criminal fines for charges relating to the manufacture and distribution of adulterated drugs (U.S. Federal Bureau of Investigation, 2011). In another case, 20 individuals were convicted for their involvement in a sophisticated scheme to defraud Medicare. The convictions involved the largest certified home health agency in Miami (Anonymous, 2007). The agency was paid more than $100 million in Medicare funds for reimbursement of services, including nursing and home aide visits. These services either had not been provided, were not necessary, or were provided to people who were not eligible. In another case, Fresenius Medical Care North America, Inc., the world's largest provider of kidney dialysis products and services, agreed to pay the U.S. government $486 million to resolve an investigation of fraud at National Medical Care, Inc., a subsidiary of Fresenius (Rowland, 2005). The list of cases could go on, but as these examples indicate, the amounts of money involved can be huge.

Health care fraud illustrates to perfection the defining characteristics of white-collar crime. All health care providers and health care organizations have legitimate access to patients and to the various government pro-grams and private companies that provide health care insurance. Even though the offenders are stealing from the government and insurance companies, they are spatially separated from them. Finally, their actions have the superficial appearance of legitimacy. Indeed, they depend on the appearance of legitimacy, because in order to get paid, those who commit fraud must submit claims that look routine and legitimate.

As we noted earlier, the key point in the opportunity structure for health care fraud is when the health care provider submits a claim to an insurer. As a thought experiment, imagine that insurers could instantly verify whether the information submitted on the claim truly represented what happened in the field and furthermore whether it was medically necessary. If this were the case, then health care providers would have no opportunity to commit fraud. However, for a number of reasons, this ideal situation is far from reality.

Part of the problem stems from the size, complexity, and structure of our heath care system. In the case of Medicare alone, about 800 million claims are filed per year. Because there are so many claims, it is impossible to review all of them carefully to make sure that they are legitimate. So, most claims are reviewed by computers. On the one hand, this is good because computers are fast and they can process claims quickly. On the other hand, it is bad because computers do only what they are told to do and in the past have not been very good at looking for unusual patterns in data, making life easy for people who want to defraud the health care programs. Another part of the problem is that controlling fraud takes time, personnel, and money away from processing claims (Sparrow, 1996). Government programs such as Medicare and Medicaid and private insur-ance companies are under a lot of pressure from physicians and the rest of the health care community to process claims as efficiently and fast as possible. Honest physicians want to be paid quickly and with a minimum of hassle. Thus, for health insurers, there is a constant tension between using resources to control fraud and using resources to process and pay claims quickly. In the past, computers could be programmed to catch simple obvious frauds, such as when a doctor claimed to have operated on 100 patients in a day, but until recently computers had been less adept at catching fraudulent claims that were not obvious. Sophisticated fraudsters could deliberately design their schemes so that they looked legitimate. They would test the system and learn from their mistakes about what is acceptable and what is not. For example, when a claim comes in that the computer recognizes as not acceptable, this does not automatically trigger an investigation that might uncover fraud. Instead, the claim is simply rejected. Unfortunately, this means that the offender would learn what does not work and get away to try another day.

However, as we discuss in Chapter 11, this situation may change in the future. Advances in both computer hardware and software may lead to strategies to improve fraud control using sophisticated data mining processes (Yang and Hwang, 2006). Big data analytics can be used to uncover potential fraud schemes by identifying unusual patterns in the number of patients seen by doctors, the number of tests ordered, overall costs of services, and so on. They could provide a more effective means of oversight than has been available in the past.

Mortgage Fraud and the Global Financial Collapse

More so than other forms of crime, white-collar crime evolves over time. New forms emerge and old ones die away. Every few years a new scandal emerges in which some previously unrecognized or underappreciated form of fraud or financial wrongdoing in the world of business explodes onto the public stage, generating widespread public outrage, fervid political posturing, and improved job security for investigative journalists and social commentators. Indeed, as we discuss in Chapter 9, the cycle of scandal, public outrage, and political response drives the evolution of legal controls over misconduct in business and the professions. In late 2008, just as we were finishing work on the first edition of this book, the most recent such scandal swelled into view. It involved a bewilderingly large variety of frauds and financial crimes arising out of the real estate, mortgage, and investment banking industries.

As with fraud in health care, to understand the crimes that occurred in these three industries, it is necessary, first, to get a handle on how these industries work, that is, how they are interconnected and how money is made in them. Change is also part of the story, because over the past three decades the home mortgage industry has changed in ways that have had both positive and negative effects on American society. On the positive side, the changes promoted greater access to homeownership for people of low to moderate incomes. However, on the negative side, the changes also created new opportunities for fraud (Barnett, 2013; Simpson, 2012). To illustrate these criminogenic conditions, we begin by tracing what typically happened when someone set out to buy a home in the early 2000s.

In the early 2000s the real estate market was hot. Homes were selling fast and home prices were rising rapidly. The process followed by the typical home buyer would go something like this. First, the prospective buyer—for example, let's say someone who owns a small business—would contact a real estate agent for help in finding homes for sale and for help in navigating the byzantine form-filled process of purchasing a home. After an acceptable home at an acceptable price was found, the buyer would get in touch with a mortgage broker, who would help the buyer find and apply for a home loan. The home buyer often needed help because applying for a loan could be a confusing process and because the variety of loan products available had expanded dramatically from what it was prior to the 1970s. Before then, most mortgages had fixed terms and required a certain size of down payment in relation to the value of the loan (called the loan to value rate), which was often 20 percent of the loan value. The loan would then be paid off over the course of a set number of years (usually 15 or 30) at a fixed interest rate. To get a loan, potential buyers would go to their local bank or savings and loan association and work with them.

However, beginning in the 1970s, lenders began to offer new forms of mortgages, such as *adjustable rate mortgages* (ARMs). As the name implies, the interest rate on an ARM loan is adjustable depending on various economic indicators. It changes over time, often starting out very low and then increasing later. ARM loans came in a number of different shapes and sizes. Other types of loans included *buy-downs* where the seller subsidizes the borrower for a short period of time. *Graduated payment mortgages* start with low payments that rise over time. *Negative amortization loans* are loans where the payment is less than is needed to pay off the loan over time and so the loan gradually gets larger over time. Another very important form of loan that developed during the 1990s was the *subprime* mortgage. These are loans made to people who would not normally qualify for regular loans because of their inadequate credit. Finally, starting around 2004, lenders developed what were called *alternative documentation loans.*

These were designed for people who had complicated finances and who could not provide traditional financial documents, such as pay stubs or W-2 forms, to verify their creditworthiness. Self-employed people, for example, might fall into this category.[1] In addition to the profusion of loan products, interest rates fluctuated dramatically during the 1990s and 2000s and lenders competed viciously to attract borrowers. The job of the mortgage broker was to help the borrower navigate this treacherous financial terrain and find the most appropriate loan product at the best price given the borrower's individual financial situation. The broker would also help organize the process of closing the loan. In return for providing these services, the broker would receive a fee, which could be paid by either the borrower or the lender.

As far as the home buyer is concerned, once the loan is closed, he or she can take possession of the house, move in, and say goodbye to the real estate agent and mortgage broker. As long as the buyer makes the monthly mortgage payments, there typically is nothing else to worry about.

Although you might think that when the buyer sends in the monthly mortgage payment it would go to the bank that made the loan, this is not what actually happens. Rather, the loan takes on a life of its own and becomes part of a flowing river of financial transactions that disappears into the hidden landscape of investment banking. To illustrate the process, let's assume that the loan was made by a local bank. The bank does not keep the loan and receive the payments from the borrower. Rather, the bank sells the loan on what is called the *secondary mortgage market*. So, for example, if the loan was for $100,000, the bank might sell it on the secondary market for $105,000. The $5,000 would be the bank's profit on the loan, and the bank would then have $100,000 to loan to a new borrower.

The secondary mortgage market involves large private financial institutions, such as Countrywide Bank, and semi-public institutions known as government sponsored entities (GSEs). Two that you might have heard of are the Federal National Mortgage Association (FNMA), popularly known as "Fannie Mae," and the Federal Home Loan Mortgage Corporation, or "Freddie Mac." These two institutions were created by the federal government to increase liquidity in the mortgage market. In simplified form, the process worked in this manner. A bank lends a home buyer

$100,000 to buy a home. The bank then sells the loan and its documentation to Fannie Mae for $100,000 plus some profit. The bank then has $100,000 available to lend to another home buyer and the process continues with subsequent buyers. Fannie Mae can hold the loan and receive the loan payments from the buyer or it can sell the loan as a security to another investor, in which case the investor would be paid interest or a dividend for as long as he or she held the security.

However, rather than selling individual loans as securities, Fannie Mae and the other institutional players in the secondary mortgage market usually would create *mortgage backed securities* (MBSs), which are securities based on a collection ("pool") of mortgages, and sell them to investors. The investors receive what is called the "pass through," that is, the interest and principal payments that the borrower makes each month on the loan. In the early 1980s, the relatively simple MBS idea was transformed when Fannie Mae and others began creating and selling *collateralized mortgage obligations* (CMOs). CMOs are complicated debt securities that can operate or perform in different ways. Simplifying greatly, a CMO is a collection of mortgage backed securities that is divided into different classes (also called "tranches") based on the creditworthiness of the borrowers and is offered for sale by what is called a *special purpose entity* (SPE). The SPE sells bonds based on the different tranches in the CMO, with the bonds paying different rates depending on the creditworthiness of the mortgages that make up each particular tranch. Some tranches are more risky than others, and so the bonds based on these more risky tranches pay higher rates. For example, the least risky tranche in a CMO might be based on mortgage loans made to people who can afford a 20 percent down payment and who have excellent credit histories, stable employment, and good incomes. The most risky tranche, on the other hand, would be based on a collection of subprime or alternative documentation loans. These are loans made to borrowers who cannot afford much in the way of a down payment, who do not have good credit, and who are at much greater risk to default. The investors in CMOs are usually large banks, hedge funds, pension funds, or insurance companies. As long as borrowers make their payments on time, CMOs represent a good investment opportunity. However, if enough borrowers in any of the tranches default on their loans, then the CMO becomes worthless and investors lose some or all of the money they have invested in the bond. This is pre-cisely what started to happen in 2008 when the housing market collapsed.

It might be helpful at this point to recap in outline form the steps involved in buying and financing a home when everything goes right.

1. The buyer works with a real estate agent to find the right home.
2. The buyer contacts a mortgage broker for help in identifying an appropriate loan product (say a subprime ARM loan) and finding a lender.
3. With the help of the mortgage broker, the buyer fills out the application for a loan and submits it to the lender.
4. After reviewing the loan application, the lender loans the money to the buyer and takes control of the title to the house and all of the loan documents.
5. The lender sells the loan and documentation on the secondary market, say to Fannie Mae.
6. Fannie Mae creates a CMO, which is then offered for sale by a SPE to investors.
7. Investors (usually large financial concerns, such as pension funds, insurance companies, or investment banks) buy shares in the CMO.
8. The buyer makes his or her loan payments on time for the life of the loan and at the end of the term gets the title to the house.
9. The investors receive the rate of return promised to them for their shares in the CMO.
10. Everyone is happy.

Unfortunately, all too often the happy scenario outlined above was not what actually happened. At any number of points along the way there were opportunities for fraud and other forms of financial malfeasance, involving in different ways all of the players in the process, from home buyers up to the investment bankers who sold MBSs and CMOs. Indeed, between roughly 1990 and 2008, the housing, mortgage, and banking markets generated a tremendous amount of lure coupled with an aston-ishing lack of oversight.

Let's start with the home buyer. In the example given above, the buyer was presented as the responsible owner of a small business who paid off the loan in a timely manner. However, in the 1990s and 2000s not all buyers were responsible or honest. Buyers could engage in what was known as "fraud for property or housing" (Financial Crimes Enforcement Network, 2006). In a fraud for property scheme, the buyer would make false statements on the application for the loan in an attempt to secure a house. The false statements might include lies about his or her income, debts, or employment. This type of fraud was relatively easy to get away with during this period because the housing market was booming and there was little oversight of the loan application process by either lenders or regulators. In other words, no one was checking carefully to see if what was on the loan application regarding the buyer's ability to repay the loan was true or accurate. Lenders were willing to make subprime loans that required no down payment, no proof of income, and interest-only payments (Barnett, 2013) because they profited not by making loans but rather by selling loans on the secondary market. The more loans they had to sell, the more profits they made.

Buyers, however, did not always act alone. Rather, they were often aided in carrying out this scheme by unscrupulous mortgage brokers who were more interested in earning a commission than in making sure the buyer could really afford the house and repay the loan. Indeed sometimes, mortgage brokers would conspire with real estate agents, appraisers, and others to engage in more sophisticated schemes, called property flipping, where the object was not property but profit. In simplified form, the scheme works like this. The real estate agent and the mortgage broker recruit a straw buyer, that is, a person who only pretends to want to buy a house. The agent, broker, and straw buyer work together to get a mortgage loan and buy the house for, say, $100,000. A little while later, the buyer puts the house up for sale, and the appraiser who is involved in the scheme appraises the house at, say, $150,000. The house is then sold at this inflated price, and after paying off the original loan, the conspirators now have $50,000 in profit (minus a few fees that have to be paid). This "flipping" of the property could continue for a few more rounds until one of two things happened. Some unsuspecting buyer is left with a house for which he or she grossly overpaid or the last buyer could also be a straw buyer and simply walk away from the house and default on the loan. Either way, the conspirators would make a nice profit for just a little paperwork. As with fraud for property schemes, property flipping was also easy to get away with because of lax oversight and competition among lenders to originate as many loans as possible. No one in the system spent much time checking the accuracy of loan documents.

In the previous two examples, the not wholly blameless victims of the fraudulent schemes were lenders, as the fraud was perpetrated against the financial institutions that made the loans. However, there were other schemes in which the victims were just ordinary people. These schemes involved mortgage brokers, banks, and other insiders who used their expertise to take advantage of unsuspecting home buyers. These schemes illustrate how legitimate financial transactions can be distorted to commit white-collar crimes. For example, consider the marketing of subprime loans in the years running up to 2008. Recall that subprime loans were developed in order to make it possible for low to moderate income people to qualify for mortgage loans and to own their own homes. Subprime loans typically required applicants to provide lower or no down payments and less proof of income than ordinary prime loans. They were often packaged as ARMs, which meant that the interest rate started out low but eventually rose to a higher rate than that charged for traditional prime loans. Compared with prime loans, subprime loans also have higher fees and prepayment penalties. Because of their higher fees, penalties, and interest rates, these types of loans are very profitable for banks and a good source of income. Although the idea of giving low income people a chance to own a home seems commendable, there is substantial evidence that this noble idea was subsequently perverted for illegal ends by many players in the mortgage and banking industry. Mortgage brokers would use fraud and deceit to entice unsophisticated low income buyers to apply for loans that they really could not afford and that would end up in default (Calem, Herschaff, and Wachter, 2004). A disproportionate number of these low income buyers were African American or Hispanic, and the targeting of minority group members to steer them toward subprime loan products was standard practice among some mortgage brokers and bankers—so much so that even middle income African Americans and Hispanics who could have qualified for normal loans were steered toward subprime products to their disadvantage (Faber, 2013). When their loan payments ballooned after the buy-down period expired, many subprime buyers could no longer afford the new monthly mortgage payment and they defaulted. Because so many of these loans targeted low income African American and Hispanic homeowners, the collateral consequences to poor urban neighborhoods were catastrophic.

But the question can be raised, why would a mortgage broker or a banker want to loan money to someone who is not likely to be able to repay it? Why would lenders seek out borrowers who posed more rather than less risk? The answer to these questions lies in the structure of the mortgage industry outlined above, especially as it relates to the securitization of mortgages, that is, the practice of bundling mortgages together and selling them as mortgage backed securities or collateralized mortgage securities. Securitization disconnected lenders from the risks posed by subprime borrowers (Faber, 2013). Banks and other mortgage lenders did not have to worry about loans defaulting, because they sold the loans to other financial institutions that then securitized them. The risks associated with subprime loans were passed onto and borne by the investors in mortgage backed securities. Thus, the broker and the lender that originated the loan would collect their fees and their profits from the sale of the loan, but they would not have to worry that the home buyer might eventually default on the loan. In addition, technological changes in the processing of loan applications that were adopted to speed up the approval process made it easier for applications based on fraudulent information to slip through unnoticed. Because competition for new loans was so fierce, many lenders adopted *automated underwriting systems*. These software systems would review the loan application and either approve or reject it based solely on the information in the application. No attempt was made to verify that the information was accurate—for example, by checking to see whether the applicant really did have the income stated on the application (Barnett, 2013).

After loans moved on to the secondary market, new opportunities for fraud and deception opened up, but they were much more complicated than the schemes cooked up by real estate agents, mortgage brokers, and appraisers. The world of mortgage backed securities, collateralized mortgage obligations, and collateralized debt obligations (CDOs) can be mind-numbingly complex. But at its core, fraud is always the same. It always involves a distortion of reality that is advantageous to one party and disadvantageous to another. In the case of mortgage backed securities, the distortion involved the description of the risks associated with the various forms of MBSs, CMOs, and CDOs. Although the legal and financial details involved here require close attention to follow, it is worth the effort in order to understand how fraud and deception in the highest ranks of the financial world put the entire American economy on the very edge of total collapse.

Recall that a CMO is a collection of mortgages that are grouped into different tranches based on the quality of the loans in the tranche. The different tranches pay different rates of return depending on their risk rating. Risk ratings are determined by big credit rating agencies, such as S&P's and Moody's. These agencies rate the risk associated with MBSs and with the different tranches in CMOs. The ratings typically range from "triple A" (Aaa) to lower ratings, such as "triple B" (Bbb). In regard to MBSs and CMOs, a rating of Aaa indicates that there is little chance that the mortgages that underlie these instruments will end in default. Ideally, investors face only a very small chance that they will lose money on instruments that are rated Aaa. On the other hand, a rating in the Bbb range indicates that there is a greater risk that some percentage of the mortgages in the instrument will end in default and investors are more likely to lose money. In theory, credit rating agencies are supposed to provide an objective and independent analysis of the risks associated with different investments so that investors can make informed decisions. However, from 2000 to 2006 the objectivity, independence, and accuracy of the judgments made by the credit rating agencies was often less reliable than the subprime mortgages that they were supposed to be evaluating. Investors who thought they were putting their money into triple A rated instruments found out later that they had been living in a fool's paradise and had been misled about the risks associated with MBSs and CMOs they had invested in.

Large investment banks, most notably Goldman Sachs, bought and then securitized subprime loans in the MBSs and CMOs it sold to investors without telling investors that a worrying percentage of the loans were likely fraudulent (Barnett, 2013), even though Goldman Sachs knew or should have known that such was the case. Of course, when Goldman Sachs and other investment banks put together MBSs and CMOs, they know that a certain percentage of the loans involved will go bad and that reality is factored into the structure of the instrument. But selling MBSs and CMOs is a highly profitable and competitive business, and the investment banks that competed in this market had little incentive and even less willingness to look deeply into the mortgages on which they were based. Since it is more difficult to sell an instrument with a rating in the B range than one with a rating in the A range, investment banks were drawn toward presenting overly optimistic views of their loan pools. To put it in simple terms, they bought junk, dressed it up, and sold it as rock-solid investments. They were aided in this process by the credit ratings agencies, which simply accepted the data provided by the investment banks to rate MBSs and CMOs and as a result underestimated the percentage of likely fraudulent subprime loans that were involved and that were likely to end up in default.

The analysis of fraud in the American mortgage market presented above tells only part of the story. There were other forms of fraud and other players involved besides appraisers, brokers, lenders, and investment banks (for a more complete description of the mortgage process, see Simpson, 2012 and Rorie and Simpson, n.d.). But regardless what role an individual or an institution played in the process, it is easy in retrospect to see that the overall structure of the mortgage industry strongly contributed to the prevalence, longevity, and seriousness of fraud. As Simpson (2012) notes, the industry was organized in a series of interlocking tiers such that pressures and constraints felt at one level influenced or affected other levels. For example, the competitive pressures felt by lenders to make as many loans as possible influenced their dealings with brokers whom they pushed and encouraged to bring in subprime borrowers.

The incentives in the system were all pointing in the wrong direction. People wanted to own their own homes. After all, owning a home is a fundamental part of the American dream, and during this period it seemed like everyone was buying a new home. As a result, many people were eager to trust the advice of brokers about the terms of complicated mortgage products that they did not understand. From the point of view of fraudsters, eager buyers make easy targets. At the same time, brokers and lenders were "incentivized" to make as many loans as possible and give little consideration to the ability of borrowers to repay their loans. Further up the food chain, investment banks needed loans to securitize, and the ratings agencies made their money by providing deceptively attractive ratings that made it easy for investment banks to sell CMOs. As long as the housing market was growing and home prices were rising, everybody, including investors in CMOs, made money. But eventually, of course, the bubble burst. The housing market started to slow, home prices stopped rising, subprime mortgage holders started defaulting, and CMOs started failing.

From the perspective of opportunity and choice theories, we can see that starting in roughly 2000 the mortgage industry became a source of lure, drawing in thousands of people seeking to work in this rapidly growing and richly rewarding industry. Between March 2001 and December 2005, employment among mortgage and nonmortgage loan brokers grew by 136 percent, more than in any other industry in the U.S. economy (Miller, 2006). Although most of the people who took up work as mortgage brokers during this period probably tried to conduct themselves honorably, it would be naive to think that all of them were saints. Rather, it seems not unreasonable to suspect that a notable proportion of the people who worked in the mortgage industry during this period either were criminal opportunists to start with or became ones after they recognized the high profit and low risk nature of many mortgage fraud opportunities (Nguyen and Pontell, 2010).

Securities Offenses

Some of the offenses discussed in the preceding section on fraud in the mortgage market involved securities, specifically mortgage backed securities and collateralized mortgage obligations. So, you already have some familiarity with the general idea of securities offenses, but the securities industry encompasses much more than just mortgage-related financial instruments. And it has long been a prominent site of high-level white-collar crime. In this section, we explicate the structure of the securities industry and identify the different forms of white-collar crime that can be found in it.

The securities industry is an extremely important part of the economy and as noted above is a major arena for white-collar crime. Let's start by getting clear on what securities are and how they work. Technically, a security is evidence of ownership, creditorship, or debt (Shapiro, 1984). To put it more simply, a security is a piece of paper, or an account number, or something that indicates that you have a financial interest or stake in some sort of economic undertaking. For example, stocks, bonds, shares in a mutual fund, promissory notes, U.S. government savings bonds are all securities. In a sense, securities are symbolic commodities.

People invest in securities to make money or to avoid losing money. For example, you can buy shares in a mutual fund and make money through dividends or increases in the share price for your fund. Or you could buy stock in an individual company and make (or lose) money the same way. When people buy securities, they are in effect making a bet or taking a gamble that the security will pay off for them. They hope that the stock will go up in value. Publicly traded securities are bought and sold on exchanges, such as the New York Stock Exchange. For our purposes, it is important to note that most of the stock in publicly held companies is owned by people who do not work in the company. Because they are outsiders, most stock owners have to trust what the company tells them when they make their buying and selling decisions. Trust is an intrinsic and unavoidable part of the system. And it is the requirement of trust that creates opportunities for white-collar crime in the securities industry, because people make their investment decisions based on what they think is trustworthy information about securities.

There are five major types of security offenses (Shapiro, 1984). They all involve taking advantage of people's trust in one way or another.

Misrepresentations involve lying about the value or condition of a security. For example, suppose I told you that I owned land out west on which oil and gas had been discovered and invited you to get in on the ground floor of a great opportunity by buying stock in my company. However, in reality, the land that I owned hadn't even been surveyed and I had no way of knowing whether there really was gas and oil out there. That would be misrepresentation.

Misappropriation is old-fashioned stealing. Many people don't actually buy securities themselves. Instead, they use an intermediary, a stockbroker, to make purchases for them. Typically, then, this offense is committed by brokers or other financial advisors who simply take the money that their clients have given them to invest and instead steal or appropriate it for their own use.

Stock manipulation involves artificially manipulating the price of a security. This can be a complex offense, but basically it involves trying to create the impression that a stock is about to increase rapidly in value. If you can create that impression, then people are likely to rush to buy the stock and hence drive up the price. If you bought when the stock was low and then sold after its price had gone up, you could make a great deal of money very quickly.

Stock manipulators typically operate in teams involving multiple co-conspirators and proceed through a series of steps to orchestrate their schemes. First, the conspirators target and take control of a small or marginal company that operates in an industry in which breakthroughs or sudden advances seem possible, such as, for example, pharmaceuticals, green technology, biotechnology, hair restoration, or other esoteric technologies, products, or services. The plausibility of the breakthrough or discovery is an important part of the scheme, because it can be used to explain any sudden increase in the trading volume or price for a company's stock. Second, once the manipulators are in control of the target company, they can engage in a variety of activities designed to make it appear as though the company has made a breakthrough that will cause the company's stock to rise rapidly in price. Fraudulent and misleading news stories can be released to or planted in the news media, or posted on the Internet; slick brochures can be sent to potential investors. To solidify the impression that the company's trading volume is starting to boom, the conspirators can set up fake accounts or use nominee buyers to trade shares back and forth. Third, as unwary investors start buying shares and as prices start to peak, the conspirators take the money and secrete it in private bank accounts rather than using it to expand or run the business. Eventually, the lack of any real breakthrough or product becomes apparent, prices start to fall, and the conspirators walk away with the investors' money.

A similar type of scheme was often used in the 1990s and 2000s when technology companies, the so-called "dot coms," were booming.

The astonishing financial success of companies such as Microsoft, Apple, Google, Oracle, and Amazon, as well as a host of other, lesser known but nevertheless wealthy technology-based companies, created the widespread impression that fortunes could be made investing in Internet startups through initial public offerings (IPOs). When these companies initially went public, investors who got in on the ground floor made millions, and many investors were frantically looking for the next big thing. Almost anything associated with technology or the Internet could be made to sound like a surefire path to riches, precisely because the technology of the Internet was so new that few people understood it. Under these conditions, unsophisticated investors made easy targets for scam artists and boiler room operators who would fraudulently market IPOs for companies that had little to no chance of succeeding (Tillman and Indergaard, 2005).

Insider trading is perhaps the most publicized security offense. It arises when people trade on the basis of nonpublic information that is relevant to the price of a stock. There is nothing wrong with insiders who work for a company buying its stock. They do this all the time. But it is illegal for insiders to buy or sell stock on the basis of information that is not available to the public.

For example, in the famous ImClone Systems case that sent Martha Stewart to prison, the leader of the company, Dr. Sam Waskal, was convicted of securities fraud for insider trading. ImClone was a biopharmaceutical firm working on a drug called Erbitux that was supposed to be a breakthrough in cancer treatment. The company's stock was being touted by analysts and was on its way up as the drug was undergoing review for approval by the Food and Drug Administration (FDA). Unfortunately for Waskal, the FDA eventually decided not to approve the drug. Waskal learned that Erbitux would not be approved on Christmas Day, December 2001, before the FDA had made a formal public announcement. He knew immediately that the price for ImClone stock would plummet as soon as the announcement was made, and anyone holding the stock would lose a lot of money. Waskal, his family, and his friends, including Martha Stewart, were among those who held significant interests in ImClone. Even though he was prohibited from doing so by law, Waskal tried to sell large blocks of his own stock holdings in ImClone to avoid losing money, and he alerted his family and friends to do the same. Word that ImClone was about to lose much of its value eventually reached Martha Stewart through an intermediary, and she sold off her holdings, too. For the record, we should note that Ms. Stewart was not actually convicted of insider trading. Rather, she went to jail for perjury because she lied to federal agents about why she sold her shares in ImClone when she did (Stewart, 2011).

The law governing insider trading is exceedingly complex and has continued to evolve through both legislation and judicial opinion since the 1930s (Perez, Cochran, and Sousa, 2008; Reichman, 1993). However, the basic moral principle underlying the prohibition of insider trading is simple. When insiders have specialized access to information that is not available to the general public, they have an unfair advantage over other traders in the market. The laws against insider trading are designed to penalize and thus deter those who would act upon this unfair advantage to the detriment of others. Although the moral principle involved here is straightforward, using the criminal law to enforce it is difficult, and insider trading is an excellent example of the problems raised by the superficial appearance of legitimacy in white-collar crimes. To convict someone of insider trading, prosecutors have to show that the person bought or sold the stock in question, *because and on the basis of* nonpublic material information. Perpetrators, of course, can claim that either they did not know about the privileged information or they traded for other reasons (Szockyj, 1993).

Investment schemes are deliberate attempts to trick people into investing so that you can steal their money. Ponzi or pyramid schemes are the classic example here. In these schemes, investors are recruited through promises of extraordinarily high returns on investments. For example, the person in charge of the scheme tells potential investors that he has a great investment opportunity and offers to let the investor get in on it for only $10,000. The schemer promises to double people's money in just 6 months. Someone invests, and soon thereafter the schemer starts sending out dividend checks. The initial investors think the investment looks great and proceed to tell their friends and relatives about this great opportunity, encouraging them to take advantage of it as well. As more people invest, the schemer is able to continue to send out dividends from the money he gets from new investors. He is also able to keep some extra for himself. But no new money is being generated from the so-called great investment opportunity. Rather, the schemer is robbing Peter to pay Paul. Eventually, as more and more investors join, the number of members grows larger than the number of new investors, and there's not enough new money to pay everyone. The charade collapses—and everybody who invested loses money, except perhaps the ones who got in early.

The most famous recent example of a Ponzi scheme, of course, is that of Bernard Madoff that we briefly discussed in Chapter 2 (Henriques, 2011). Madoff's case is unusual for several reasons. First, Bernie Madoff was not a fly-by-night operator. Rather, he was a well-known and highly respected trader, investment advisor, and money manager on Wall Street, who once served as chairman of the Board of the National Association of Securities Dealers. Second, he did not actively recruit individual investors. Indeed, many people heard about Bernard L. Madoff Investment Securities (the name of his company) by word of mouth. Madoff was Jewish, as were many of his investors who learned about him through informal networks. Third, rather than trying to recruit clients with promises of high returns, Madoff offered very steady returns to an exclusive clientele. Many of the investors in his company were money managers and investment firms, who were handling the money for unions, pension funds, and the retirement savings of ordinary citizens. Fourth, while it is difficult to know the exact date at which Madoff's frauds began, it is clear that they lasted for at least a decade and perhaps much longer. This is unusual for Ponzi schemes, which usually collapse under their own weight much more quickly. The longevity of Madoff's scheme may have been facilitated by the high level of trust that his investors had in him because they shared a Jewish identity. Madoff's reputation and his ability to hide his scheme from regulators enabled him to continue to get new clients and to persist in fraud. Finally, there is the sheer size of Madoff's scheme, which eventually resulted in losses in the tens of billions of dollars (Henriques, 2011).

Like almost all Ponzi schemes, Madoff's case illustrates all of the defining characteristics of white-collar crime. His reputation on Wall Street gave him both the superficial appearance of legitimacy and legitimate access to other people's money, most of whom he never met or had any face-to-face contact with. He would send fraudulent statements to his clients indicating that their accounts were growing steadily despite the inevitable ups and downs of the stock market. If anyone demanded to withdraw a large amount of their funds, Madoff would threaten to kick the investor out of his fund. Astonishingly, even though the Securities and Exchange Commission (SEC) was warned in 2000 by an analyst named Harry Markopolos that Madoff's returns could not possibly be that consistent, the SEC never rigorously investigated his activities (Henriques, 2011), and his scheme continued until December 2008, when it finally collapsed. It had started to come apart earlier in the year as the economy was crashing and as more and more of his clients demanded to take their money out of the market. Madoff eventually realized he could never fulfill all of the redemption requests and called his lawyer.

Opportunity and Securities Fraud

Some types of securities offenses have opportunity structures that are quite similar to consumer frauds. Misrepresentations and investment schemes, for example, rely on the deception of individuals. They are in a sense like mislabeled products or misleading advertising. The offender presents misleading information about a security, and the victim falls for it. Whether the offense succeeds or not depends on who is contacted and how skillful the offender is in presenting a distorted picture of reality. Although the Madoff case is unique because of its complexity, size, and longevity, at bottom it is like all Ponzi schemes. To their detriment, the victims trusted Madoff and believed in the picture of reality that he presented. Madoff was also fortunate to be operating in a regulatory environment that provided little oversight of his activities and in an economy that was growing rapidly. This combination of economic growth and regulatory ineptitude were crucial to his success.

Other types of securities offenses have different structures. Insider trading, for example, does not require the offender to deceive an individual in order to take advantage of her. Rather, the offender is attempting to hide or disguise a prohibited transaction. Whether the offense succeeds depends on how well the offender can hide his involvement in transactions that are illegal but that benefit him. The offender must hide his involvement from outside observers, such as the SEC. The evolution of insider trading and the legal prohibitions against it provide an excellent illustration of how opportunity structures evolve and how offenders adapt to changes in their environment.

Antitrust Offenses

Antitrust offenses are sometimes called *offenses of the marketplace.* They depend on the market in the sense that they are impossible to commit without a free market or something close to it being present. Hence, to begin our discussion of antitrust offenses, we first have to say a few things about this so-called free market. What exactly is a free market? Technically, a free market is one in which the prices of goods and services are arranged by the mutual non-coerced consent of sellers and buyers. In theory, prices are determined by the law of supply and demand with no government interference in the regulation of costs, supply, or demand (Downes and Goodman, 2006). Free market economies can be contrasted with controlled economies, in which prices are set by a central authority. Soviet-style communism was an example of a controlled economy.

Although we call ourselves a free-market society, there is no such thing as a totally free market. As you have already seen in previous sections, there are all sorts of laws and regulations governing what and how things are produced, marketed, and sold. But relatively speaking, ours is a free-market economy, and that is one reason why we have antitrust laws and outlaw certain practices in the marketplace. We outlaw certain activities because we think that they somehow damage or negatively affect how the free market operates.

In theory, the free market is the most efficient form of economic organization. Businesses produce based on what they think the market (i.e., buyers) want, and buyers have the freedom to spend their money as they see fit. Businesses compete with one another for the attention of buyers. If a business firm meets the needs of buyers, they will buy its products or services and it will make money. The firm's competitors will have to match or better its performance if they want to stay in business. Everybody is supposed to benefit from this arrangement, but it often does not seem to work out that way.

Antitrust violations can be divided into two broad groups: restrictive trade agreements and monopolies or monopolistic practices.

Restrictive trade agreements are often called *restraints of trade*. A restrictive trade agreement is just that: some form of illegal agreement between producers or sellers in an industry to restrict how the industry works. Recall that in a free market, prices are supposed to be determined by the mutual non-coerced consent of *sellers and buyers*. In theory, this means that sellers are not supposed to cooperate or work together to determine prices. There are three basic forms of restrictive trade agreements: price fixing, bid rigging, and market division or allocation schemes. Price fixing refers to agreements between competitors to set or in some way manipulate prices so that they are held at a certain level. For example, Apple Inc. and five major book publishers were recently accused of conspiring to raise the prices of e-books. According to a civil lawsuit filed by the U.S. Department of Justice, Apple and the book publishers were unhappy that Amazon was offering e-books at deeply discounted prices. The conspirators were alleged to have agreed among themselves to raise the price of many of the most popular books from $9.99 to $12.99 or $14.99 and then to force this model on Amazon (Catan, Trachtenberg, and Bray, 2012). In another recent case, nine Japanese automotive suppliers pleaded guilty to fixing the prices of auto parts sold in the United States and paid $740 million in criminal fines (Trop, 2013). Bid rigging occurs when competitors agree in advance who will submit the lowest bid as part of a competitive bid process for a contract. The purchasers in bid rigging cases often are federal, state, or local governments. Finally, market allocation occurs when competitors get together and divvy up an area so that only one of them operates in any one area at a time. For example, in the late 1970s and early 1980s, much of the collection of residential and commercial waste in and around New York City was controlled by a cartel made up of small cartage companies. These companies were often family owned and passed on from one generation to the next. The carters engaged in a sophisticated and long-running customer allocation scheme in which customers were treated as assets that could be bought and sold. Prices were established and enforced by the cartel, and this conspiracy is estimated to have raised the prices paid by commercial customers by as much as 50 percent. An interesting feature of this market allocation scheme was that organized crime was involved in enforcing the allocation of customers, and knowledge that it was involved helped to restrict the access of large national waste collection firms to the local market (Reuter, 1993).

Monopolies and monopolistic practices are unfair attempts to corner a market or to drive out competitors from a marketplace. A monopoly is said to exist if one company controls an entire market, but a company can have monopolistic control even though it has competitors if it controls a large enough share of a market. Microsoft's Windows, for example, was recently declared to be a monopoly even though there are other operating systems available. The other systems have such a small market share and Windows has such a large share that it effectively controls the market. Not all monopolies are illegal. Indeed, some monopolies are explicitly created and sanctioned by the government, such as power and water utilities. We permit monopolies in these industries because it seems to make sense. You wouldn't want ten different water companies digging trenches and putting in water mains in your neighborhood.

Opportunity and Antitrust Offenses

Restrictive trade agreements are based on collusion between competitors in an industry, and they are more likely to arise under certain conditions. To be successful in their collusion, competitors must communicate, ensure compliance, and maintain secrecy. They must share information regarding how prices are to be set, markets divided, or bids rigged. The participants to the conspiracy also must have some method of ensuring that everyone complies with the terms of the agreement. Finally, they have to somehow hide their activities from purchasers and the government. Because of these requirements, restrictive trade agreements are more likely to arise in industries where there are few rather than many competitors. It is easier to share information, ensure compliance, and maintain secrecy among a small number of participants than it is among a large number.

Collusion is also more likely with some types of products than with others. For example, the probability of collusion increases if the product or service in question is standardized and if other products cannot be easily substituted for it. The more standardized the product is, the easier it is for competing firms to reach an agreement on prices. If other products cannot be easily substituted for the product in question, then the sellers do not have to worry that purchasers will simply buy something else if the price gets too high. Consider, for example, the natural gas industry and the retail pizza industry. Natural gas is natural gas. There is not much to differentiate between one kilogram of gas and another. Pizza, on the other hand, comes in an extraordinarily large number of permutations. It would be very difficult to agree upon a standard price, and even if the owners of pizza joints in a town could agree on a common price pattern, there would be limits on how high the price could be set. If it gets too unreasonable, consumers can simply switch to frozen pizza or another food entirely. For homeowners, however, switching from natural gas to some other form of energy is certainly a much more difficult undertaking than switching from pizza to spaghetti.

Finally, the nature of the relationships between competitors in an industry influences the likelihood of collusion. If competitors know one another well through social connections, trade associations, business contacts, or the movement of employees from one company to another, collusion becomes easier. For example, if a governmental agency makes repetitive purchases of a particular product or service, then over time vendors may come to know one another and decide to share the work for future contracts.

Summary

In this chapter, we have applied our opportunity perspective to a small selection of white-collar crimes. There are many other types that could have been chosen, and even among those that we did explore, there are subtypes and variants that we did not address. The typological approach that we used here, however, should not be overemphasized. Although each of the various crimes that we have discussed is based on a specific opportunity structure, there are, nevertheless, general themes that pertain to all of them. In this concluding section, we identify and explore these themes and touch briefly on their implications for the problem of controlling white-collar crime.

As Marcus Felson (2002, p. 99) has correctly pointed out, all predatory offenders have to solve the basic problem of gaining access to their intended crime target or victim. White-collar offenders have an advantage over street criminals in this regard, because by virtue of their occupational position, they have legitimate access to their target or victim (Felson, 2002). In none of the offenses examined here did the offenders have to break down a door or jimmy a lock or hide in the bushes and grab passersby. Rather, their access to the crime target was perfectly legal and normal.

The offender's specialized access to the crime target has profound implications for the problem of preventing these offenses. One of the major strategies used to prevent other forms of crime is to block the offender's access to the target. The whole point of locks, fences, and walls is to keep people with bad intentions away from you or something you value. For white-collar offenses, however, this strategy often is not feasible for obvious reasons. At least, it is not feasible in the form of physically blocking offenders from getting to a physical target. However, as we discuss in later chapters, there are ways to reconfigure the strategy of blocking access as applied to white-collar crime. Nevertheless, the problem of controlling white-collar crime remains enormously complicated.

All of the crimes that we have discussed in this chapter depend on the offender's conveying for some period of time a superficial appearance of legitimacy. The offenses involve behaviors or activities that look normal or routine when viewed from the outside. They somehow mimic or are based in normal economic activities. For example, during the housing boom of the 2000s, hundreds of thousands of subprime loans were made, packaged, and sold as mortgaged backed securities. Many, indeed probably a majority, of these activities were perfectly legal and appropriate, but a certain percentage was not. In these cases, buyers, brokers, lenders, and investment banks engaged in fraud—on their loan applications, via broker and lender targeting and deception of buyers, and by selling securities that held a much greater investment risk than advertised. In many health care frauds, a health care provider submits a claim to a health care insurer. There is nothing unusual about that. Illegality arises when the claim does not reflect what actually happened in the field. In price fixing, a product or service is offered for sale, which is perfectly normal. It becomes a crime when the price of the product has been set by collusion among sellers rather than by free and open competition. Thus, white-collar crime depends on and is intimately linked to legitimate economic activities.

Like specialized access, the superficial appearance of legitimacy has implications for crime prevention and control. Besides blocking access, another major prevention strategy is surveillance. Security cameras, private guards, and neighborhood watches are all based on the idea that offenders will refrain from committing crimes if they think they are under surveillance. In the case of white-collar crimes, however, surveillance is problematic. The problem is that what the offender is doing physically is not obviously illegal or perhaps even suspicious-looking. Thus, although surveillance can play an important role in white-collar crime prevention, it involves more than simply looking for something that is obviously out of place or suspicious. It requires piercing the appearance of legitimacy.

Earlier we defined deception as the "advantageous distortion of reality," with the advantage devolving to the offender. All of the offenses examined here somehow involve an advantageous distortion of reality, but the nature of the distortion and the way in which it is advantageous to the offender differ among crimes. There are two broad types of deception. They involve the presentation of misleading information and the concealment of information.

First, in many of the white-collar offenses examined here, the offenders in some way present misleading or false information about some aspect of a product or service. On the basis of that information, victims make decisions to relinquish control over economic resources to the benefit of offenders. The term *victims* needs to be construed broadly to include individuals, other organizations, and governmental programs. For example, in mortgage fraud, the victim may be an individual who buys a loan based on misleading information. Although they may seem different, many health care frauds work the same way, but here the victim is a health care insurer that pays for (in effect, buys) a service from a health care provider based on bad information.

Second, offenders can hide their activities and benefit by gaining control over economic resources that arise through the natural operation of the marketplace. For example, in price-fixing cases, offenders collude to set the price of some product or service above what it would be if the price were determined by competition. After the artificial price is set, the offenders benefit through the normal decisions of purchasers to buy products or services. Similarly, in stock manipulations, the offenders engage in clandestine actions that create a misleading image of the value of a stock or other type of security. They benefit if other players in the market behave normally in terms of their buying decisions.

Both kinds of deception—presenting misleading information and hiding information—have implications for the problem of control, which we briefly identify here and discuss more fully in future chapters. White-collar crimes based on the presentation of misleading information can be reduced if those who receive the information become better able to see through the misleading image that offenders try to create. To reduce offenses based on hiding information, we must become better at recognizing patterns of activities or at making the hiding of information riskier.

Note

1   The idea behind the creation of these new loan products was at the start commendable. It was hoped that ARMs, subprime loans, and all of the other new products would expand the housing market to previously underserved segments of the population. They were designed to make it possible for people of low to moderate incomes to buy their own homes.

6

CORPORATE VIOLENCE
Environmental, Workplace, and
Manufacturing Offenses

In the previous chapter, we examined crimes that impose financial or pecuniary costs on their victims, be they individuals, government agencies, or other businesses. In this chapter, we apply the opportunity perspective to environmental, workplace safety, and manufacturing crimes. These offenses are potentially much more serious. They may impose real physical costs on individuals. This is not to say that the perpetrators deliberately set out to harm other people. They do not. The physical harms that they cause are unintended in the sense that they are not what the offender is trying to achieve. The motivation for the offense is not to impose harm on others but rather to gain a financial advantage. Physical harm, however, is always a potential side effect. Thus, we examine what has been called the "quiet violence" of corporations (Frank, 1985).

In addition to the nature of the harm that they impose, the offenses discussed in this chapter differ from those examined earlier in another way as well. Their legal status as crimes is more ambiguous. In the previous chapter, we applied the opportunity perspectives to offenses that involve some kind of fraud. Recognition of the harmfulness of fraud and of the need to proscribe fraudulent behavior has deep roots in legal history, going back to biblical times and probably farther (Podgor, 1999). Although many of the specific offenses that we discussed earlier, such as subprime mortgage fraud and fraudulent billing in the health care industry, are new in the sense that they have come into being only relatively recently, their underlying illegality, nevertheless, is based on ancient legal principles. In this chapter, we deal with offenses that do not have such long historical pedigrees. These are modern offenses in the sense that they developed out of the industrialization and modernization of production in the past few centuries. Their legal status as crimes is still evolving. Many environmental, manufacturing, and workplace-related offenses are illegal in the sense that they violate various regulations, but they are not necessarily criminal. Indeed, an important part of the opportunity structures for these sorts of offenses is their status as regulatory as opposed to criminal violations.

Environmental Crime

In an influential book, *The Closing Circle: Nature, Men, and Technology*, environmental activist Barry Commoner linked rising levels of industrial pollution to the development of new technologies (Commoner, 1971). He observed that though new technological developments typically increase profits for business, they frequently are accompanied by detrimental environmental side effects. Extra profit for business was often at the expense of environmental degradation, and the costs of this degradation was borne by society as a whole and not the business per se. Commoner's work gave rise to a form of environmentalism that has affected *what* is defined as environmental crime and *how*-to "fight" the crime problem.

During the 1970s, Americans started to become increasingly sensitive to the high costs of pollution and to demand action against it. The case against the agricultural pesticide DDT for its harmful effects on wildlife and human health (documented in *Silent Spring* by Rachel Carson [1962]); the unforgettable sight of the Cuyahoga River, a tributary of Lake Erie, catching fire in 1969 as a result of petrochemical dumping by Cleveland and other Ohio cities; and the headlines garnered by 20 million Americans celebrating Earth Day in 1970 led the federal government (with President Nixon leading the charge) to mandate the creation of a centralized regulatory agency for environmental affairs, the U.S. Environmental Protection Agency (EPA). Joining the Environmental and Natural Resources Division (created in 1909) and the Environmental Crimes Section of the Department of Justice, this federal agency was given control over the enforcement of federal environmental statutes. The

EPA was designed to assist and cooperate with state-level enforcement or, if pollution laws were not sufficiently enforced, to supersede state authority with federal enforcement efforts. Under this collaborative model, the states handle the bulk of environmental enforcement today. In 1997, for instance, while the federal EPA initiated 4,129 actions, state environmental agencies initiated 10,515 administrative actions and referred 379 cases to state courts (Scalia, 1999). In Figure 6.1, looking just at enforcement of the Clean Air Act and pollution from stationary sources like chemical plants, utilities, and steel mills, we can see that federal enforcement efforts in fiscal year (FY) 2013 are dwarfed by those of the states. This distributional split is replicated for other types of pollution, such as hazardous waste disposal and water pollution.

The primary responsibility of the EPA is to clean up existing pollution problems and protect the environment and human health by enforcing environmental laws enacted by Congress. The EPA has criminal investigative and civil enforcement powers, which means that violators may be prosecuted and jailed for environmental crimes or brought into statutory compliance through civil/administrative enforcement of regulations. Criminal enforcement is rare, especially for corporations. For instance, between 1994 and 1997, a total of 1,846 defendants were charged with a criminal environmental offense. Yet, only 314 (17%) of those criminally charged were *organizational* defendants, most of which were charged with an environmental protection violation (Scalia, 1999). Criminal prosecution is typically reserved for the most egregious violations in which laws are knowingly and intentionally broken. In these kinds of cases, the goals of enforcement are to achieve both special and general deterrence.

Compliance is the main goal of civil and administrative enforcement under the assumption that highly punitive sanctions are unnecessary (or because, as we discuss later, criminal legal standards are too difficult to meet). It is a much more common form of regulatory intervention. For example, of the 4,129 federal environmental enforcement actions initiated in 1997, 88 percent (3,634) were administrative or civil in nature (Scalia, 1999). Data from FY 2013 also reveal a split heavily weighted toward noncriminal cases: 3,297 cases were opened but 2,418 were handled via civil judicial and administrative proceedings (U.S. Environmental Protection Agency, 2013).

Number of Facilities with Alleged Violations

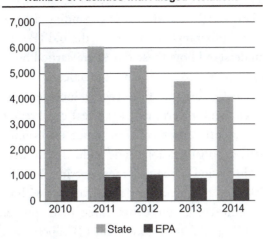

Number of Facilities Subject to Formal Enforcement

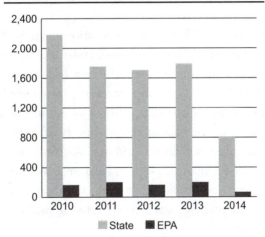

Figure 6.1 Clean Air Act facility alleged violations and formal enforcement, by federal and state agencies
Source: U.S. Environmental Protection Agency, 2014.

These statistics demonstrate that criminal intervention is relatively rare in the enforcement mix when violations are discovered. Yet, because we know so little about the hidden figure of environmental crime, it is difficult to estimate whether environmental enforcement effectively deters companies. The EPA, along with other federal agencies, is responsible for enforcing the law, which is continually expanding as new responsibilities and regulatory programs are added to the old (Portney, 2000). It is important to understand how these duties are carried out because criminal opportunities are tied to enforcement practices.

Individuals as well as organizations (which include not only businesses but also nonprofits and government agencies) can break environmental laws. Yet, until recently, most concern about environmental pollution has concentrated on organizational and industrial sources of pollution. Therefore, our discussion of environmental crime and the opportunity framework focuses on companies and the managers within them.

Recall that white-collar crime has three main properties: (1) specialized access, (2) spatial separation, and (3) superficial appearance of legitimacy. All of these characteristics are illustrated in the tragic 1980s case of the W.R. Grace Corporation and a small working-class town in Massachusetts.

The case against the W.R. Grace Corporation began in the mid-1970s when the residents of Woburn, Massachusetts started to realize that an abnormally large number of local children had contracted leukemia (Brown and Mikkelsen, 1990). For decades, the townspeople had noticed that a local lake, Lake Mishawum, often had a foul smell and an odd reddish color. They worried about the possibility of contaminated water because of the number of chemical and manufacturing plants in the area that produced toxic wastes. In 1978, two local wells were tested and had to be closed because of dangerously high levels of carbon-chloroform extract (CCE). At first, the problem was attributed to the method the town used to chlorinate water.

The problem with the water in Woburn, however, was much worse than an odd color and bad smell. The parents of the children diagnosed with leukemia eventually formed a committee to press for more testing. In 1979, the EPA tested the wetlands surrounding the two wells that had been closed and found elevated levels of arsenic, chromium, and lead—all known carcinogens. With help from researchers at the Harvard School of Public Health, the citizens group was able to document a statistically improbable cluster of leukemia cases in the Woburn area.

Eight families eventually filed a $100 million class action lawsuit against W.R. Grace. Of course, the company denied any wrongdoing. However, at the trial, it came out that the company's Cryovac Division had dumped toxic wastes on its property. The waste products eventually had filtered into the groundwater and from there into the homes and bodies of the people of Woburn. After a few years of legal maneuvering, W.R. Grace eventually settled with the families. In 1988, it was indicted and pled guilty in U.S. District Court of the crime of providing false statements to the EPA about its toxic waste disposal practices.

Unfortunately, what happened in Woburn, Massachusetts is not an isolated case (for additional examples, see Rosoff, Pontell, and Tillman, 2013, pp. 149–210). There are literally hundreds if not thousands of similar pollution scenarios involving other companies and other communities. In fact, an end of FY 2013 report by the Environmental and Natural Resources Division of the Department of Justice highlighted one of these cases as a major accomplishment of the division:

> In October 2012, following a three-week jury trial, Dominick Mazza, his company, Mazza & Sons, Inc., and Cross Nicastro, were convicted of conspiracy, Clean Water Act, Superfund, and false statement violations. Defendants conspired to fill Nicastro's 28-acre property on the Mohawk River in upstate New York, over the course of five years, with pulverized construction and demolition debris that was processed at New Jersey solid waste management facilities and then transported to the property. Law enforcement officials uncovered the plot just months after defendants began the operation, when they had already dumped at least 400 truckloads of debris at the site. Much of the material that was dumped was placed in and around waters of the United States and some of the material was found to be contaminated with asbestos. The conspirators then concealed the illegal dumping by fabricating a New York State Department of Environmental Conservation (DEC) permit and forged the name of a DEC official on the fraudulent permit. In June 2013, Dominick Mazza was sentenced to 51 months in prison to be followed by three years of supervised

release, and to pay a $75,000 criminal fine and $492,000 in res-
titution. Mazza & Sons, Inc., was sentenced to pay a $100,000
criminal fine and $494,000 in restitution and clean-up costs to
EPA, and received five years of corporate probation. The court
also ordered Mazza & Sons to fund and implement an environmental compliance plan administered by a third-party auditor
to prevent future environmental violations at their Tinton Falls,
New Jersey, recycling operation. Cross Nicastro was sentenced to
33 months in prison and three years of supervised release and
to pay $492,494 in restitution and a $25,000 criminal fine. (U.S.
Department of Justice, Environmental and Natural Resources
Division, 2013)

In all of these cases, a legitimate business produces some type of toxic
waste that it is supposed to handle and dispose of in a particular manner.
However, instead of doing that, the company disposes of the waste illegally in some other way. There are a number of different ways. Like W.R.
Grace, a company may simply dump the toxic waste on its own property.
Alternatively, the company can truck the waste somewhere else and dump
it, or more likely, hire someone else to do the same thing. Another strategy
is to mix the toxic waste with other, nontoxic waste and dispose of all of it
as nontoxic waste, which is much less stringently regulated and much less
costly to handle (Rebovich, 1992).

These cases display all of the characteristic features of white-collar
crime. The company has a legitimate right to use whatever chemicals or
materials are involved and is, in effect, on its honor to dispose of them
properly. Thus, it has specialized access. Those who will eventually be
harmed may be miles away from where the offense, the illegal dumping,
occurs. Finally, because there often are no obvious signs that something
bad has happened, the company appears to be doing nothing wrong, at
least as viewed from the outside. Indeed, in the Woburn case, the families had to spend an extraordinary amount of time and effort gathering
evidence to show that something illegal had happened. First, they had
to demonstrate that there was a statistically improbable cluster of leukemia cases in Woburn. Then they had to prove that toxic waste from
the Cryovac plant could filter into the groundwater and eventually into
the drinking water of residents. Finally, they had to show that employees

and managers at Cryovac did indeed improperly dispose of toxic waste. Although all of these facts were proved, it was a complicated and difficult process to do so (Brown and Mikkelsen, 1990).

The opportunity structure of illegal hazardous waste disposal has two key features. First, companies are trusted to be responsible for disposing of waste in a legal manner. Hence, they are in control regarding whether they do so or not. Second, if they choose to dispose of toxic waste illegally, the effects of their illegal actions are not immediately obvious and indeed are often delayed for considerable periods of time.

Companies such as W.R. Grace are able to engage in illegal disposal practices, primarily because of a lack of credible oversight (Shover and Hochstetler, 2006). As we noted at the start of this section, the enforcement system is an integral part of the opportunity structure for environmental crime. There are literally hundreds of thousands of business enterprises that produce some form of hazardous waste as a by-product of their normal operations. They range in size from behemoth corporations like the W.R. Grace Corporation to tiny mom-and-pop dry cleaning establishments. All of these enterprises are supposed to handle and dispose of their waste as specified by law and regulations. And herein lies the problem. It is impossible to watch all of these organizations to make sure that they actually do follow the law in disposing of their hazardous waste. The opportunity for environmental crime arises because it is difficult and costly to monitor whether companies are or are not complying with the law. Hence, the risk of the offense being exposed is low. Unfortunately, we do not really know how low the risk may be.

On the other side of the risk equation, many businesses—especially those in manufacturing sectors—are engaged in "productive" activities in which risk is an elemental component. For instance, the current manufacture of paper involves the use of bleach in pulp to strengthen paper and to keep it from yellowing when exposed to sunlight (www. paperonline.org/paper-making/paper-production/pulping/bleaching). Thus, pulp and paper facilities must store large amounts of the chemical on site and, because the bleaching process also requires the use of sizable amounts of water, companies must successfully manage potentially hazardous contamination on a daily basis. Although firms are moving away from using bleach in pulp and paper processing by substituting less toxic chemicals and new technologies that offer better environmental options

(U.S. Environmental Protection Agency, 2001), these still pose risks that need to be assessed and managed.

Conservation criminology (Herbig and Joubert, 2006), a newly developed theoretical framework, emphasizes this important link between environmental risks and crime. This approach, which integrates criminology, natural resource management, risks and decision science, offers insight into why environmental offending occurs; how enforcement and compliance operate (including the politicized process through which law is created and applied); the relationship between human and natural ecosystems, along with the governance and management of natural resources; and the technical and perceived risks related to human and natural systems (Gibbs, Gore, McGarrell, and Rivers, 2010; McGarrell and Gibbs, forthcoming).

Conservation criminology ties in nicely with our opportunity perspective in several ways. First, both recognize that opportunities are shaped and distributed according to the nature of economic and productive activities of different industries. Second, as these legitimate opportunities expand and new laws emerge, so too do unintended criminal opportunity structures. Third, risks are often unknown (but conservation criminology offers tools to systematically assess risks and vulnerabilities). Fourth, in the environmental realm not all harms are legally designated as crimes or even as offenses per se.

Keeping these similarities in mind, we now turn to a recent case of environmental crime where a relatively new opportunity[1] in an established industry resulted in death and extensive environmental degradation. The April 2010 oil spill that occurred when the oil rig Deepwater Horizon exploded and sank into the Gulf of Mexico is considered the largest spill in U.S. history (Congressional Research Service, 2014). The explosion killed 11 people and injured many others, and the pipe leaked oil and gas on the ocean floor for 87 days until the Macondo well was capped. In the interim, an estimated 4.9 million barrels of oil leaked into the Gulf, resulting in substantial deterioration of the ecosystem.

The primary corporate players in this disaster were British Petroleum (BP) PLC, the Swiss company Transocean Ltd., and Halliburton. Several lesser known companies were also named in court documents. BP pleaded guilty to criminal charges, admitting 11 counts of felony manslaughter, obstruction of Congress, and a series of environmental crimes, and agreed to a $4 billion fine. Class action claims by individuals and businesses who were economically harmed by the spill were settled by BP (which then challenged the settlement and lost). The company ultimately agreed to put aside $9.2 billion for claims (Trefis Team, 2014). Civil cases related to violation of environmental statutes are still pending and could cost BP additional billions of dollars in fines. Transocean agreed to pay $1.4 billion in civil and criminal fines and penalties, primarily related to federal Clean Water Act civil penalty claims. In a move to settle most claims against the company and avoid future liability regarding legal claims filed on behalf of thousands of potential victims whose "lives and livelihoods were ruined by the spill," Halliburton pled guilty to destroying evidence after the incident and agreed to settle claims for $1.1 billion without admitting negligence. Halliburton contracted with BP to provide cement for the Macondo well (*USA Today*, 2014).

Only four individuals have been charged in the Deepwater Horizon oil spill case. Prosecutors brought criminal charges ranging from obstruction of justice (deleting e-mails and voice mail communications) and lying to Congress, to seaman's manslaughter and involuntary manslaughter. Seaman's manslaughter is a special type of manslaughter charge in which criminal penalties (fines or up to 10 years imprisonment, or both) may be levied when loss of life results from a wrongful act related to misconduct, negligence, or inattention to duties by "captains, engineers, pilots or other persons" (Akpinar, 2010). In addition, some defendants were also charged with violation of the federal Clean Water Act (Thompson and Galafaro, 2013). Kurt Mix was found guilty in 2013 of obstructing justice but was granted a new trial based on his claim of juror misconduct (Fisk, 2014). The two supervisors charged with manslaughter (Robert Kaluza and Donald Vidrine) brought a motion to dismiss the manslaughter charges, but a judge ruled against their argument. The judge did agree, however, to drop the seaman's manslaughter charges, as neither Kaluza nor Vidrine had navigation functions in their jobs (Stempel, 2014). After two postponements, the trial of David Rainey (BP's former vice president of exploration for the Gulf of Mexico), charged with lying to Congress and making false statements to investigators, is scheduled to begin October 24, 2014 (Huffington Post, 2014).

The cause of the disaster has been linked to several factors: (1) a corporate culture of recklessness, (2) failure to utilize proper safety procedures once indicators of well instability were identified and noted by supervisors (Kaluza and Vidrine), and (3) a weak system of regulation. The culture of recklessness is apparent in e-mail communications exchanged between the well engineer and his boss during the construction of the Macondo well. The engineer noted significant production problems. He observed that the drilling crew was "flying by the seat of our pants" under a "huge level of paranoia" that was "driving chaos," concluding that "the operation is not going to succeed if we continue in this manner" (Rushe, 2013). Because of its depth and use of new technology, the risks of the Macondo well were relatively unknown. Yet, these very characteristics *should* have produced a full environmental assessment and review—at least according to the 2004 Minerals Management Service (MMS) Guidelines. The MMS is the federal regulatory agency in charge of overseeing the offshore oil and gas industry. However, the MMS granted a "categorical exclusion" from the National Environmental Policy Act (NEPA) to certain oil and gas activities in the Gulf of Mexico during the Bush administration, which exempted this site (along with others) from extensive environmental review. The MMS also discounted any substantial environmental damage from oil spills in the region where the future well would be located. For instance, the agency predicted that offshore oil spills resulting from a proposed action would not likely damage significantly any wetlands along the Gulf Coast; that impacts to wetland habitats from an oil spill would be expected to be low and temporary; and that at the expected level of impact, the influence on commercial fishing activities would be negligible and indistinguishable from variations due to natural causes. Taking extant empirical data on loss of well control and blowouts into account, they concluded that these were rare events and of short duration—thus, their potential impacts to marine water quality were not expected to be significant (Cleveland, 2013). It would be belaboring the obvious to note that this assessment was wrong in every regard. Of course even if a full environmental report had been submitted and assessed, and the well approved in spite of its deficiencies, it is not at all clear that the regulatory system could have prevented the disaster given that the MMS has about 60 inspectors to cover nearly 4,000 offshore facilities in the Gulf of Mexico (Cleveland, 2013).

In a commissioned postmortem report by the National Academy of Engineering, it was revealed that the blowout preventer technology utilized by Deepwater Horizon "was neither designed nor tested for the dynamic conditions that most likely existed at the time that attempts were made to recapture well control." The report also suggests that the shortcomings of Deepwater's equipment "may be present" at other deepwater drilling operations (National Academy of Engineering, 2011, p. 71). Although the Obama administration put a moratorium on Gulf drilling and committed to following the recommendations of experts (including those of the National Academy of Engineering), at this time, drilling has resumed at an accelerated pace in the Gulf, while few of the recommendations have been implemented—especially those related to blowout preventers (Birnbaum and Savitz, 2014).

The conservation criminology perspective offers analytic insight into the Deepwater Horizon case (McGarrell and Gibbs, forthcoming) by providing answers to some critical questions such as: (1) Why were the MMS regulations regarding deep water drilling in the Gulf mitigated during the Bush administration? and (2) Why did the MMS discredit the risks associated with drilling? The risk literature suggests that political action depends on an alignment between actuarial and public perception of risk. In effect, effective legislation requires strong public support. Because environmental regulators operate in a politically charged sphere with powerful corporate actors (and jobs) on one side and environmentalists on the other, it would appear that public opinion had not been swayed in the direction of legislative restrictions. In fact, the "evidence" presented by MMS suggested little risk associated with the deep-well drilling and the potential for blowouts. The risk assessments that were conducted did not appear to balance the likely costs to people, wildlife, and the environment (i.e., the natural resources perspective) but instead focused primarily on the consequences for commercial fishing interests. Finally, in the wake of the disaster, conservation criminology would expect fraud and other crimes to accompany new regulations and controls. Evidence clearly suggests that this has occurred. The Department of Justice, for instance, has committed to thoroughly investigate "all meritorious reports of fraud related to the oil spill and its aftermath, including fraudulent claims, charity fraud, identity theft, insurance fraud, and procurement and government-benefit fraud" (U.S. Department of Justice, 2014).

The BP case was discovered only after a spectacularly noticeable explosion. But environmental offenses may be exposed in a variety of different ways, including self-reports, inspections, whistle-blowing, and accidental discovery. Companies are required to keep track of how they handle hazardous waste and to self-report any instances of noncompliance. Although W.R. Grace certainly did not disclose its offense, some companies do make such reports, perhaps because they fear the negative publicity that would result if the offense were to come to light via other means. The ratio of reported to nonreported instances of noncompliance, however, is not known. Offenses can also be discovered by the EPA inspectors. Unfortunately, though, inspections are relatively rare because waste-producing enterprises vastly outnumber inspectors. Two other mechanisms of exposure are accidental discovery by the general public, such as an oil spill or fish kill, and whistle-blowing by knowledgeable employees.

Whistle-blowing is a potentially important source of exposure and hence risk for companies that violate environmental regulations. When a company *knowingly* engages in environmental crime, efforts are made, of course, to conceal the activity. Yet, within the company, multiple parties may be privy to the knowledge that a crime has occurred. From the point of view of company managers, all of these individuals are potential sources of risk because they could expose the offense. Because businesses vary greatly in size and structure, who and how many within a company may know about illegal activity also varies. Larger companies, compared with smaller ones, are more likely to be divided into specialized areas that make it easier to hide illegality from managers and employees in other areas. Smaller firms, on the other hand, are more likely to have a "flat" management structure (Barlow, 1993; Makkai and Braithwaite, 1994). Such a structure increases the likelihood that top managers will have actual knowledge of an illegal activity when it occurs. Legally, however, top managers are held liable for illegal activities that they *should* have known about but did not (Cohen, 1998).

Finally, it is important to recognize that in the case of environmental crimes, the potential offenders—businesses—have a great deal of influence over the nature of the oversight that is imposed on them. The system of enforcement that we have now came about as a result of a negotiated political process. The business community resisted the establishment of the EPA, and since they failed, they have continually attempted to restrict its size and legal mandate (Burns and Lynch, 2004, p. 71). Indeed, in the 1980s, during the Reagan administration, efforts were made to deregulate the environment and to reduce the EPA's budget (Burns and Lynch, 2004). To a degree, then, businesses can shape the opportunity structures for their offenses through their influence over the enforcement process. Large, well-established companies generally have more economic and political power than those that are smaller and newer. This translates into influential congressional and corporate friends, community leaders, and other stakeholders who make it more difficult for regulators to investigate and pursue offenders even if violations somehow come to light (Shover and Hochstetler, 2006).

All of these mechanisms produce a certain number of known instances of environmental crime every year. Yet, because many environmental offenses are not obvious, we never know how many offenses go undiscovered. The executives at W. R. Grace may have reasonably assumed that the benefit of their "crime" (saving money that would normally be spent on environmentally sound disposal of toxic waste) outweighed its costs (low risk of discovery). Yet, it is important to recognize that there are countervailing forces that business must contend with and that can potentially raise the costs of environmental deviance. As we know from the Deepwater Horizon/BP oil spill, the victims of environmental crimes are not always just individuals. Other organizations or groups may be harmed as well as wildlife. For instance, the Love Canal section of Niagara Falls in New York and the city of Times Beach, Missouri were evacuated and, in the case of Times Beach, purchased by the government and destroyed after toxic chemicals were found in the soil. Illegal use, storage, and disposal of toxic chemicals by companies (Hooker Chemical and Northeastern Pharmaceutical and Chemical Company) were implicated in both cases. The municipal, state, and federal governments got involved—as they did in the 2010 BP oil spill, suing the industrial giants for redress on behalf of the victims and for financial assistance to help the federal government clean up the waste sites (Superfund). In these cases, the power relationship between offenders and victims is more balanced and less asymmetric than is often the case between environmental offenders and their victims. For example, an employee of a large petroleum company accused of illegal waste disposal once acknowledged that power asymmetries can vary when he observed, "I don't think the company is too awfully worried about suits filed by their own employees. They were more worried about the state because it has clout" (Trost, 2008).

Finally, we note that the cost of pollution weighs more heavily on some segments of society than others. Research has suggested, for instance, that minorities and the poor are disproportionately affected by pollution (Checker, 2005). Indeed, some suggest that victimization occurs precisely because these groups have less economic and political power to protect their communities from environmental polluters in the first place, and these same groups lack the resources to force environmental cleanup once pollution has occurred (or to move out of areas that have higher pollution levels). The term *environmental injustice* has been coined to describe the unequal distribution of environmental risks and hazards to which members of disadvantaged groups are subjected. We talk more about environmental injustice in Chapter 8.

Workplace Crimes

Many different kinds of crimes occur in the workplace, but only some of these fit with our definition of white-collar offending (Friedrichs, 2002). For instance, an angry spouse can shoot his wife while she is working or one worker may steal another's wallet. These are more traditional kinds of crimes that can occur anywhere. The workplace is merely the setting in which the event transpires. However, some kinds of white-collar offenses arise out of the unique opportunities that are presented by a particular organizational structure or by a particular occupational position. In this section, we focus on work conditions that are hazardous for employee health and safety.

Many, but not all, workplace safety and health violations are regulated by the Occupational Safety and Health Administration (OSHA). Others may fall under more specialized agencies, such as the Mine Safety and Health Administration (MSHA) (Shover, Clelland, and Lynxwiler, 1986) or the Nuclear Regulatory Commission. Like the EPA, OSHA is a fairly new regulatory agency. The Occupational Safety and Health Act of 1970 established a federal program to protect most workers from job-related deaths, injuries, and illnesses. Established by the then Secretary of Labor, James Hodgson, on April 28, 1971, the task of the new agency was to administer the provisions of the OSH Act (MacLaury, 2008).

Although OSHA was established less than 40 years ago, the dangers associated with working conditions were recognized long before that. In this country, laws governing the safety of working conditions started to appear during the mid-19th century (Frank, 1993) and served as a rallying point for organized labor in the United States in the 1900s. Sadly, however, despite the laws and OSHA, work-related diseases, injuries, and deaths are estimated to number in the hundreds of thousands (if not higher) annually (Reiman, 1990). Some of these tragic outcomes are accidents or due to negligence on the part of workers; yet, evidence suggests that firms too often fail to properly warn employees about hazardous conditions and neglect to train or equip them to safely negotiate the workplace. One estimate holds that up to one-third of all on-the-job injuries are due to illegal working conditions (Reasons, Ross, and Paterson, 1981). Unfortunately, taking precautions to protect workers is viewed by some firms as overly burdensome and costly to the company's bottom line (Clinard and Yeager, 1980, p. 69; Szasz, 1984).

When workplace violations do occur, there are regulatory, civil (tort), and criminal enforcement actions that can be brought against offenders (Frank, 1993). However, as is true in the case of environmental enforcement, criminal prosecution of OSHA cases is the legal intervention of last resort (Hawkins, 2002). For example, a careful review of OSHA data by the *New York Times* found that between 1982 and 2002, there were 2,197 cases in which a worker had died because of a willful violation of safety laws by the employer. Only 196 of these cases (less than 10%) were referred for criminal prosecution. Of these, only half led to convictions, and only 20 percent of the convictions led to sentences of incarceration. All in all, the likelihood that someone will be imprisoned when a worker dies as a result of a willful safety violation is less than 1 in 100 (Cullen et al., 2006).

In many ways, the opportunity structure for workplace offenses is similar to that for environmental crime, but there are some unique characteristics as well. As with most environmental crimes, in the case of workplace crimes, the criminal actors (whether the firm or officers of the company) are engaged in legitimate economic activity. Since a primary goal of owners and managers is to make a profit, they are always looking for ways to reduce the costs of production. Holding everything else constant, if costs can be reduced, then profits go up. For most businesses, the cost of labor has a significant impact on overall profitability. Hence, there is a built-in incentive to cut labor costs whenever possible. One way of doing this is by skimping on safety and in the process endangering workers.

For example, a case exposed by the *New York Times* involving McWane Inc., a privately held company headquartered in Birmingham, Alabama, provides a textbook example of the link between cutting costs and dangerous workplaces (Barstow and Bergman, 2003). McWane Inc. makes pipes, and it has profited enormously using "the McWane way" of running things. The McWane way is to cut labor costs to the bone by reducing the number of workers to the bare minimum, requiring the workers who are left to work extended hours, and avoiding as many safety-related costs as possible. These measures have made McWane one of the most profitable pipe manufacturers in America and one of the most dangerous employers in America. According to the *Times*, between 1995 and 2003, at least 4,600 injuries have been recorded in McWane foundries. Nine workers have been killed, and the company was cited for more than 400 federal health and safety violations. This is far more than all six of their major competitors combined (Barstow and Bergman, 2003).

Let's consider the story of McWane and the Tyler Pipe Company in more detail. In 1995, McWane bought Tyler Pipe, a foundry located in Tyler, Texas, and using the McWane way, turned it into a hellhole for the most disadvantaged and vulnerable of workers. After McWane bought the plant, it cut nearly two-thirds of employees while insisting that productivity remain the same. Safety inspectors, pollution control personnel, relief workers, cleaning crews, and maintenance workers were all eliminated. Rather than have three 8-hour shifts, the company instituted two 12-hour shifts and often required employees to work even more hours 7 days a week. Conditions at the plant in Tyler got so bad that the company had to recruit employees from local prisons, and "only the desperate" would seek work at Tyler Pipe (Barstow and Bergman, 2003).

Not all types of work carry the same potential for harm. Generally speaking, employment in unskilled jobs, especially those in mining, manufacturing, and production, increases the risk of illegal exposure to hazardous substances or unsafe conditions on the job (although repetitive stress injuries can occur in clerical/secretarial and other forms of service work). Because these jobs are stratified by gender, race, and class, the chances of victimization are not distributed evenly within society, nor is the opportunity or means for redress (Szockyj and Fox, 1996)—a point we return to in Chapter 9.

A key property of white-collar offending is the spatial separation of victim and offender. In our environmental crime example, we noted how difficult it can be to trace victimization to its source. In the workplace, there is less separation between offenders and victims than in the case of environmental crime because both work for the same organization. Yet, the top managers who make health and safety decisions are unlikely to work "on the floor" in a plant or in the mine, where exposure risks are greatest. And in cases where the corporation is separated into divisions, top management may work in a corporate headquarters located hundreds or thousands of miles away from manufacturing facilities. Moreover, because the risks of working with hazardous and toxic substances may not be apparent for many years and may be confounded by other "risk" factors (e.g., smoking), employees may never know that their ill health is caused by unsafe working conditions (Calhoun and Hiller, 1992). In mining and textiles, black and brown lung disease has been firmly established as an occupational health hazard associated with these lines of work. This risk has been ascertained after decades of medical research. Thus, for this type of white-collar crime, there is a physical and symbolic division of labor between the offender and victim that is akin to the kind of spatial separation that we have discussed earlier.

Our framework suggests that companies that violate OSHA regulations will try to maintain the appearance of legal compliance. They try to do so in a variety of different ways. Some may provide limited, but not sufficient, training or safety equipment to employees, perpetrating the illusion that health and safety provisions for employees have been met and are taken seriously. A firm also may purposely keep knowledge about toxic exposure and its consequences from employees, in some cases referring workers to "company" doctors who dismiss illnesses or fail to "connect the dots" that implicate toxic exposure in the workplace (e.g., liver cancer is caused by alcohol consumption and not by exposure to vinyl chloride). Indeed, corporations have a long history of knowingly exposing their employees to hazardous substances on the job while maintaining the illusion of ignorance (Calhoun and Hiller, 1992).

A famous example in this regard involves the Johns-Manville Corporation and asbestos (Brodeur, 1985). The potential dangers of exposure to asbestos, a mineral highly valued and useful for its resistance to heat, have been recognized since the first century of the common era. Breathing asbestos-laden dust can lead to asbestosis, a crippling and usually fatal lung disease. The Johns-Manville Corporation produced and marketed asbestos products for decades. Since at least the 1930s, the company had internal medical reports of asbestosis among its workers. Yet, it hid this information about health hazards from its own workers for decades (Brodeur, 1985; Calhoun and Hiller, 1992). By the 1970s, thousands of former Johns-Manville workers were dead or dying as a result of asbestos exposure (Friedrichs, 2010).

Knowingly exposing employees to unsafe working conditions also seems to be more common in certain industries—both within the United States and globally. For instance, unsafe conditions are a feature of mining operations. The Sago mine in West Virginia, where twelve miners were killed in an explosion underground in 2006, was issued more than 270 safety citations in the 2 years prior to the explosion. Some of these citations were known to management in the Massey Energy Company and were related to problems that could result in shaft collapse and explosions. Several years before the Sago mine exploded—an incident that was followed 2 weeks later by a fire with two fatalities at another mine also owned by Massey—the U.S. Mine Safety and Health Administration adopted a cooperative health and safety partnership with labor, mine operators, and industry associations ostensibly coupled with strong enforcement against unsafe operators. But critics of the cooperative tactic suggested that the regulatory strategy adopted by MSHA failed. It failed to effectively step up enforcement after cooperative interventions failed; the agency became less transparent as the cooperative strategy was implemented; and MSHA may not have effectively condemned the violations—i.e., it was overly lenient in its regulatory style (Simpson, 2006). A *New York Times* (2006) editorial noted, "[S]adly, in the way mines are often run, the $24,000 in fines paid by the Sago managers last year constituted little more than the cost of doing business. In the Appalachian routine, miners balking at risky conditions down below can quickly forfeit their livelihood if they have no union protection."

The U.S. record, however, is much better than mining operations in other countries. The MSHA realized a 35 percent decrease in fatal accidents after 2000 (Simpson, 2006). In Turkey, on the other hand, there have been 1,308 fatal accidents since 2000; in 2013, 13,000 miners were involved in accidents and 10.4 percent of all work-related accidents in Turkey were in the mining industry (Senerdem, 2014). However, unlike in the United States, where supervisors and executives are rarely criminally prosecuted for negligence and manslaughter, in 2014 after 301 miners were killed in a mining explosion in Turkey, prosecutors arrested and charged 7 mine executives and supervisors with negligent death. This occurred in the context of significant public protest amid news reports that high levels of toxic gas were noted by sensors inside the mine several days before the disaster but company officials took no action (Associated Press, 2014).

The opportunity perspective, thus, can be usefully applied to workplace safety offenses. Next, we see how the techniques of white-collar crime (deception, abuse of trust, and concealment) are utilized by OSHA violators. To do so, we draw from a well-known corporate crime case involving Occidental Chemical Company. Occidental workers were found to be sterile as a result of handling the pesticide DBCP (Simon and Etizen, 1990), a chemical used to control fruit pests.

DBCP was banned by the EPA in the late 1970s, but the damage had already been done. The company knew DBCP caused testicular atrophy in animals but took no action to warn its employees of potential consequences. A lawsuit was brought against the three largest producers of the chemical (Dow, Shell, and Occidental) by 57 employees. Twenty-five of these claims were ultimately settled by Occidental for $425,000 (Gold, 1989).

This case demonstrates how the white-collar offending techniques discussed throughout this book can inform our understanding of unsafe production. From all accounts Occidental management knew the results from numerous studies by scientists at Shell and Dow Chemical that suggested alarming reproductive consequences associated with DBCP exposure. Occidental deceived its employees, failing to "connect the dots" even after an unusually high level of childlessness was noticed among male workers. The callous disregard for the safety of its employees is obvious in a remark made by one Occidental official in a film made about the case, *The Song of the Canary*. He said, "Heck, we just didn't draw the conclusion that there'd be sterility from the fact that the testicles were shriveling up."

Concealment, the last technique to be discussed, is a critical element of unsafe productions. In the Occidental case, management knew of the hazards but concealed the evidence. If the true dangers of the workplace were revealed to employees, it might be hard to attract and keep them, or firms might need to raise wages in order to attract willing workers. The cost of cleanup, added safety training and equipment, and the risk of medical bills and potential lawsuits almost guarantee that many, if not most, companies will conceal rather than reveal violations and employee risks.

There are two key features to the opportunity structure for workplace crimes. First, like environmental offenses, they occur incidentally to and as a by-product of legitimate economic activities that are conducted for the most part in private spaces, that is, within a private company's workplace. Hence, the offense is difficult to observe from the outside. The enforcement of workplace safety laws suffers from the same weakness as environmental enforcement. OHSA, like the EPA and the MMS, is not up to the task. There are too many potential offenders and far too few inspectors. Second, the victims are either not aware that they are being exposed to a hazardous substance or workplace condition or they are powerless to do anything about it. Workers may be powerless simply because they have no other employment opportunities and are desperate for work. From the perspective of the company, both of these factors reduce the risk that their illegal and harmful treatment of workers will be exposed.

The twin problems of ignorance and powerlessness often are exacerbated for workers outside of the United States, particularly those in less developed countries (recall the 2013 building collapse in Bangladesh in which more than 1,000 garment workers, mostly poor young women, were killed). The size and scale of business operations affect economic and political power not just in this country but worldwide. Large and profitable companies from the United States and other capitalist industrialized nations that stoke the economic engines of the developed world have significant environmental and workplace safety consequences in lesser developed countries.

To illustrate this point, we draw from the legal case in Nicaragua against Occidental (shipping DBCP overseas). In 1958, unpublished initial studies of the chemicals' toxicity by Dow Chemical and Shell Oil revealed adverse effects to the endocrine system. Yet, in 1964, the chemical companies received approval for the commercial distribution and sale of Nemagon without modification and without any recommendations for protective clothing or special handling of the chemical.

When the EPA banned Nemagon in the United States, the agency pulled the chemical off the market here, citing its toxic effects on human chromosomes. DBCP does not dissipate easily. Rather, according to EPA reports, the chemical can persist in the air, soil, and water—contaminating multiple generations. Costa Rica also banned Nemagon, and as a consequence, two of the three major banana-producing companies in Central America switched to other, more expensive nematicides. One company, Standard Fruit, continued using Nemagon. Farmworkers and others in Nicaragua believe that DBCP is still being used in some pesticides. In addition, seepage from buried tanks of the pesticide into the environment continues to expose Nicaraguans to extremely hazardous conditions. As one might expect, it is difficult for host-country citizens to seek legal redress for wrongs done to them by multinational corporations. Some legal groundwork has been laid by the Nicaraguan National Assembly that would allow farmworkers to sue foreign corporations, and in December 2002, three U.S. corporations (Dole, Dow, and Shell) were found liable under Nicaraguan Law 364. The companies were ordered to pay $490 million in a class action lawsuit filed by 583 farm laborers who were exposed to the chemical while picking bananas (International Committee in Solidarity with the Victims of Nemagon, 2008). As is typical in these kinds of cases, U.S. companies have denied the legality of the case on technical grounds and have asked for a new trial in the United States.

Manufacturing Crimes

The foundations of early capitalism rested on the idiom "buyer beware," implying that the ultimate responsibility for protecting oneself from flawed products in the marketplace rested with the customer. In the United States, Americans most likely were formally and collectively introduced to manufacturing wrongdoings when Upton Sinclair published his treatise on the trials of working-class and immigrant life in the United States. In *The Jungle*, Sinclair (1906) exposed how the meat packing industry sold rotten and diseased meat to unsuspecting customers. Not long after the book was published, the 1906 Pure Food and Drug Act was passed and a fledgling consumer movement was given momentum that did not fully materialize until the 1960s (Mayer, 2012).

Manufacturing crimes are those in which unsafe products are knowingly marketed to consumers (Clinard and Yeager, 1980) or those in which manufacturers put products on the market before they have been properly tested and their safety established. Pharmaceutical companies may, for instance, falsify drug testing results or even fabricate them (Braithwaite, 1984). These kinds of offenses are consistent with our definition of white-collar crime in that: (1) there is spatial separation between the offenders and victims, (2) the production of the flawed product occurs under the guise of legitimacy, and (3) the manufacturer has specialized access to consumers.

There are many known instances of manufacturing crimes, but, as we have discussed earlier, known cases are likely a small percentage of the total number of offenses that occur in any given year. The discovery of manufacturing crime often depends on someone getting injured and being able to track that injury back to its source. Oftentimes, making this connection—especially against powerful corporate actors—is difficult.

Although one of the most infamous cases of manufacturing crime is the Ford Pinto case (Cullen et al., 2006; Dowie, 1987; Swigert and Farrell, 1981), nearly 40 years later General Motors Corporation finds itself in the midst of its own scandal. GM has issued a recall for 2.6 million vehicles that have a dangerous defect associated with the ignition switch, including the popular Saturn, Pontiac, and Chevrolet brands and an additional 3 million or more larger automobiles thought to have a separate ignition defect. According to the National Highway Transportation and Safety

Administration—the regulatory agency charged with investigating safety defects and setting and enforcing safety and performance standards for motor vehicles (see the NHTSA website)—the faulty automobiles marketed by GM are responsible for 31 crashes, with 13 related fatalities. This number is likely to increase before the GM case is concluded. Research by the Center for Auto Safety (CAS), for instance, has identified a total of 303 fatalities associated with airbags that failed to deploy—a likely consequence of the defective ignition switch (Boudette and Fuller, 2014).

GM chief executive officer Mary Barra, who in testimony to Congress cited results from an internal investigation, identified a single engineer in the firm who was able to approve the use of a switch that didn't meet company specifications, and who, years later, ordered a change to that switch without anyone else at GM being aware (Click On Detroit, 2014). In her testimony, Barra repeatedly noted that the "culture of secrecy" that gave rise to the production and dissemination of faulty automobiles was a problem in the "old GM" but not in the 2014 GM.

The GM case highlights a tactic often adopted by companies that are under litigation threat. General Motors filed for bankruptcy in 2009, which puts any lawsuits brought against the firm on hold until the bankruptcy is complete. Lawyers for GM will likely argue that the defective ignition was a "product of the old GM" and that the new GM should not be liable. In this way, the new corporate entity would avoid the costs associated with any lawsuits (Boudette and Fuller, 2014).

Summary

In this chapter, we have explored three forms of corporate violence. Like the property crimes that we examined in the previous chapter, environmental, workplace-safety, and manufacturing crimes have their own opportunity structures that are based on the characteristics that we have identified as important for white-collar crime. These characteristics include specialized access, spatial separation, and superficial appearance of legitimacy. In addition, like all white-collar crimes, these offenses involve the use of deception, concealment, and the abuse of trust. Yet, these offenses also have several unique features that need to be noted. These features influence our ability to detect and control these forms of white-collar crime.

First, even though manufacturing offenses, workplace-safety violations, and environmental crimes can have potentially devastating physical effects, they are, oddly enough, not predatory crimes. That is, the offenders do not intend to deliberately harm another person or persons. Indeed, the offenders would prefer that no one be physically harmed because the lack of obvious physical harm makes it easier to conceal the offense. When consumers die, as happened in the GM recall case, or children fall ill with leukemia, as happened in Woburn, it draws attention and may eventually lead to the discovery of the offense. One implication of this feature is that if the crimes do come to light and are brought into court, the offenders can reasonably claim that they never intended to harm anyone.

Second, the offenses may be hidden within the businesses, making their discovery especially difficult. For example, the safety violations that plagued the workers in McWane's pipe foundries all occurred on premises controlled by McWane. The Cryovac Division of W.R. Grace dumped toxic waste on land that it owned. In both of these cases, the offenses were shielded from the scrutiny of outsiders. Unless and until something obviously bad happens, the only ways in which the offense is going to be discovered is through either a regulatory inspection or a complaint by an inside whistle-blower. For employers like McWane, who attract only the most vulnerable and desperate employees, the likelihood of a whistle-blower stepping forward is low. Also low is the likelihood of frequent and vigorous regulatory inspections. Thus, the offender's ability to control the space within which the offenses occur is an important feature of the opportunity structures for workplace safety and environmental offenses.

A third, and final, feature of these offenses also involves the opportunity structure. In a sense, the opportunity structure is shaped at least in part by the offenders themselves through their influence over the regulatory regime that governs their activities. We elaborate on this idea in more detail in Chapter 9, where we focus on legal remedies for corporate crime. So here we provide only a brief overview.

One way to see how the business community shapes the very opportunity structures that it takes advantage of is to consider how lawmaking in regard to street crime differs from law making for white-collar crimes. Have you ever seen or heard of your state legislature inviting in burglars or robbers to comment on proposed changes in the law governing burglary or robbery, such as, for example, an increase in penalties? Of course not. Indeed, we are sure the question strikes you as ludicrous. Yet, something very similar to this happens whenever legislative authorities contemplate changing the laws or implementing new criminal laws regarding business activities. CEOs, industry representatives, and lobbyists are invited or invite themselves to meet with legislators or to address committees to give their input on how the law should be written and enforced. The influence of the business community over regulatory agencies and the development of regulatory codes is even more pronounced, and this is especially the case with respect to the EPA and OSHA (Burns and Lynch, 2004; Calavita, 1983). In effect, the business community exerts a direct influence on the degree of the oversight that will be imposed on it. Less oversight equals better opportunities for crime. Ordinary street criminals should be so lucky.

Note

1 The first successful 3,000-meter well was drilled in 2003 (www.visiongain.com/ Report/955/The-Deepwater-Ultra-Deepwater-Exploration-Production-Market-2013–2023). The Deepwater Horizon well was substantially deeper: 18,360 feet— or approximately 5,596 meters below sea level (www.justice.gov/opa/documents/ transocean-plea-agreement.pdf).

PART IV
THE SYMBOLIC CONSTRUCTION AND SOCIAL DISTRIBUTION OF OPPORTUNITIES

The opportunity perspective assumes that white-collar crime opportunities arise out of legitimate business activities and that all business or areas of economic activity create some type of opportunity for white-collar crime. That is, opportunities appear to be ubiquitous, or to put it another way, lure is everywhere. Even though opportunities to engage in white-collar crimes would appear to be all around us, not everyone (thankfully for society) avails themselves of these opportunities. Rather, most people obey the law most of the time. That conformity to the law is widespread throughout society raises an important question for the opportunity perspective advanced here and for any criminological theory based on rational choice. If opportunities are ubiquitous, then why do only some people take advantage of them, while other similarly situated individuals do not?

In Chapter 7, we argue that one answer to this question can be found in how potential white-collar offenders conceive or symbolically construct opportunities, paying particular attention to the processes of neutralization and normalization of deviance. In Chapter 8, we present a different answer to the question, one that focuses on how the sociodemographic characteristics of social class, gender, and race influence access to white-collar crime opportunities. Opportunities for white-collar crime may, indeed, be ubiquitous throughout the business world, but access to these opportunities is not the same for everyone. People of a certain social class (high-level executives), gender (male), or race (white) are more likely to end up in occupational positions that provide access to white-collar crime opportunities than people of other class backgrounds (low-level employees), gender (female), and racial or ethnic identities (African American or Hispanic).

7

THE SYMBOLIC CONSTRUCTION OF OPPORTUNITY
The Neutralization and Normalization of Deviance

One of the main points made in the preceding chapters is that white-collar crime arises out of legitimate business activities. Indeed, it is the structure and organization of particular business activities that create opportunities for particular types of white-collar crime. The types of fraud that we see today in the health care system, for example, are possible in part because of the way in which health care in the United States is organized. Imagine for a moment that consumers paid for health care directly out of their own pockets instead of having costs paid mainly by insurance companies and government programs. There would still be opportunities for fraud, but they would not be the same types of opportunities that we have today. For instance, it is difficult to imagine how one could carry off the "rent-a-patient" scheme described in Chapter 5 if individual consumers paid for doctors' visits. All businesses and industries present opportunities for white-collar crime, and opportunities are, in a very real sense, everywhere.

Even though all businesses and industries create opportunities for white-collar crime, this does not mean that everyone involved in those economic activities is a white-collar criminal. We assume, or at least we hope, that a large majority of businessmen and women obey the law as best they can. Not everyone is an offender. Some individuals who, because of their occupational positions, have access to particular white-collar crime opportunities do not take advantage of them, but other individuals do take advantage.

Exactly how large or small the ratio of offenders to non-offenders is with respect to white-collar crime is a hotly debated issue. According to self-control theory, we should expect the proportion of individuals who *do not* take advantage of their access to white-collar crime opportunities to be relatively large (Hirschi and Gottfredson, 1987a, 1987b). That is, controlling for access to opportunity, the rate of white-collar offending is predicted to be low according to self-control theory, because the people who occupy white-collar types of positions are presumed to be high in self-control and hence able to resist the seductions of criminal opportunities (Hirschi and Gottfredson, 1987a). As noted in Chapter 3, other scholars disagree with self-control theory on this and other points (Benson and Moore, 1992; Geis, 2000; Reed and Yeager, 1996; Simpson and Piquero, 2002; Steffensmeier, 1989). Although we cannot settle the debate here, we note that both sides implicitly agree on a couple of points. Not everyone is an offender, and not all opportunities are taken advantage of. They disagree, of course, on the proportion of potential offenders who become real offenders and the proportion of potential opportunities that result in real offenses.

If we assume that opportunities for white-collar crime are ubiquitous in the business world, then why do some potential offenders take advantage of them, whereas other individuals in similar situations do not? Why do some people decide to act on some white-collar crime opportunities but not others, at some times but not others, and in some places but not others? As we showed in Chapter 2, white-collar offenders come from a social strata that is not the same as that of ordinary street criminals. Though they may not all be members of the elite class, a large majority of the people who commit white-collar offenses are nevertheless solid middle-class citizens. They don't appear to suffer from the personal or social pathologies that plague so many of the people who commit street offenses. However, as we discussed in Chapter 2, there is a growing body of evidence that suggests that at least some people may be predisposed to white-collar crime because of their innate psychological traits. Thus, individual differences in personality may explain in part why some people become involved in white-collar crime while others who have the same opportunity do not succumb to its seductions. However, even though people may vary in their susceptibility to the lure of white-collar crime and even though this variation may explain differential involvement to a degree, we do not think that individual differences are all that matters. White-collar offenders often have intact families, financial assets, ties to their communities, and good reputations as law-abiding, upstanding citizens. In short, they have a lot to lose if they are caught committing a white-collar or any other sort of offense (Wheeler, 1992). So, the question remains, how do they become involved in white-collar offending?

In this chapter, we argue that part of the answer to this question lies in how white-collar offenders conceive or symbolically construct opportunities. For many white-collar offenders, it is not enough merely to have access to an illegal opportunity to enrich themselves, or to avoid losing money, or to gain a business advantage. Rather, before committing the offense, many white-collar offenders need to be able to somehow justify their illegal actions to themselves so that they can maintain a noncriminal identity. That is, they must symbolically represent their situation to themselves in such a way that they see their behavior as somehow justified or as at least not improper. We also argue that, like so many things related to white-collar crime, symbolic constructions are influenced by gender, race, and social class (Klenowski, Copes, and Mullins, 2011; Maruna and Copes, 2005; Shover and Hochstetler, 2006; Willott, Griffen, and Torrance, 2001).

The White-Collar Offender's Sense of Identity

While testifying before a congressional committee, one of the executives involved in the heavy electrical equipment antitrust case of 1961 was asked whether he knew that his meetings with his co-conspirators were illegal. He replied, "Illegal? Yes, but not criminal. I didn't find that out until I read the indictment. . . . I assumed that criminal action meant damaging someone and we did not do that" (Geis, 1977). This executive is typical of a large majority of the people involved in white-collar crime. He did not define his actions as criminal, even though he knew, as he admits in his testimony, that they were illegal. Most certainly he did not see himself as a criminal.

Almost all white-collar offenders are like the electrical executive who testified before Congress. Even after they have been convicted, most white-collar offenders are loath to admit that they actually have committed a crime. They go to great lengths to deny having a criminal mind (Benson, 1985). They say that they really did not intend to harm anyone and did not have a criminal intent. Although most will grudgingly admit that their actions may have violated the law somehow, they nevertheless describe their offenses as "oversights," "mistakes," or "technical violations." They present themselves as upstanding, law-abiding, moral individuals. They are committed to conventional moral values and have a respectable self-identity (Box, 1983). In their own eyes, they are not like "real criminals" (Benson, 1985). Indeed, because they see themselves as upstanding citizens, white-collar offenders often argue that they should be spared harsh punishments for their crimes because they have "suffered enough" as a result of having their name and reputation dragged through the mud during the criminal justice process (Benson, 1984, 1985; Benson and Cullen, 1988).

It is easy, of course, to pass off white-collar offenders' protestations as merely after-the-fact rationalizations and as attempts to put their seemingly untoward behavior in the best possible light. Undoubtedly, this interpretation is correct in some cases. Some white-collar offenders surely know that what they are doing is criminal, and they decide to go ahead and do it anyway. After they are caught, they try to lessen the stigma attached to their behavior by presenting an account of it that puts them in a favorable light. But we do not think this is true of all white-collar offenders or even very many of them. We believe that most people most of the time accept the major conventions of the moral order. Before they can violate these conventions they must first convince themselves that the violations are for some reason acceptable (Sykes and Matza, 1957). White-collar offenders do this by using accounts and techniques of neutralization.

An account is a statement made by someone to explain unanticipated or untoward behavior (Scott and Lyman, 1968). There are two general forms of accounts: excuses and justifications. In making an excuse, the person admits that he or she did something wrong but denies having full responsibility for the action. For example, someone who is convicted of income tax evasion might try to excuse his behavior by saying that he was confused by the complexity of the tax codes and his violation was just an accident.

The second general form of accounts—the justification—is important for understanding white-collar crime from an opportunity perspective. In justifying untoward behavior, the person accepts responsibility for the act but denies its pejorative content. For example, a teller who embezzles money from a bank might contend that she was really owed the money because she had worked overtime earlier and her boss had refused to pay her for it. Although justifications are typically delivered after the untoward action has occurred, they nevertheless reveal something about how actors view their situations before committing their offenses. For white-collar offenders, it tells us something about how they symbolically understood or conceived of the criminal opportunities that they took advantage of. White-collar crime opportunities have a cognitive dimension in the sense that offenders must conceive of the opportunity in such a way that they can maintain a noncriminal identity.

Cognitive Dimensions of Opportunities: Neutralizations

The world of business is imbued with a set of values and ideologies that can be used to define illegal behavior in favorable terms (Box, 1983; Sutherland, 1983). Businesspeople follow norms, customs, and precepts that are balanced between convention and crime. These values and norms are not directly antisocial, and they do not actively endorse law breaking. Rather, they operate as extenuating conditions under which crime becomes permissible (Box, 1983, p. 54). The availability of these norms and customs is important, because they enable potential white-collar offenders to interpret their criminal intentions and behavior in non-criminal terms. They help offenders soften the harshness of their criminal acts so as to make them appear either as "not really" against the law or as somehow justified by a higher morality than that contained in the criminal law (Box, 1983, p. 54). In short, they help offenders symbolically construct the opportunities they confront as part of their normal occupational activities in ways that make illegal behavior seem acceptable.

It is possible for white-collar offenders to paint their illegal behavior in saintly colors, because their environment provides them with an inventory of verbal techniques for avoiding and undercutting the moral bind of the law (Box, 1983, p. 54). These techniques are called *neutralizations* (Sykes and Matza, 1957). They permit offenders to engage in illegal behavior while at the same time not thinking of themselves as criminals. The type of neutralization used by offenders depends in part on the nature of the opportunity structure they confront. As we illustrate next, certain types of neutralizations are more likely to be used for some white-collar crimes than for others.

A technique often used by white-collar offenders is similar to what has been called, with respect to juvenile delinquents, *denying responsibility* (Sykes and Matza, 1957). In these cases, offenders know or suspect that what they are doing is illegal, but they do not conceive of themselves as directly responsible for the act or its consequences. Two ways of doing this are by maintaining "concerted ignorance" (Katz, 1979) and "acting under orders." Both of these practices allow individuals to prepare what Katz (1979) calls "metaphysical escape" plans so that they can engage in illegal activity but protect themselves in advance if it should later be exposed.

The laws regulating practices in many industries can be enormously complex and difficult to interpret. They often are vague and contain ambiguous definitions that can be interpreted in different ways, especially by individuals who would prefer not to be bothered with the trouble of conforming to regulatory requirements. Small business owners in particular may find the regulations governing their enterprises daunting and troublesome. They may feel overwhelmed by regulatory unreasonableness (Bardach and Kagan, 1982). Rather than spending time and energy to learn and understand the regulations, it is simply easier and more convenient not to know what is condoned and what is condemned. Even the officials who run well-endowed corporations often complain about the complexity of the regulatory environment and contend that any violations their companies committed were done out of ignorance and not intentionally. If you do not really know what the law is, then you cannot really intentionally break it.

Corporate leaders can also avoid taking responsibility for their actions by maintaining ignorance about the risks that they are imposing on others (Friedrichs, 2010, p. 11). As we noted in Chapter 6, it is certainly fair to assume that in most cases where workers are sickened, injured, or killed by their work, their bosses do not intend for these tragedies to occur. Neither do corporate executives intentionally put dangerous products and drugs on the market. Their primary motive when these unfortunate events happen is always for the good of the company. They want to make the company more efficient and more profitable. Surely, efficiency and profitability are worthy objectives in a society governed by free-market principles. These objectives can be achieved by cutting costs, delaying repairs to equipment, avoiding unnecessary testing, and a host of other means. If these cost-cutting measures mean that someone accidentally gets hurt in the process, well—that is unfortunate, but it was not intended. From the executive's point of view, without intention there can be no crime. By focusing on their intentions and interpreting all harmful consequences as accidents, corporate officials can commit corporate crimes without even acknowledging that they are crimes in the first place (Box, 1983, p. 55; Friedrichs, 2010).

Those in leadership positions in large corporations can practice concerted ignorance in another way besides failing to learn regulatory requirements and ignoring risks. They can simply deliberately avoid knowing what their subordinates are doing. As corporations grow larger and more complex, lines of communication between different levels in the corporate hierarchy become longer and more difficult to maintain (Vaughan, 1990). Corporate leaders cannot be expected to directly supervise everyone under their command or to have an intimate knowledge of everything that goes on in their organization. What leaders can do is set general goals and objectives for the organization and hold their subordinates accountable for achieving them. Exactly how the subordinates go about achieving the objectives is not the leader's concern. If someone in the organization breaks the law while pursuing a corporate goal, corporate leaders can, with a clear conscience, claim that they never intended that to happen. With some plausibility, they can claim that they never directly ordered or authorized lawbreaking. Hence, they should not be held responsible for somebody else's misdeeds.

For example, in many of the corporate accounting scandals of the past decade, the chief executives asserted that they were not responsible for the fraudulent accounting practices of their companies. The lawyers for Kenneth Lay, former CEO of Enron, for instance, argued during his trial that Mr. Lay was unaware of what Andrew Fastow (the chief financial officer for Enron) and others were doing with respect to accounting. Furthermore, in the Enron case, executives argued that what they did was not a crime at all because they relied on the advice of lawyers and accountants (Coffee, 2002; Eichenwald, 2002). Similarly, Bernard Ebbers, convicted CEO of WorldCom, put the blame for his company's collapse squarely on the shoulders of his subordinates and claimed that he did not really understand the complex accounting rules and regulations (Ackman, 2005). Both Lay's and Ebbers's claims of ignorance were rejected by their respective juries, and both men were found guilty. However, it has worked in other cases, and the frequency with which it is invoked at trial suggests that in the upper reaches of many corporate hierarchies, concerted ignorance is standard practice.

Employees and subordinates, on the other hand, can avoid responsibility by using another means. They can view themselves as simply subjects who have to obey any orders they receive from those above them. Though corporate leaders may claim that they did not know what was going on, subordinates feel that they are simply following orders. They are doing what their bosses want and what the corporation needs. Thus, employees may engage in actions that they know or strongly suspect are illegal without feeling responsible for the consequences. They are simply doing their jobs and if they don't do so, then the company will find others who will. In this way, the underlings who commit white-collar crimes in organizational settings can still think of themselves as essentially law-abiding and morally upstanding people.

This pattern of behavior may be common in large organizations and may result from subtle negotiations between the occupants of different ranks in the organizational hierarchy as to how they are going to relate to one another. Both supervisors and their subordinates may exercise information control as a means of managing their relationships and avoiding culpability for illegal behavior. For example, managers and supervisors sometimes have a vested interest in not knowing too much about what their subordinates are doing, because if deviance should come to light, it could reflect poorly on their leadership. In addition, there may be times when managers really do not want to know if their subordinates are not following company policies exactly as written, because if they did know, then they would have to do something to enforce the policies and this might make them unpopular with their subordinates. Similarly, subordinates might not want to know exactly what their boss is thinking, because then they would be responsible for conforming to his or her wishes. Such "bilateral information control" in hierarchical organizations facilitates the continuation and cover-up of organizational deviance (Katz, 1979, p. 303).

A second general technique for sanitizing criminal opportunities in business settings is to *deny the victim*. The burglar who breaks into a home knows that he is taking someone else's property. Likewise, the robber who accosts someone on the street can see the fear in the victim's eyes. These offenders know in advance of their crimes that they are going to cause an innocent person to suffer some sort of harm or loss. White-collar offenders, however, often do not have to look their victims in the eye. Indeed, the "victim" may not be an individual at all but rather a vast governmental agency, such as Medicare in the case of health care fraud. In price-fixing cases, there may be millions of victims, each of whom loses only a trivial amount of money, or the victim may be another large corporate entity. Similarly, in some types of securities offenses, such as insider trading, it may be difficult to identify victims in the traditional sense at all. Rather, the victim, to the extent that there is one, is an amorphous class of individuals whose investment decisions might have been different if they had had access to the inside information. In all of these cases, it is possible for white-collar offenders to convince themselves that no real person will suffer as a result of their actions, and therefore there is no real criminal victim. For example, a businessman convicted of price fixing looked at his offense in this manner:

> It certainly wasn't a premeditated type of thing in our case as far as I can see. . . . To me it's different than [his partner] and I sitting down and we plan, well, we're going to rob this bank tomorrow and premeditatedly go in there. . . . That wasn't the case at all. . . . It wasn't like sitting down and planning I'm to rob this bank type of thing.
>
> (Benson, 1985)

This reasoning is plausible because it conforms to our commonsense construction of crime as involving a premeditated act that harms a real person. Many white-collar offenses fail to match this commonsense stereotype because the offenders do not set out intentionally to harm any specific individual. Rather, the consequences of their illegal acts fall upon impersonal organizations or a diffuse and unseen mass of people.

As Sutherland noted long ago, the laws that govern and regulate business behaviors in the United States define what lawyers call *mala prohibita* rather than *mala in se* offenses. That is, the behaviors are considered crimes only because they have been declared so by a legislative authority, as opposed to being universally recognized as innately evil and wrong. The laws that define *mala prohibita* offenses are not universally endorsed. Rather, there is, as Sutherland put it, a conflict of standards regarding just how much the government should intervene in a free-market society (Sutherland, 1983). People disagree about the need for government regulations in a whole host of areas and about how much businesspeople can be trusted to voluntarily regulate themselves. This conflict in standards gives rise to a third technique used by white-collar offenders to maintain a noncriminal identity: *condemning the condemners*. If the law itself is not legitimate or necessary and if those who enforce it are not competent or trustworthy, then our moral obligation to obey the law is seriously undermined. Particularly in a free-enterprise system, businesspeople can argue to themselves that government has no business regulating economic behavior. In their view, the competitive processes of the market should decide what is or is not acceptable, not some bureaucrat who has never had to make a profit. If business executives think that the law is unfair and that it unreasonably restricts the freeplay of economic forces, then they are free to violate the law (Conklin, 1977, p. 94).

Another technique used by corporate leaders is to cast their behavior within a different context by claiming allegiance to a higher morality than that contained in the narrow legalisms of the law. There are several different forms that this *appeal to higher loyalties* can take. Employees who are asked to do something illegal may recognize that their behavior is wrong but argue to themselves that being loyal to their employer or organization is more important. Offenders can also make a distinction between morality and the technical requirements of the law and claim that it is more important to do the "right" thing than the legal thing. An example of this reasoning comes from one of the executives in the great electrical conspiracy:

One faces a decision, I guess, at such times, about how far to go with company instructions, and since the spirit of such meetings only appeared to be correcting a horrible price level situation, that there was not an attempt to damage customers, charge excessive prices, there was no personal gain in it for me, the company did not seem actually to be defrauding . . . morally it did not seem quite so bad as might be inferred by the definition of the activity itself.

(Geis, 1977)

The key point is that the offenders see themselves as doing something for the good of the company while not directly harming or taking unfair advantage of anyone else. From this point of view, saving or protecting the company is the moral thing to do, and it claims a higher allegiance than obeying technical requirements of the law.

Businesspeople sometimes take an even broader view of the relationship between the law and business ethics. In a free-enterprise system, the pursuit of profit is seen as the generator of employment and wealth. It is the engine that drives our standard of living upward and ensures social welfare. Thus, the pursuit of profit can be viewed by businesspeople as the ethical thing to do. Indeed, it is the primary ethic on which our free-enterprise system operates. It can at times supersede the ethical imperatives of the law. If obeying the law would undermine or retard the pursuit of fair profit, then the law itself is contrary to our country's most basic values and is morally inferior to business ethics. By viewing the pursuit of fair profit as the true reflection of our country's values, businesspeople can free themselves from the moral constraints of the law and maintain a noncriminal identity even while breaking the law.

Although both males and females use the various techniques of neutralizations, they tend to construct them in slightly different ways. In a recent study, Klenowski and colleagues interviewed 40 convicted white-collar offenders equally divided between men and women and found gender-based differences in the use of accounts. For example, for both the men and the women in the study, one of the most frequently used neutralizations was the appeal to higher loyalties. The subjects claimed that their crimes were committed out of a need to support their families. But when women used this technique, they made it clear that they had to do so because there was no male available to provide the support their families needed. Men, on the other hand, referred to their responsibility as men to provide for their families by any means necessary (Klenowski et al., 2011). Following Klenowski and colleagues, we suggest that for men, committing a white-collar crime may sometimes be consistent with their sense of identity and with the process of doing gender; but for women, committing a crime requires them to step outside the normal parameters of their gender roles. As another example of gender differences in accounting, some men in the study used the technique of denying responsibility, but when they did so they "presented accounts rooted in psychological-medical ways that allowed them to invoke the sick role" (Klenowski et al., 2011, p. 63). The authors speculate that adopting the sick role was more comfortable for men than it would be to admit that they were not in control of their own actions. Women, however, are not expected to be in charge and in control of all their actions. Thus, the loss of agency implied when one denies responsibility for one's actions is not as threatening to women's gender identities as it is to men's. Accordingly, the women in the study were more likely to simply deny responsibility than men.

A recent study of gender differences in intentions to not comply with environmental regulations lends support to the idea that gender influences how actors subjectively perceive opportunities (Simpson, 2012). The study involved environmental decision makers in U.S.-based organizations. The male and female subjects were asked to respond to a series of scenarios that described an actor not complying with environmental regulations under different organizational conditions. In one scenario, a superior asked a subordinate to violate the law. For the men in the study, being asked to put themselves in the situation of someone who was asked to violate the law decreased the desirability of the behavior and increased the perceived shame associated with the behavior. This was not the case for women, where being asked to do something increased the social desirability of the act. The results here are consistent with the idea that the potential loss of agency is more threatening to men than to women and that it may influence how both groups subjectively construct potential criminal opportunities. These and other subtle differences in the way in which gender identities align with criminal behavior may play some role in the generally lower levels of female participation in white-collar crime.

All of these techniques—denying responsibility, denying the victim, condemning the condemners, and appealing to higher loyalties—are available to potential white-collar offenders. They provide offenders with a perspective or viewpoint on their behavior that enables them to violate the law without feeling guilt or tarnishing their self-images as respectable people. In addition, the white-collar offender's efforts to maintain a noncriminal identity benefit from the stereotypical view of crime as a lower-class phenomenon in which predatory men directly prey upon innocent victims. For white-collar offenders, neither they nor their offenses look like the official portrait of crime. The white-collar offender's crimes are, in his or her view, different from street crimes. They are technical violations that harm no one and are committed for good reasons. Hence, white-collar offenders can view their actions as not tainted by the moral stigma that attaches to lower-class crime.

Combining the Symbolic and Structural Dimensions of Opportunity

White-collar crime opportunities thus have a symbolic dimension in addition to their structural aspects. As we noted in Chapter 2, two key features of the structure of white-collar crime opportunities include (1) the ease with which criminal behavior can be disguised as legitimate or in some way hidden from view and (2) the inability of victims to recognize or be aware of their victimization. Together, these features ensure that the probability of detection is low. Because of these general structural features, white-collar crime opportunities are attractive. From a purely rational point of view, an offender's decision to take advantage of the opportunity is certainly understandable. The potential benefits of the crime seem high while the potential costs seem low. Why not take advantage of the opportunity?

In this situation, the only thing holding a white-collar offender back is his or her personal sense of morality and integrity. If committing a white-collar crime would violate the offender's personal morality, then even if he or she can escape official detection, there is still a price to be paid—the loss of one's self-image as a respectable person. However, the availability of neutralizations provides white-collar offenders with a means of overcoming this last symbolic obstacle. The white-collar offense is symbolically transformed from an evil act into an act that is understandable, justifiable, and perhaps even morally acceptable.

Risk and the Normalization of Deviance

A weakness of the opportunity perspective as applied to white-collar crime, particularly crimes committed in organizational settings, is that it implies that offenders are on some level aware that their actions are wrong or illegal. Indeed, to say that offenders must use techniques of neutralization to protect their sense of identity implies that they are aware that their behavior could be construed as illegal or morally objectionable. Neutralizations imply intentionality. Potential offenders are seen as convincing themselves that no one really will be hurt, or it's not really my fault, or the law is unfair to begin with, or it's more important to save the company and the workers' jobs than obey the law. However, this image of the offender as intentionally and knowingly violating the law may not be accurate in regard to some types of deviance that occur in large organizations.

Some white-collar crime scholars argue that large organizations are characterized by situations in which deviance can become normalized (Vaughan, 2005). Normalized deviance is deviant behavior that is not recognized by actors as being deviant. Rather, according to Diane Vaughan, the leading proponent of this view, when making decisions about what to do in a risky situation the individuals involved reinterpret information that could be seen as a sign of potential danger. The information is reinterpreted in such a way that the dangerousness of the situation is obscured or disappears altogether. And a potential course of action that might have originally appeared as quite risky is transformed into one that appears acceptable and nondeviant. This reinterpretation of evidence leads to a decision that has unintended but very harmful outcomes and that in retrospect looks very foolish if not criminally negligent on the part of the decision makers.

There is a difference between neutralized deviance and normalized deviance. In neutralized deviance, actors recognize that at some level what they are doing could be viewed as deviant or illegal, but they convince themselves that they have a good reason or an excuse for going ahead anyway. In contrast, normalized deviance arises out of a more profound process of collective self-deception, in which actors, for complex reasons, really do not see their decisions as being potentially very risky with potentially very harmful consequences. How does this happen?

The best example of the process of normalizing deviance comes from the Space Shuttle *Challenger* tragedy. In 1986, *Challenger* exploded shortly after takeoff, killing all astronauts on board. After the tragedy, an investigation discovered evidence that appeared to indicate that officials at the U.S. National Space and Aeronautics Administration (NASA) had been forewarned about the possibility of a catastrophic failure on the shuttle. Yet, in spite of the warnings, they decided to authorize the launch anyway. In retrospect, it appeared that because they were under a lot of pressure to keep the shuttle program on schedule, NASA officials had deliberately decided to ignore warnings and launch *Challenger* even though they knew it was risky. If this scenario were true, then all those involved in the *Challenger* decision would at a minimum be guilty of misconduct if not of criminally negligent behavior. After a detailed investigation of the events leading up to the launch decision, however, Diane Vaughan argues that this interpretation is not accurate. In her view, the disaster was the result of mistakes in judgment rather than misconduct.

The explosion that doomed *Challenger* was caused by cold weather and a faulty O-ring. The O-rings were part of the solid rocket booster that launched the space shuttle into space. The boosters were made in sections that were connected at joints that were sealed by O-rings. In the *Challenger* disaster, the O-rings failed, allowing hot gases from the solid rocket boosters to escape, leading to the explosion. The rubber O-rings failed in part because they had become stiff owing to the cold temperature. Later in the post-tragedy investigation, it was learned that during a pre-launch conference call, some engineers at Morton Thiokol, the company that manufactured the solid rocket boosters, had argued against the launch. The engineers had protested that the cold temperatures that were predicted for launch time could cause the O-rings to fail. NASA managers, however, overrode the recommendations of the engineers and authorized the launch. It was also suggested after the tragedy that NASA had been under a great deal of political pressure to keep the space shuttles going on schedule. Thus, the original interpretation of the tragedy was that NASA managers had been warned that the launch was risky but had nevertheless succumbed to political pressure and violated safety rules by going ahead and authorizing the launch.

In contrast to this damning interpretation, Vaughan argues that the decision to launch *Challenger* was taken within an historical and structural context in which it was not seen as being unreasonably risky. Rather, the risks involved were seen as normal and therefore acceptable by official NASA decision makers. The decision makers came to this erroneous conclusion as a result of a complex set of factors that included: (1) the context within which they received the information about the potentially faulty O-rings, (2) the organizational culture and political environment of NASA, and (3) the structural secrecy inherent in large organizations.

The context within which the information about the potential risks posed by the O-rings was received influenced how it was interpreted. First, everyone knew that building and launching the space shuttle was an inherently risky undertaking. Much of the technology involved was new, and the overall design of the shuttle vehicle had never been tried before. In this context, technical problems were expected, and it was understood that the risks associated with flying into space could never be reduced to zero. As a result, when technical problems arose in any of the shuttle's many interactive systems, they were not interpreted as signs of potential danger. To handle the problems that occurred continually throughout the shuttle program, NASA established standardized procedures to analyze and correct them so that risk would be reduced to an acceptable, but not zero, level. Therefore, the problem with the O-rings was simply one of many technical problems that NASA engineers had encountered and handled before.

A second aspect of the context that influenced how the problems with the O-rings were interpreted involved the accumulation of information on this issue over time. *Challenger* had completed nine missions before the explosion. When previous shuttle flights had returned from space, they had, of course, been examined carefully for signs of wear and failure. Erosion of the O-rings had been observed in some of the flights that preceded *Challenger*, but not in all of them. Sometimes the cause of the erosion was identified, such as, for example, a piece of lint on an O-ring, and corrected. After the fix, O-ring erosion in subsequent flights was either reduced or not observed for a while. Importantly, there was no convincing evidence that cold temperatures could cause the O-rings to fail. In 1985, erosion began occurring regularly but did not result in any explosions. NASA engineers interpreted these results as evidence that they understood and had learned how to handle the potential risks posed by the O-rings. Taken together, the tacit assumption that a certain level of risk was unavoidable and the pattern of information that appeared to indicate that this particular risk was being managed acceptably led NASA officials to grossly underestimate the risks posed by the faulty O-ring design.

In addition to the information context, the organizational culture and political environment of NASA played a role in the *Challenger* disaster. During the Apollo era, NASA prided itself on technological excellence. Risk assessments were made on the basis of watertight quantitative engineering analyses. By the time the space shuttle program began, however, two other cultural mandates besides technological excellence were operating: political accountability and bureaucratic accountability.

First, NASA had to be accountable to Congress, which agreed to fund the space shuttle program in part because NASA argued that it would eventually pay for itself. Thus, in making decisions to launch or not to launch the shuttle, NASA officials had to be sensitive to how these decisions would play to Congress. If the shuttle launches fell too far behind schedule, Congress presumably would not be happy and might reconsider its decision to fund the shuttle program.

Second, NASA became much more bureaucratic than it had been during the Apollo days. To build, launch, and maintain the shuttle was an enormously complex task, involving hundreds of contractors. To keep track of the contractors, the millions of components that made up the shuttle, and the thousands of pre-launch activities, NASA managers and engineers had to process mountains of paperwork. They had to follow rules. Following the rules contributed in an odd way to the normalization of deviance. Over time, the rules came to convey a sense of safety and security. The seductive, but flawed, logic at work here is understandable. If you follow all the rules and the shuttle flies successfully (which it had in all previous flights), then obviously following the rules meant that the shuttle is safe to fly. This kind of thinking led managers and engineers to downplay the significance of anomalies (such as warning signs that the O-rings were not working properly) that cropped up periodically in the shuttle program.

These cultural mandates—technological excellence, political accountability, and reliance on bureaucratic procedures to ensure consistency—shaped how managers interpreted signs of potential danger in general in the shuttle program and specifically how they interpreted the conditions preceding the launch of *Challenger*. Based on what had happened during previous flights, everything looked normal or at least acceptably close to normal. At the time it was made, the decision to launch represented conformity. Only afterward, in retrospect, did it appear to indicate deviance and rule breaking.

Like all large organizations, NASA is a complex place, and it suffers from a problem that is common to large organizations: structural secrecy. According to Diane Vaughan (2005, p. 264):

> [S]tructural secrecy refers . . . to how organizational structure—division of labor, hierarchy, complexity, geographic dispersion of parts—systematically undermines the ability of people situated in one part of an organization to fully understand what happens in other parts.

Inevitably, as organizations grow large, knowledge about what is going on becomes compartmentalized in subunits. One unit handles one thing, and another unit is in charge of something else. Communication between subunits becomes difficult, as the people in one unit lack the expertise to really understand what people in the other unit are doing. Even within subunits, individuals may have only partial knowledge about tasks and goals because of the specialized division of labor. One person is an expert in one thing, and another person is an expert in something else. The problem of structural secrecy becomes particularly pronounced when the people at the bottom of the organizational hierarchy are highly specialized experts. It is difficult for organizational leaders to be fully aware of all of the information and views that those below them have on any given issue. Of course, organizations try to develop mechanisms for keeping track of what is going on and for exchanging information. They require people to fill out forms and file reports regularly. But these efforts, though they may create the appearance that everything is under control, often only add to the problem. As the flow of reports and files grows ever larger, the time that organizational leaders have to devote to reading and mastering information overload remains fixed. The more information there is, the less that can be mastered. Ironically, too much information can be as bad for organizational decision making as too little.

In the case of the *Challenger* disaster, structural secrecy contributed to the normalization of deviance because it helped to conceal from decision makers the seriousness of the O-ring problem. As you might expect, the actual process by which NASA made launch decisions at the time was very formal and rigorous. It involved a four-tiered hierarchical process called a Flight Readiness Review. The various work groups in charge of different components on the shuttle would submit their reports on the readiness of their particular component. These reports, based on careful engineering analyses, could be challenged at every stage of the Flight Readiness Review, but the engineering analyses were not replicated outside of the work group.

This was a key weakness in the decision-making process. The people who actually made the decision to launch were dependent on information they received from those below them. They could criticize the information in a general way, and they could ask tough questions, but they did not analyze each component in the same detail as did the work groups. That is, they could not produce their own information based on their own analyses. Most of the time, the process worked. Errors were caught and corrected. Engineers were sometimes asked to redo their analyses and make them more rigorous. Unfortunately, however, if a work group made a fundamental error but still recommended a launch that was based on tight engineering analyses, no one outside the work group was likely to see the mistake and intervene.

The *Challenger* disaster involved a combination of all of these factors— complex and ambiguous information, political and bureaucratic pressures, and structural secrecy. Together they created a situation in which a decision was taken that seemed reasonable at the time but that had disastrous consequences, which no one intended and very few thought were remotely possible. According to Vaughan, the conventional interpretation that the disaster was caused by reckless NASA officials who repeatedly ignored obvious warning signals because they wanted to keep the shuttle program on schedule is simply misguided. It does not accurately reflect what actually happened.

We end up, then, with two contrasting perspectives on the role of risk and responsibility in the *Challenger* disaster. The conventional interpretation holds NASA officials responsible. They recklessly ignored risks that they knew existed, because they were more concerned with the success of the shuttle program than the safety of the crew. Known risks were knowingly imposed on unknowing victims, that is, the seven astronauts who made up the shuttle's crew. The alternative interpretation puts the blame on faulty organizational structures and dynamics. The risks posed by the faulty O-ring design were not fully recognized or appreciated because of organizational factors outside of the control and understanding of anyone. In other words, unknown risks were mistakenly imposed on the shuttle's crew.

The Normalization of Deviance in Other Organizations

The space shuttle program officially ended on August 31, 2011 with only one other major accident, the breakup of *Columbia* on February 1, 2003 when it was returning to earth. The shuttle program was obviously an enormously complex, risky, and one-of-a-kind undertaking, which involved thousands of individual components that had to be integrated into a complex whole to accomplish a task that had never been achieved before. Much of the technology on which the shuttle was based had to be invented and tested along the way. Because of the unique nature of the shuttle program in general and the *Challenger* disaster in particular, it is difficult to know how much we can generalize from what happened at NASA to other organizations. Yet, it is certainly possible that something like the normalization of deviance that occurred at NASA happens in other large organizations.

All large organizations suffer to some degree from the problem of structural secrecy. As they grow large, organizations tend to divide into specialized subunits and become more hierarchical, and these tendencies apply to organizations regardless of the country or culture in which they are located (Miller, 1987). Hierarchy and the division of tasks among subunits make it more difficult for information to flow and be accurately interpreted throughout the organizational structure. What happens in one part of an organization may be neither known nor fully understood in another part. Although organizational leaders can try to set up mechanisms to ensure that they know what is going on, there are limits to the amount of information that they, as fallible human beings, can absorb and interpret.

All large organizations also suffer from the problem of being account-able to parties and forces that are external to the organization. For NASA, the external accountability came from Congress, which expected a return on its investment of taxpayers' dollars in the shuttle program. Large private business organizations are accountable to their investors and stockhold-ers, who also expect a return on their money. Having to live up to the expectations of the marketplace does not make organizational leaders into completely amoral calculators, but it does color their interpretation of information. Being accountable to external parties influences how they interpret information. The need to make a profit, to satisfy stockhold-ers and investors, must always be taken into account in decision making. Private, for-profit organizations must always balance the fundamental requirement to make money against the risks and harms that may be imposed on others in the process of making money.

The degree to which large organizations have to contend with an infor-mational context similar to the one that confronted NASA depends on whether they are developing new products as opposed to simply market-ing tried and true ones. New products always pose potential risks. These risks must be evaluated through testing. The testing process produces information that must be distributed throughout the organization and interpreted by decision makers prior to putting the product on the market. Even after a new product is placed on the market, it continues to generate information in the form of feedback regarding problems and complaints from salespeople, customers, and users. Similarly, each time the space shuttle flew, it generated new information regarding how components were performing. The interpretation of this information may be skewed by its context. Whether a product is regarded as posing acceptable versus unacceptable risks depends on how information about its performance is captured and interpreted relative to all sorts of other feedback that an organization is receiving.

One of the most tragic examples that appears to illustrate the impor-tance of information context, and also of structural secrecy and external accountability, involves the Ford Pinto. The complete story of the Pinto is complex and involves technical details beyond the scope of this book. Accordingly, as its rise and fall has been ably reviewed elsewhere (Cullen et al., 2006), we present only a brief summary of events here.

The Pinto was a subcompact car that the Ford Motor Company introduced in 1970. It was designed to compete with small cars produced by Volkswagen and Japanese manufacturers, such as Honda and Toyota. Lee Iacocca, then chairman of Ford, had instructed his engineers to design a car that weighed less than 2,000 pounds and that cost less than $2,000. To get the car to market quickly, the normal production time of 43 months was slashed to only 25 months (Cullen et al., 2006).

The Pinto was a popular car with consumers, with more than 1.5 million units sold in its first 6 years of production. It suffered, however, from a potentially fatal design flaw. The gas tank had been placed too close to the back of the car near the rear wheel axle. It was in a position where it could be easily ruptured in a rear-end collision of moderate speed. Under the right conditions, a ruptured fuel tank could leak gasoline, leading to a devastating fire in the vehicle. Tragically, this happened repeatedly during the years that the Pinto was in production, and thousands of people died or were grotesquely disfigured in fiery crashes (Cullen et al., 2006, p. 146). The most famous accident and the one that led to the landmark criminal prosecution of Ford occurred in Elkhart, Indiana. Three teenage girls were burned to death after the Pinto they were driving was hit from behind by a van.

In retrospect, what made the Pinto story seem so outrageous was the discovery that Ford apparently had known since early in the production process that the design of the gas tank was flawed. Like all new vehicles, the Pinto was crash tested, and the results of some tests indicated that fuel tank ruptures were likely to occur at moderate speeds. It also appeared that Ford had known that several relatively cheap technological fixes were available that could have made the car much safer. Officials at Ford, however, appeared to have chosen not to make any changes to the design of the gas tank after a cost-benefit analysis indicated that improved safety was not warranted financially. To put it bluntly, in Ford's view, it was cheaper to pay off crash victims than to fix the gas tank.

The conventional interpretation of the Pinto case is in many ways similar to how the *Challenger* disaster was interpreted. In both cases, decision makers appear to have ignored obvious warning signs and put lives in danger in pursuit of organizational goals. Yet, there is an alternative interpretation of the Pinto decision that resembles Vaughan's reanalysis of the *Challenger* decision (Gioia, 1992; Lee and Ermann, 1999). The Pinto was brought to market after a lengthy process of development that involved hundreds of employees working in different subunits. Although some crash tests indicated that the gas tank design was flawed, the results of other tests fell within the normal range. In short, the crash tests were inconclusive. In addition, the car met federal safety standards that were in force at the time and appeared to be as safe as other subcompacts then on the road.

Thus, according to the alternative interpretation, the employees and managers at Ford were subject to organizational forces and situational factors that resembled those involved in the *Challenger* disaster—structural secrecy, ambiguous information, and external environmental pressures. Caught up in the rush to produce the Pinto on time, managers simply did not see the problems with the gas tank design as serious safety anomalies. They followed standard procedures. The car's problematic features were assessed according to routine practices. Unfortunately, however, by following standard practices, the people at Ford ended up "normalizing" the rear-end crash test results, that is, defining them as acceptable risks rather than recognizing them as serious safety anomalies.

The *Challenger* and Pinto cases should alert us to the potential limits of the opportunity perspective in the context of large organizations. The opportunity perspective assumes that rationality lies behind the decision to commit a white-collar crime. It assumes that people see or recognize criminal opportunities and choose to take advantage of them for their own benefit (or, in the case of some people in organizations, for the benefit of their organizations). Yet, in large organizations, people may make decisions in situations where they do not truly understand the implications of those decisions. There is a difference between ignoring or neutralizing a risk and simply not seeing the risk in the first place. There is also a difference between concerted ignorance and structural secrecy. Concerted ignorance arises when organizational leaders deliberately try to avoid learning about certain types of information in hopes of thereby reducing or eliminating their legal culpability. Structural secrecy, on the other hand, arises when certain types of information do not circulate through an organization and, as a result, organizational leaders are unaware of them. Both the *Challenger* case and the Pinto case raise the possibility that under some circumstances, people in organizations simply do not see that their decisions may impose unacceptable risks on others. They misinterpret and normalize warning signs.

Of course, this exculpatory reasoning should not be carried too far. We are not suggesting, as do many corporate executives when confronted with charges of illegality, that it was all just a big mistake or a big misunderstanding. As we showed in Chapter 5, people who work in large corporations often knowingly take advantage of criminal opportunities for their own benefit or the benefit of their companies. Likewise, it is certainly not uncommon for corporate executives to try to hide behind the sham of concerted ignorance.

Cases of what appears to be deviance or criminality in large organizations seem to generate competing narratives almost automatically. These narratives provide wildly different interpretations of the intentionality of actors in large organizations regardless of whether the case concerns an unsafe consumer product or a dangerous workplace or a large-scale financial fraud. On one side are narratives produced by consumer advocates, unions, investigative journalists, and white-collar crime scholars that interpret the behavior of corporate executives in terms of the greedy and criminal pursuit of profits over people (Barnett, 2013; Cullen et al., 2006; McLean and Elkind, 2004; Pontell and Geis, 2014; Shover and Hochstetler, 2006). On the other side are corporate apologists who contend that mistakes happen and that untoward events are the result of some sort of system failure as opposed to intentional wrongdoing (Gioia, 1992; Lee and Ermann, 1999; Vaughan, 2005). Exactly which of the two narratives is correct in any given case depends, of course, on the facts. But regardless of whether any given case involves a criminal act or an unfortunate accident, the organizational setting greatly complicates its moral and legal interpretation both in the courtroom and in the arena of public opinion.

We suggest that this structurally induced ambiguity plays an important role in the continuation of corporate crime in modern society for several reasons. First, ambiguity makes it possible for corporate leaders to construct metaphysical escapes that reduce if not eliminate their culpability.

Of course, executives may be mistaken in their belief that no one will hold them accountable, but that simply means that they have misjudged the potential costs or risks of their actions, as any offender may do. What matters is not that metaphysical escapes or efforts at concerted ignorance always have to work, but that corporate leaders have reason to believe that they work most of the time. This belief makes it easier for corporate criminals to take risky actions than would be the case if they knew that discovery would often bring individual culpability. Second, ambiguity contributes to the factual complexity of corporate crimes. Consider, for example, a case involving the deaths of 51 workers who were killed when scaffolding for a water tower that they were working on collapsed. It was clear that OSHA regulations had been violated when the scaffolding was constructed and it was clear that the 51 workers had died, but it was not clear that the regulatory violations actually caused the scaffolding to collapse. Other factors, such as weather conditions, may also have been involved. Prosecutors looking into the case eventually decided that the case was so complex that they did not believe they could convince a jury beyond a reasonable doubt that the company or any executive in it was guilty of a crime (Braithwaite and Geis, 1982). More recently, it is instructive that so far no one in the investment banks involved in the financial collapse of 2008 has been charged with criminal fraud. Despite the widespread public outrage over the public bailout of investment banks, the lack of prosecutions certainly sends a message to corporate insiders that there is safety behind corporate walls (Pontell and Geis, 2014).

Summary

In this chapter, we have argued that white-collar crime opportunities have symbolic as well as structural dimensions. The structure of a white-collar crime opportunity is determined primarily by the way in which a business or industry is organized. As we described in earlier chapters, different forms of organization create different types of opportunities. The symbolic dimension of white-collar crime opportunities refers to how potential offenders interpret their illegal activities. Most white-collar offenders do not conceive of themselves as criminals. Rather, they think of themselves as upstanding, law-abiding, and morally upright individuals. To break the law deliberately for one's personal benefit without having some sort of excuse or justification for doing so would be inconsistent with a conventional self-image. To avoid this inconsistency, white-collar offenders often use neutralizations to excuse or justify their involvement in illegal activity.

The neutralizations that are most prominently used to justify white-collar crime can be divided into four main types: denying responsibility, denying the victims, condemning the condemners, and appealing to higher loyalties. Because of the complex nature of large corporations, both those at the top and those at the bottom can deny to themselves that they are individually responsible for untoward behavior. Those at the bottom can say that they are just following orders; those at the top can argue that they cannot really be expected to know and to be held responsible for every little thing that goes wrong in a huge organization. Similarly, it is easy for white-collar offenders to think that their actions do not really harm anyone, that there are no victims in the traditional sense of an individual who suffers some sort of loss or harm. Denying the victim is not hard when the "victim" is a faceless government bureaucracy such as the Medicare system. In the eyes of business executives and professionals, government bureaucracies deserve to be condemned because they create burdensome regulations that get in the way of honest people's trying to make an honest living. Finally, white-collar offenders can rationalize to themselves that sometimes obedience to the law is not their most important moral obligation. They have obligations to their employees and customers. It is more important to make a profit and to stay in business in order to protect people's jobs than it is to obey some obscure and probably misguided government regulation. All of these techniques of neutralization serve the same function. They help make it morally acceptable to offenders to take advantage of white-collar criminal opportunities.

Techniques of neutralization are necessary for white-collar offenders if they are aware that their actions could be characterized as illegal or unreasonably risky. It is the awareness of potential illegality that provokes the offender's use of neutralizations to undermine the moral stigma that would accompany involvement in criminal activity. However, as the cases of the space shuttle *Challenger* and perhaps the Ford Pinto show, sometimes it is not clear that organizational leaders have this level of awareness. In large organizations, deviance may, under certain circumstances, become normalized. That is, deviant or risky behavior may not be recognized as such. Rather, information that should be interpreted as a warning signal is misunderstood or reinterpreted as normal.

The normalization of deviance involves three factors. First, there is an information context that makes it difficult to separate out important messages and signals from those that can be safely ignored. This problem may arise because the information itself is ambiguous or because there is simply too much of it for people to assimilate and evaluate effectively. Second, structural secrecy hinders the flow of information to decision makers and throughout the organization. Because of the division of labor among subunits and because of task specialization, people in one part of an organization may not really understand the significance of what people in another part are doing. Third, the organization is subject to environmentally generated pressures or expectations to achieve some goal. For business corporations the pressure comes mainly from the market and the need to make a profit. For other types of organizations, such as NASA, the expectations may be political in nature, but organizations are always under some type of pressure to perform (Gross, 1978). Regardless of the source, externally generated expectations shape the way that organizations evaluate information and make decisions. They may lead decision makers to downplay risks, particularly when the risks are imposed on someone else (Friedrichs, 2010). Taken together, these factors—information context, structural secrecy, and the pressure to perform—can create conditions in which people in large organizations make decisions that from the outside appear to be obviously deviant or criminal. Yet, from the inside, they appear normal or routine and not out of the ordinary.

8

THE SOCIAL DISTRIBUTION OF OPPORTUNITY
Class, Gender, and Race

In the preceding chapters, we have argued that opportunities for white-collar crime are shaped and distributed according to the nature of the economic and productive activities of different industries. Certain types of white-collar crime are more common in some industries than others because the opportunity to commit those types of crime is built into the organization of the industry. For example, the structure of the health care insurance system makes possible certain types of fraud, deception, and abuse of trust that would be difficult if not impossible to carry out in the retail clothing industry. As a general rule that has only a few exceptions, white-collar crimes are not spread evenly across industries or occupations. The exceptions involve activities that are common to all business undertakings. For example, all businesses must engage in accounting, and in recent years, accounting fraud appears to have spread to all types of businesses and industries, indeed even to some municipal authorities (Partnoy, 2003).

Just as opportunities for white-collar crime are not distributed evenly across industries, they are also not distributed evenly across people. Some people are more likely to have access to opportunities for white-collar crime than others. In this chapter, we argue that access to opportunities for white-collar crime are powerfully influenced by social class, gender, and race. The reason why these social characteristics matter is not complicated.

Most white-collar crimes are committed within occupational settings. Indeed, it is the offender's occupation that gives rise to the opportunity to commit different types of white-collar crime. Insider trading, for example, requires that one be an organizational insider of some sort or have access to inside information, which has to come from some source inside the organization. Access to most white-collar crime opportunities is based, therefore, on having access to an occupational position. It follows that any characteristic that influences access to occupational positions will also, indirectly, influence access to opportunities to commit white-collar crime. This general rule is true even for occupational positions within the illicit markets of the underworld (Steffensmeier, 1983). Social class, gender, and race are just such characteristics.

You do not need an advanced academic degree to know that the occupational structure has long been stratified along class, gender, and racial lines (Kalev, 2009). Opportunities to commit white-collar crime also are stratified along these same lines. Individuals, depending on their gender, class, and race, will have more or less opportunity to offend. These characteristics, alone or in conjunction with one another, affect the white-collar crime opportunity structure.

Consider, for example, gender and the "glass ceiling." The glass ceiling refers to the barriers that women face moving into management-level positions within business. In 1991, the Department of Labor put together a group called the Glass Ceiling Commission to study the problem of women in business. The commission's report issued in 1995 found that in spite of more women moving into the labor force and in spite of substantial advances in educational attainment by women (e.g., women held more than half the master's degrees awarded), 95 percent of senior managers were male. A decade later, little had changed. According to data reported in *The Economist* a few years ago, women are still largely frozen out of the top management positions. In 2005, for instance, only 8 percent of top managers were women. Booz Allen Hamilton, a consulting firm that tracks the comings and goings of top managers, reports that the number of senior women executives is "very low and not getting larger" (Economist, 2005).

Women are not the only ones who bump their heads against the glass ceiling. Minorities also often find their way to the top blocked. The report of the Glass Ceiling Commission (1995) noted that African Americans, Latinos, and Asians were nearly nonexistent in senior management positions, with whites holding fully 97 percent of those positions. Thus, race, class, and gender are tightly coupled social characteristics that "reflect our nation's entire social history . . . [and] our nation's present social structure, with income inequality and occupational immobility for some, but new levels of well-being and material success for others" (Harris, 1991, pp. 97–98). Although the position of women and minorities in the workplace has not remained entirely static and there is evidence of some improvement in some companies and industries (Kalev, 2009), it is still the case that both groups are often segregated into low-level and undervalued positions.

Of course, not all occupations are equally stratified. Some occupations are more open to women and minorities than others. In this chapter, we explore how opportunities to commit white-collar crimes are stratified along class, gender, and racial lines. We also explore how these characteristics shape the risk of white-collar crime victimization.

Class, Status, and White-Collar Crime

Sutherland originally defined white-collar crime as crime committed by persons of "respectability and social status." He set out to focus on "persons of the upper socioeconomic classes" (Sutherland, 1983, p. 7). Most of the examples and case studies presented in *White-Collar Crime* involved powerful men, including the leaders of such stalwarts of American capitalism as the U.S. Steel Corporation, Standard Oil Company, Proctor and Gamble, and Dupont Chemicals (Sutherland, 1983, pp. 64–65). Sutherland's influential imagery resonated throughout the following decades. Even today, the common stereotype of the white-collar offender pictures him (yes, *him*) as a white businessman who occupies a position of power and prestige, a wealthy member of America's corporate elite. There is no shortage of examples of white male corporate elites involved in white-collar crime. Except perhaps for Martha Stewart, the ringleaders in the most recent string of corporate scandals are almost exclusively upper-class white males (Steffensmeier et al., 2013).

People from other class and status backgrounds, however, are involved in white-collar crime. As we showed in Chapter 2, in the mid-1970s, most of the people convicted of white-collar types of crimes in the federal court system could not be described as upper-class corporate elites. Rather, they appeared to come primarily from the middle classes of American society (Weisburd et al., 1991). Many of the subjects in the Yale and the Forst and Rhodes samples were not exactly what Sutherland had in mind when he coined the term *white-collar crime.* The difference between Sutherland's white-collar offenders and those of more recent studies is explained in part by the changing nature of work in American society. In Sutherland's day, white-collar office work was high-status work, but that is no longer the case. Today, the labor market is dominated by low-status clerical and technical jobs. Wearing nice clothes to work and spending most of your working day in an office no longer guarantees high social status or financial success. Many white-collar jobs are little more than poorly paid dead-ends—known as "pink collar" positions for their tendency to be disproportionately filled by women (Weisburd et al., 1991).

Sutherland used the terms *status* and *class* interchangeably and did not make any sharp conceptual distinction between them. The contemporary view, however, is that although status and class are related, they are not exactly the same thing. *Social status* is a relative term in the sense that people can be ranked as having more or less of it, depending on their income, education, and occupation. A standard tool for measuring social status is the Duncan Socioeconomic Index (SEI). It assigns a numerical status score to an occupation based on the salary, education, and prestige associated with it. SEI scores range from 0 to 99. Professionals such as doctors and lawyers have higher SEI scores (92 and 93, respectively) than manual laborers such as truck drivers and farmworkers (15 and 6, respectively).

In contrast to social status, *social class* refers to the nature and structural relationships of the occupational positions that people hold, not their standing relative to others. A widely used typology of class was developed by Erik Olin Wright. In Wright's typology, class position is based on three criteria: (1) ownership of capital assets, (2) control of organizational assets, and (3) possession of skill or credential assets (Wright, 1997). Wright distinguishes the owners of the means of production from non-owners, and managers and supervisors from others. Most of us fall into the non-owners class because we are simply employees who work for others and have no control over the means of production. Owners do have control over the means of production, but in advanced capitalistic economies such as ours, they often do not actually exercise much day-to-day control. Rather, in most modern corporations, control is exercised by professional managers and supervisors. In regard to white-collar crime, the distinction between owners and managers is important. The most serious white-collar crimes are not necessarily committed by those who own corporations but rather by those who have access to and control over organizational resources, for instance chief executive officers (CEOs), chief financial officers (CFOs), or even upper-level line managers and supervisors (Wheeler and Rothman, 1980).

White-collar crimes vary in organizational complexity and in the severity of their consequences. More complex offenses have a discernible pattern, involve the use of organizational resources, are committed by multiple participants, and last for a long period of time. The severity of an offense is determined by how many victims it has, the dollar value of the victims' losses, and the geographical impact of the offense. In the Yale study, the researchers found that the eight offenses they examined could be divided into a hierarchy with three levels based on the components of organizational complexity (Weisburd et al., 1991, pp. 39–42). The offenses with high complexity included antitrust violations and securities fraud. Mail fraud, false claims, and bribery were moderately complex, while tax fraud, credit fraud, and bank embezzlement were usually of low complexity. Antitrust and securities offenses also ranked highest in severity, whereas false claims, credit fraud, bribery, tax fraud, and bank embezzlement ranked lowest. Mail fraud on average tended to have consequences for victims that fell between these two groups.

In the Yale study, then, the most serious and organizationally complex offenses were antitrust violations and securities fraud. Access to opportunities to commit these offenses appears to be heavily influenced by class position (see Table 8.1). Just over seven of ten of the antitrust offenders in the Yale sample were either owners or officers of their companies (71.3%). Among those convicted of securities fraud, a very similar percentage were owners or officers (68.4%). For all other offenses, only a third or less of those convicted were owners or officers (Weisburd et al., 1991, pp. 50–51). In other words, most of them were employees who probably had little or no supervisory authority and little or no power in the

Table 8.1 Class position and socioeconomic status of white-collar offenders (adapted from Table 3.1 in Weisburd et al., 1991, pp. 50–51)

	Social Class	*Average Duncan SEI*
Antitrust	71.3	61.1
Securities fraud	68.4	67.4
Tax	33.3	56.2
Bribery	36.8	57.3
Credit fraud	31.8	57.3
False claims	16.4	52.6
Mail fraud	28.0	55.7
Bank embezzlement	15.9	57.3

workplace. Opportunities to commit serious white-collar offenses, then, appear to be greatly enhanced for those who hold certain organizational positions.

The Yale study suggests that class position is more important than social status in determining access to white-collar crime opportunities. Although the antitrust and securities offenders had on average the highest SEI scores, they were not markedly higher than the SEI scores for the offenders who committed other types of offenses. For example, as shown in Table 8.1, the average SEI score for the antitrust offenders was 61.1, and for all other offense types it was more than 52.6. Recall that SEI scores range from 0 (no occupation) to 99. So, in the Yale sample, the average SEI scores for the different types of offenders fall within a fairly narrow range of the possible scores (Weisburd et al., 1991, pp. 50–51).

Social status and class position are linked in that social status provides access to organizational positions where there is greater potential for large-scale white-collar offending (Wheeler and Rothman, 1980). Attending a prestigious university or professional school and garnering a law or business degree do not by themselves put one in a position to be a big-time white-collar criminal—but they may open the door to such positions.

The importance of getting access to such a position is clearly shown in Stanton Wheeler's and Mitchell Rothman's careful analysis of the Yale data. Wheeler and Rothman (1980) divided the defendants in their sample into three groups according to whether they used an occupational or organizational role in committing their offenses. Those who did not use either an occupational or organizational role were called *individual offenders* (e.g., someone who files a fraudulent personal income tax return). Those who used their occupational role were called *occupational offenders* (e.g., a bank teller who embezzles). Finally, those who committed offenses using both their occupational and organizational positions were called *organizational offenders* (e.g., an executive who violates antitrust laws). Wheeler and Rothman then examined the nature and consequences of the offenses that the different types of offenders committed. The results showed that the organizational offenders committed more complex and longer-lasting offenses than did either individual or occupational offenders. Importantly, organizational offenders also committed offenses that were significantly more costly. For individual offenders, the median take—that is, the dollar value of the offense—was $7,523, whereas for occupational offenders, it was $8,018. Organizational offenders, however, had a median take of $387,274. As Wheeler and Rothman (1980, pp. 1410–1414) put it, those who use a formal organization to commit their offense accrue an enormous financial advantage.

Wheeler and Rothman recognized that other variables related to both the offense and the offender might be correlated with their organizational dimension that would also influence offense magnitude. They examined this possibility and found that many characteristics of the offenses did affect the size of the take. These characteristics included the duration of the offense and its geographic spread, complexity, and sophistication. In regard to characteristics of the offender, the only variables that appeared to matter were the defendant's gender and, notably, organizational position. Age, race, education, and occupational prestige, however, were not important. Even after controlling for all of these individual and offense characteristics, the use of organizational resources still significantly predicted the dollar value of the offense (Wheeler and Rothman, 1980, p. 1416).

The organizational offenders were different from the individual and occupational offenders on a number of dimensions. On average, they were more highly educated and slightly older. They had higher occupational status and greater "impeccability," which was a composite variable that reflected the defendant's social background. It included indicators of conventionality such as employment history, religious affiliation and attendance, community group affiliations, and community reputation. As a group, the organizational offenders looked more socially accomplished, reputable, and upstanding than either the individual or occupational offenders. Wheeler and Rothman (1980, pp. 1420–1421) speculate on how organizational position and individual status combine to facilitate and augment white-collar offending:

> [A] portion of the organizational defendant's advantage accrues not through his organizational affiliation per se, but because the defendant's stature lends credibility to their claims. Occupational and organizational status tend to go together in our society—the stockbroker, for example, is also a vice-president of the firm and the lawyer is also general counsel to the corporation. This combination of organizational status and occupational position facilitates the theft of vastly greater sums of money than in the case of almost any other kind of crime, white-collar or not.

Large-scale white-collar offending depends on access to organizational resources, and access is facilitated by class position. Thus, professional managers and supervisors have the most opportunity to commit serious white-collar offenses.

The Gender Gap in White-Collar Crime: Offending

One of the oldest and most widely accepted findings in criminology is that males are more likely to be offenders than females. Indeed, gender is regarded as the single best predictor of crime. This generalization appears to apply in all societies and in all historical periods (Steffensmeier and Allan, 2000). In regard to traditional street crimes, the gap between male and female offending is not the same for all offenses. It is smaller for some offenses than it is for others. For example, in 1995, the female percentage of arrests for minor property crimes was 35 percent. In other words, more than one-third of all the arrests for these offenses involved women. However, for crimes such as robbery, females accounted for only about 8 percent of arrestees (i.e., less than one in ten; Steffensmeier and Allan, 2000). The gender gap is narrower for minor property offenses and wider for more violent offenses. It is also wider for adults than it is for juveniles (Smith and Visher, 1980).

Gender is also a strong predictor of white-collar crime, and like traditional street crimes, the size of the gender gap depends on the type of white-collar crime. Recall from Chapter 2 that whereas women made up less than 5 percent of those convicted of antitrust or securities fraud in the Yale study, they accounted for almost half of the convicted bank embezzlers. And the data reported in Chapter 2 from the U.S. Sentencing Commission clearly indicate that this pattern has not changed recently. Between 2006 and 2012, women made up less than 1 percent of those convicted of antitrust offenses (see Table 2.4 in Chapter 2). In the Yale study, women offenders also were more apt to be unemployed, less educated, and single heads of households compared with their male counterparts. Their lower status vis-à-vis male offenders translated into less complex offenses, usually without co-offenders, that yielded lower financial benefits (Daly, 1989).

Data from other studies show similar variations in the gender gap but they also suggest that for some types of offenses, the gender gap may be closing slightly. Recall that in the Forst and Rhodes study, women constituted just under 50 percent of the bank embezzlers but only about 10 percent of those convicted of bribery and tax offenses. More recent data from the Sentencing Commission suggests that women's involvement in tax and bribery offenses has increased somewhat so that women now account for about 20 percent of those convicted for tax violations and over 50 percent of those convicted for embezzlement (see Table 2.4 in Chapter 2).

While women's involvement in some forms of white-collar crime appears to be increasing slightly, they are still dramatically underrepresented in white-collar offenses that involve access to or control over organizational resources. For example, a recent study examined three different types of fraud (asset misappropriation, corruption, and fraudulent statements) using survey data collected by the Association of Certified Fraud Examiners (Holtfreter, 2005). Asset misappropriation is defined as the theft or misuse of organizational assets by employees. It is similar to embezzlement. Corruption involves the wrongful use of business influence for personal gain. Fraudulent statements involve the falsification of organizational records or documents. Of the three types of fraud, fraudulent statements require greater access to organizational resources and are more similar to organizational as opposed to occupational offenses. In regard to gender differences and consistent with the Yale study, Holtfreter (2005, p. 359) found that individuals who committed asset misappropriation "were significantly less likely to be male than those who committed fraudulent statements." In other words, females were more significantly represented among those charged with asset misappropriation as compared with those charged with fraudulent statements. However, she did not find any gender differences between asset misappropriation and corruption, or corruption and fraudulent statements.

Holtfreter's research reinforces the important link between the structure of organizations and white-collar offending opportunities. The three types of fraud differed with respect to organizational characteristics such as size, public versus privately traded firms, and internal compliance systems. For instance, she found that asset misappropriation was committed more often in smaller organizations, whereas corruption took place more often in larger (and generally publicly traded) companies. Audits and anonymous reporting systems discovered corruption (but not false statements or asset misappropriation) within firms.

Another study looked at the gender breakdown of defendants in the Enron and post-Enron financial scandals. It revealed an even smaller percentage of female defendants. Kathleen Brickey (2008) has collected data on all companies and their officers against whom fraud charges were brought in the post-Enron era (i.e., between March 2002 and July 2007). Of the 355 total defendants in these cases, only 26 (7%) were women. A cursory glance at Brickey's data shows that the majority of cases had only one or no female defendant. A case involving an impropriety by KPMG, the big accounting firm, for instance, had 1 lone female among 22 male defendants. The well-known Aldelphia case had six defendants, all of whom were male. The firm with the most women defendants in Brickey's study was Health-South, which also had a large number of individual defendants (25). One-fifth of these (5) were female. The Enron scandal, perhaps the most infamous financial fraud of the past decade, produced 33 individual codefendants, but only 3 of these were female, including Lea Fastow, Enron assistant treasurer and wife of the former CFO (and codefendant) Andrew Fastow.

Brickey's analysis has been expanded and deepened in a recent study by Darrell Steffensmeier and colleagues that sheds even more light on the gender gap in high-level corporate frauds in the post-Enron era (Steffensmeier, Schwartz, and Roche, 2013). This study looked at 83 post-Enron corporate frauds that resulted in indictments and were prosecuted by the Department of Justice's Corporate Fraud Task Force (CFTF). The CFTF was formed after the Enron and WorldCom scandals, and it was explicitly focused on high-level corporate frauds. The CFTF compiled a database of indictments that contained rich data on the 83 cases and the 436 offenders involved in them. The researchers supplemented the information in the indictments with other data gathered from news sources as well as other government reports and press releases. They were able to identify the gender of the defendants, their occupational positions, and their roles in the various offenses. Of the 436 defendants, only 37 were women, that is, 9 percent of the sample.

A more significant finding perhaps than the small number of women involved in these cases concerns their roles in the fraud conspiracies. These high-level frauds always involved multiple conspirators who played different roles in the criminal networks. The researchers divided the roles into four levels—ringleader, major role, in-between role, and minor role. Of the 37 women, only 3 were ringleaders and only 7 played a major role. The remaining 27 women played in-between (8) or minor (19) roles. Indeed, in over 70 percent of the cases, there were no women involved in the criminal group at all. This study is the first systematic gender-based analysis of high-level corporate frauds, the kind of white-collar crimes that would have interested Sutherland, and the results could not be more telling in regard to the gender gap in serious white-collar crimes.

As the studies cited clearly show, women are underrepresented in official statistics for certain types of organizationally based white-collar crimes. However, exactly what causes this pattern is open to interpretation. There are several possibilities. One interpretation is that because access to occupational and organizational positions is stratified by gender, women have fewer opportunities to engage in certain types of white-collar crime, specifically those types that allow offenders to use the organization as a weapon to deceive and conspire against victims; that is, criminal opportunities could be due to job incumbency. Hence, restricted access explains why it is unusual to find women charged with these types of white-collar crimes. Restricted access or lack of job incumbency may explain some of the underrepresentation of women in high-level corporate frauds, but it is not the whole story. Steffensmeier and colleagues (2013) argue that the proportion of women involved in post-Enron corporate frauds is considerably lower than the proportion of mid- and upper-level management positions held by women. In other words, based on their representation in management positions, more women should have been involved in these frauds if simple access to opportunity were the deciding factor. Since job incumbency does not seem to be the issue, some other factor or factors must explain the relatively low level of participation of women in these high-level frauds. Another possible explanation raised by Steffensmeier and colleagues (2013) is that women have restricted access to the informal networks that are found throughout large organizations. Thus, even though women's formal access to management positions is improving, they may still be discriminated against by men in regard to their inclusion in informal networks of power and, consequently, illegal activity.

The relationship between gender and crime is often treated in individualistic terms, but this ignores that many crimes are group undertakings that involve networks of people working together. Individuals not involved in these networks have reduced access to criminal opportunities. Research on street-level crime indicates that access to criminal networks is sex segregated, with women being largely excluded from networks or restricted to playing subordinate supporting roles (Maher, 1997; Miller, 2001; Mullins and Wright, 2003; Steffensmeier, 1983). The same sex segregation of roles appears to happen in white-collar crime, too. In the CFTF study, most of the women played only supporting roles and were included primarily for utilitarian reasons. The women who were included held strategic financial positions in the companies that were necessary for the frauds to be carried out. For example, since many of the frauds involved false statements about financial data that had to be made on official documents and reports, it was sometimes necessary for the ringleaders to secure the cooperation of women who held subordinate positions in the accounting department in order to carry out their crimes. Thus, the same processes of sex segregation found in street crime groups appear to be operating in regard to white-collar crime networks. Many white-collar crimes committed within organizational settings involve networks of people working in a conspiratorial fashion, and organizational research indicates that even when women attain high status positions in organizations, they are often excluded from male-dominated informal social networks (Gorman and Kmec, 2009). If the exclusion of women from informal networks extends to illegal networks, then this would explain lower rates of participation in white-collar crime for women even when they hold the same occupational positions as men.

To put it bluntly, while men may be willing to tolerate having women in leadership roles in the workplace, they still may not trust women and exclude them from "old boy" networks. Hence, women would be less likely to be invited to participate in criminal conspiracies than men. This is a variation on the "restricted access" interpretation of the low level of female involvement in corporate crimes in that it argues that it is women's access to informal networks that is restricted rather than their access to particular organizational roles.

Regardless which form of "restricted access" is at work, we note that this interpretation implicitly assumes that women would behave as men do if they had access to similar positions or networks (Adler, 1975; Simon, 1975). However, it is also possible that even if they occupied the same positions and had the same opportunities, women would behave differently from men. Perhaps women are simply more law-abiding than men. Another possibility, reviewed further on, is that men and women offend at similar rates but the criminal justice system and internal compliance programs are more chivalrous toward women offenders (Pollock, 1950).

Research suggests that though access to opportunities is important, it is not the only factor involved in the gender gap in white-collar crime. Men and women share some of the same pathways into crime and contact with the criminal justice system, but it is also clear that some routes into crime are gendered. Motivations for white-collar offending appear to differ by gender (Daly, 1989; Zietz, 1981). And in their analysis of the post-Enron frauds, the researchers found that one of the main pathways into white-collar crime for women arose out of their close personal or romantic ties to a male co-offender. This relational pathway was characteristic for many of the women involved in the post-Enron era of corporate frauds and it suggests that women's motivations for their involvement in high-level corporate frauds may be substantially different from men's (Steffensmeier et al., 2013).

Another possible explanation for the paucity of women in white-collar crime is that women are treated differently than men by investigators and prosecutors. According to this line of reasoning, investigators and prosecutors do not think of women as potential criminal predators and hence treat them in a chivalrous manner. While the evidence on women's different motivations and pathways into white-collar crime is fairly consistent, the evidence regarding the so-called chivalry effect is more mixed. What appears to be chivalry toward women offenders may actually reflect stereotypical ideas on the part of criminal justice agents about "typical" offenders being male (Silberman, 1978), judicial concerns about family responsibilities (Daly, 1994), or differences in criminal history records that favor women in sentencing. Some studies have found that women offenders are actually treated more harshly than males when the crimes they commit are nonstereotypical (Chesney-Lind, 1989; Sealock and Simpson, 1998).

Taken together, these studies suggest that it is more than mere opportunity to offend that creates the gender differences in white-collar offending. Numerous books have been written about this very topic, and there are many different points of view. We suggest that there are gender differences in how men and women view opportunities for white-collar crime. These perceptual differences may arise from a number of sources. For instance, women who move into top management positions—by virtue of their uniqueness—are more visible to others. They are probably watched more carefully than males in these positions, are less "trusted" by others to go along with illicit activity, and thus are more apt to blow the whistle when illegality occurs than their male counterparts. Indeed, some argue that women may be better suited for "positions of trust and security" than men because they are better socialized, have more self-control, and score better on measures of integrity (Atkinson, 2006). Do women have a different conception of morality than males, that is, a "different voice" (Gilligan, 1993)? If so, this would affect many facets of crime, including women's willingness to engage in illegal behavior, their motivations for doing so, and how they respond when they learn about criminal activity by others.

In their gendered theory of focal concerns, Steffensmeier and Allan (2000) contend that women are socialized to accept nurturant role obligations that emphasize the importance of social relationships and communalistic orientations toward others. Through the assimilation of these obligations, women develop identities as caregivers. In addition, women's concern with beauty and virtue contrasts with the sordidness of stereotypical images of criminals, making the role of criminal or lawbreaker inconsistent with the taken-for-granted female identity (Steffensmeier et al., 2013). According to the theory of gendered focal concerns, women's adoption of identities based on beauty, virtue, and caregiving also affects their risk preferences, making them less willing to take risks than men. Hence, excluding only certain sex-related crimes such as prostitution or illegal abortions, women are expected to be less involved in all forms of crime than men.

There are no studies that directly test some of these contentions, but statistics and results from other research on crime are informative. We know, for instance, that female participation in white-collar offending has been on the rise for over 30 years (Atkinson, 2006; Simon, 1975) and that this risk is concurrent with the entry of more women into positions of trust, primarily in lower-level service positions. If women are becoming the norm rather than just tokens in lower-level positions (say, as tellers in banks), they should stand out less and socialize more with others in similar positions that may increase their knowledge of and exposure to white-collar crime opportunities and neutralizations about this type of illegality. Recall that our review of Brickey's (2008) data showed that Health-South had the most female codefendants. The health care industry is not as gender stratified as other industries. Yet these may not be the best data to address how industry structure affects offending opportunities because most of the companies in the database are service industry providers (telecommunications, financial services, retail). The absence of women as codefendants for most corporate defendants may suggest a relatively high level of vertical stratification in the service industry such that women are unwilling to participate in or have been left out of the illegal "loop."

Indeed, the data collected by Brickey (2008) and Steffensmeier et al. (2013) may even over-represent women's involvement in corporate crime. If their data included cases involving environmental illegality or health and safety violations, which are typically associated with basic manu-facturing industries that are much more stratified by gender, they might have found an even smaller number of female codefendants. Though the Brickey data and the CFTF data are intriguing, they do not tell us whether women and men in similar positions are equally likely to take advantage of illicit opportunities. Work by Michelle Howe (2003) gives us some clues about this question. She looked at whether a group of 77 survey respondents (including students and managers) were willing to engage in three types of corporate crime: price fixing, bribery, and environmental offending (Howe, 2003). Offending conditions were experimentally var-ied across the offense types. Her research revealed that gender per se did not affect the overall offending decision (i.e., females and males appeared to be equally willing to offend). However, the decision to offend was influ-enced by different factors for males and females (e.g., religiosity was more important for females), and the magnitude of the effects of different fac-tors varied by gender.

The Gender Gap in White-Collar Crime: Victimization

We have argued and presented evidence to suggest that white-collar offending opportunities are structured by gender. What we have not yet discussed is how white-collar victimization can also vary by gender. Ger-ber and Weeks (1992) first called attention to the lack of research on this subject by noting their inability "to locate even a single study that focuses specifically on women as victims of corporate crime." Shortly thereafter, Szockyj and Fox (1996) collected a group of original essays from schol-ars in the field who drew on case studies focusing on how differences in gender roles (e.g., employment, consumption), male and female socializa-tion, and legal protections, exclusions, and access to redress (such as union membership) affect contemporary patterns of corporate victimization. The historical record in Great Britain has been examined and found to show that rigid stereotypes and institutional sexism in the Victorian era increased the risk of fraud victimization for middle-class white women. Robb (2006, p. 1062) suggests that these women were almost certainly targeted for victimization because they were inexperienced (and therefore "easily duped") and because women shareholders were excluded from any board of director oversight:

> Considerable evidence exists that women were sought out as vic-
> tims by frauds and embezzlers who well understood their vul-
> nerability. During the 1860s, for example, the shady company
> promoter Albert Grant compiled lists of widows, unmarried
> women and other small investors to whom he sent circulars adver-
> tising his dubious speculations. . . . Not only were these women
> lacking in business experience and acumen, but they were ill-
> placed to fight him in court should it come to that.

Women's vulnerability was emphasized in Victorian society—and women
were warned away from the unregulated capital markets at the same time
their investments were highly sought.

Just as women's risk of fraud victimization in the Victorian era was
exacerbated by gender stereotypes and institutional sexism, these same
factors continue to play a role in gendered patterns of white-collar victimization in the modern era. Obviously, both men and women can be victims
of white-collar crime, but the types of white-collar harms that they experience are not entirely the same. Rather, differential exposure to types of
white-collar victimizations is influenced by cultural norms and gender-
based stereotypes. For example, pharmaceutical and consumer products
and services related to birth control, health, and beauty, such as cosmet-
ics, diet products, and cosmetic surgery, are marketed much more heavily
toward women than men. Certainly, this happens in part because market-
ers recognize and wish to take advantage of the culturally conditioned
concern and sensitivity that women have toward physical appearance. To
the extent that these products and services are dangerous or advertised in
misleading ways, women are correspondingly more likely to be harmed
than men (Croall, 2009). Unfortunately and despite the protestations of
pharmaceutical and cosmetic manufacturers concerning the safety of their
products, there are many examples of misleading advertising and dangerous products (Lister, 2005). Dow Corning was found in civil proceedings
to have acted with "fraud, malice and oppression" in regard to the way that
it marketed silicone breast implants that harmed many women (Croall,
2009, p. 134). Likewise, the Dalkon shield, an intrauterine device for birth
control manufactured by A.H. Robins, "exposed millions of women to
serious infection, sterility, and even death" (Mintz, 1995, p. 191). A 2011

survey conducted by the U.S. Federal Trade Commission (2013) revealed that women were almost 20 percent more likely to be consumer fraud victims compared with men, a difference mostly due to fraudulent weight loss products (2.6% of women were victims of this type of fraud compared with 1.6% of men). Men, of course, also consume weight loss and "grooming products" and elective plastic surgery, but not at the same rate as women. Their susceptibility to these types of white-collar victimizations is correspondingly lower. In contrast, compared with women, men are more likely to be employed in high risk occupations, such as construction and mining, where their exposure to workplace safety violations is elevated.

In summary, the gendered nature of white-collar victimization patterns mirror the gendered nature of white-collar offending. Women's differential access to particular types of occupations, professions, and organizational positions is shaped by culturally based focal concerns and institutional sex segregation, which in turn influences women's exposure to white-collar offending opportunities. These same focal concerns and institutional practices influence the types of products and services that women consume and the types of interactions that they experience in the marketplace. These patterns of consumption and interaction, in turn, make them differentially susceptible to some forms of white-collar victimization more so than others. And the same is true for men. Their patterns of consumption and the types of economic activities that they engage in differentially expose them to some forms of white-collar victimization more so than others.

Race and White-Collar Crime: Offending

Like gender, race is a characteristic that is highly correlated with traditional offending regardless of how the data are collected (e.g., self-reports, victimization reports, official statistics). The strength of the association between race and crime varies by offense type, crime seriousness, and whether participation or frequency of offending is considered. Generally, compared with whites, members of racial minority groups have higher rates of crime, are more likely to engage in more serious types of crime, and are more apt to be chronic offenders (Harris and Shaw, 2000). Yet, when the lens is shifted from traditional street crime to white-collar crime, the relationship between race and crime changes dramatically.

The typical Gestalt of crime in the United States is one of a minority offender in the foreground framed against a sea of conforming white faces (Harris and Shaw, 2000). However, as the Yale study demonstrated, the higher one moves toward Sutherland's "elite" offenders, the more that image changes, shifts, and permutates. This is not to say that white-collar crime is an exclusively "white" form of crime. As we showed in Chapter 2, for certain types of lower-level white-collar offenses, such as false claims, mail fraud, and credit fraud, significant proportions of offenders are nonwhite, and there is some evidence that nonwhites are becoming more involved in middle- and upper-level white-collar offenses such as antitrust violations and securities fraud (see Chapter 2). However, it is still the case that a substantial majority of those involved in antitrust violations and securities frauds are white males. Indeed, when it comes to the high level corporate frauds of the post-Enron era, the number of nonwhite offenders is almost zero. Of the 436 defendants studied by Steffensmeier and colleagues (2013), only six were African American, that is, just a little more than 1 percent (Steffensmeier, personal communication). No doubt, this is primarily because corporate CEOs, presidents, and other top managers are overwhelmingly white and male.

Harris and Shaw (2000) found that blacks were overrepresented among lower-level offenders in the Yale data by a factor of about 2.5 to 1 at the same time that whites were overrepresented among middle-level offenders by a factor of about 2.7 to 1. The middle-level offenders were also much more likely to have a college education than the lower-level offenders. Figure 8.1 (taken from Harris and Shaw, 2000, p. 156) demonstrates the hypothetical race ratios as one compares traditional street crime with white-collar crime.

Again, one might wonder whether opportunity alone accounts for these racial disparities in crime patterns. Harris's earlier work on gender, race, and typescripts suggests that there is more than mere opportunity at play here (Harris, 1976, 1977; Harris and Hill, 1982). Societal stereotypes about who commits crime are likely to affect the perceptions of potential offenders about criminal opportunities and whether they should take advantage of them. Stereotypes also influence how people respond to the illegal behavior of others when it occurs (as a leader, a business peer or associate, or justice agent). The parabolic relationship depicted in Figure 8.1 demonstrates, according to Harris and Shaw (2000, p. 156):

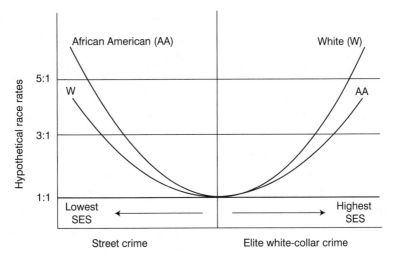

Figure 8.1 Possible relationships among crime, race, and socioeconomic status (SES)

[R]ace or caste differences net of class have the greatest impact at the extreme edges of the class spectrum. Ironically, upper class whites and underclass blacks may well have something rare but theoretically very important in common: a pronounced, and perhaps highly rational, lack of fear when it comes to committing crime. On the one hand, elite whites are likely to believe that their chances of being caught or severely punished for committing crimes are very low. On the other hand, if, as an underclass black, one feels that 'the joint is like the projects, except they feed you free,' then one is likely to believe that, in getting caught for crime, you do not have very much left to lose.

An important question regarding the connection between race and white-collar crime is whether it can be reduced to social class. Perhaps African Americans are so underrepresented among elite white-collar offenders simply because there are so relatively few African Americans in the middle and upper social classes. In other words, can the association between race and white-collar crime be reduced to the association between social class and white-collar crime? Although this is still an open question, some believe that it will eventually be answered in the negative (Harris and Shaw, 2000). Class-advantaged whites have greater opportunities to commit certain types of white-collar crime than do class-advantaged African Americans.

There are a couple of possible reasons why class-advantaged whites may have more opportunities. First, like women, African Americans who make it to the top of the corporate hierarchy are exceptional. Similar to women, they may feel that because of their uniqueness, they are subject to additional scrutiny and supervision: Someone is watching every move they make. Hence, for them, the possibility of detection and exposure must be weighted more heavily in their calculations of the costs and benefits of potential white-collar crime opportunities. White managers and executives, on the other hand, do not have to worry as much about being watched because they do not stand out from the crowd. Second, for reasons of race, African American managers may not have access to as much social capital as white managers. Like women, they may not be as embedded in informal occupational and organizational networks as whites. Research on occupational mobility in organizations certainly supports this interpretation. Compared with white males, African American males do not have access to the same networking and sponsorship opportunities that people use to advance into managerial positions. Rather, they have to rely on more formal mechanisms for advancement, such as accumulating human capital through education and workforce experience in order to advance (Smith, 2005; Wilson, 2012). Since African Americans lack access to informal networks for organizational advancement, it seems likely that they also are denied access to the informal networks of high-level white-collar crime. Access to these networks is a source of freedom and power, power to commit large-scale white-collar crimes (Hagan, 1994, p. 101).

Race and White-Collar Crime: Victimization

The link between social class and race also has implications for white-collar victimization. Because African Americans are disproportionately represented among the lower social classes, they are also disproportionately subject to the types of white-collar crime that target the poor and disadvantaged. Regrettably, some of these are among the most serious forms of white-collar crime, including environmental offenses and work-place safety violations as well as the more mundane forms of consumer fraud.

Not all communities are created equal. In the United States, garbage dumps, hazardous waste collection facilities, incinerators, chemical plants, paper mills, and other polluting industries are almost never located in upper-class communities. Rather, for decades, they have been situated in economically disadvantaged and politically powerless minority communities (Bullard, 1990). The residents of these communities face elevated risks of exposure to environmental toxins and hazardous wastes.

The term that has been coined to describe this situation is *environmental racism*, and it is clear that race and social class play a key role in environmental planning and decision making (Bullard, 2000). The most polluted urban environments are, not surprisingly, those that are poorest and largely inhabited by minorities. For example, in the Los Angeles area, more than 70 percent of African Americans and 50 percent of Latinos live in areas of heavy air pollution compared with only a third of whites (Bullard, 2000, p. 224). This pattern is not unique to Los Angeles or even California but rather is found nationwide. Air pollution is not the only environmental risk facing minority communities. The U.S. General Accounting Office found a strong relationship between the siting of hazardous waste facilities and the race and socioeconomic status of an area (Bullard, 2000, p. 32). The siting of a hazardous waste facility or any potentially polluting industry near a minority community does not necessarily mean that the residents of that particular community have been victimized by environmental crime. However, as environmental crimes are found more often in some industries than others (Epstein and Hammett, 1995; Hammett and Epstein, 1993), the people who live nearby necessarily face elevated risks of victimization. More often than not, those people are minorities.

Similarly, minorities are more likely to work in occupations and industries that expose them to elevated risks of work-related disease, injury, and death (Leeth and Ruser, 2006). Using data from the Bureau of Labor Statistics, Leeth and Ruser recently found that the rate of work-related fatalities for African American and Hispanic men was 35 percent higher than it was for white men. To put it another way, for every three white men killed at work, four African American and Hispanic workers die. This gap in fatality rates is largely, but not entirely, accounted for by occupational differences between minorities and whites (Leeth and Ruser, 2006). Even within dangerous occupations, African Americans and Hispanics suffer proportionately more fatalities than whites. As we noted in Chapter 6, not all work-related injuries and fatalities are the result of occupational safety violations. Most result from accidents. However, to the extent that work-related fatalities are caused by safety violations, minority workers are more likely to be the victims of those violations than white workers. As Leeth and Ruser put it, safety is segregated.

What accounts for the elevated risk of environmental and occupational victimization for minorities? Our opportunity perspective suggests two important factors: proximity and lack of access to guardianship. As implied earlier, minorities suffer proportionately more than whites from environmental and occupational violations simply because they often are in closer proximity to the places or settings in which these violations occur. For reasons of class and race, they are more likely than whites to live in the communities or work in the industries where these violations are concentrated. By lack of access to guardianship, we mean the relatively low capacity of minority group members and minority communities to call upon the state to exert control and oversight over potential offenders. Minority communities often lack economic and political power. Because of this lack of power, they are ill-equipped to resist the siting of polluting industries nearby, and potential offenders take this into account when making decisions. A particularly bald example of such thinking is provided by Bullard (2000). He quotes from a report prepared by a company called Cerrell Associates for the California Waste Management Board. This report, which focused on the siting of hazardous waste incinerators, presented a detailed profile of the types of communities most likely to organize effective resistance against incinerators. According to the report by Cerrell Associates:

> All socioeconomic groupings tend to resent the nearby siting of major facilities, but middle and upper socioeconomic strata possess better resources to effectuate their opposition. Middle and higher socioeconomic strata neighborhoods should not fall within the one-mile and five-mile radius of the proposed site.
>
> (quoted in Bullard, 2000, p. 225)

As Bullard notes, if incinerators aren't sited near middle and upper socioeconomic neighborhoods, the only place left for them to go is low socioeconomic communities. And these are disproportionately minority communities.

Summary

This chapter has addressed how the distribution of white-collar crime opportunities is influenced by social class, gender, and race. That these demographic characteristics are strongly related to white-collar offending and victimization should not come as a big surprise. All three have obvious connections to the occupational structure, and occupations determine access to white-collar crime opportunities. Separating out the unique effects of class, race, and gender is difficult because both gender and race are closely related to class position. As a result, it is often hard to establish what is a race or gender effect independent of social class (Harris and Shaw, 2000). It seems likely that the importance of race and gender on white-collar offending depends on the circumstances. For example, within organizations, gender may have an indirect effect on white-collar offending via its effects on access to class-linked occupational positions. Because of the glass ceiling, not many women or minorities hold top management positions and hence they do not have access to the criminal opportunities available to top managers, and even when they advance to senior management positions, women and minorities may still be excluded from the informal networks that carry out high-level corporate frauds. However, outside of organizations, gender may have a direct influence on offending. Women are excluded from certain types of crime groups precisely because they are women, not because of their class position (Steffensmeier, 1983; Steffensmeier et al., 2013). Members of racial minorities may face similar obstacles. The effects of class, race, and gender on criminal offending, then, are complex and variable.

Social class has long been recognized as an important influence on individual involvement in crime. Prior to Sutherland, it was commonplace for criminologists to think that crime was concentrated in the lower social classes. However, as Sutherland and those who followed him have shown, the traditional view is mistaken. Crime is spread throughout the class structure, but different classes engage in different forms of crime.

Although research on the connection between class and crime is complicated by many methodological difficulties, insofar as can be determined, traditional forms of serious predatory street crime do appear to be more common in the lower social classes (Braithwaite, 1981; Harris and Shaw, 2000). However, the connection between class and crime is reversed for serious white-collar crimes, wherein people from the upper class clearly predominate.

Although social status and social class are related, they are not exactly the same thing. Social status is a relative concept in the sense that one can have more or less of it based on certain criteria, such as education, income, and occupational prestige. Social class, on the other hand, at least as used here, is a relational concept. It refers to whether one has or does not have control over organizational assets and resources. The most serious and complex white-collar crimes tend to be committed by those who have control over organizational assets and resources, that is, by owners, managers, and supervisors (Wheeler and Rothman, 1980). Thus, what really matters in white-collar crime is organizational position rather than social status per se. Attending a prestigious university and getting a business or law degree does not necessarily put one in position to commit a big-time white-collar crime, but on the other hand, it may provide access to an occupation or organizational position that does.

As the data reviewed in this chapter and previously in Chapter 2 show, women are now and have been for some time severely underrepresented in big-time white-collar crime. By "big-time," we mean crimes that are organizationally complex and have serious and widespread consequences for victims. Antitrust violations, securities fraud, and, in more recent times, accounting fraud are classic examples of big-time white-collar crime. According to the Yale data, in the 1970s, women accounted for less than 1 percent of antitrust offenders, and according to the data collected by Kathleen Brickey and Darrell Steffensmeier, they make up a similarly small percentage of the individuals charged in the spate of accounting frauds that have come to light since the year 2000. Women make a better showing in low-level unsophisticated white-collar offenses, such as bank embezzlement.

Although a good deal of the gender gap in white-collar offending can be explained by the relative paucity of women in high-level corporate positions, this may not account for all of the disparity. Other differences between men and women may be involved besides their relative levels of access to leadership positions. Even when men and women do commit the same type of white-collar crime, research has found that they do so for different reasons (Daly, 1989; Zietz, 1981). That is, at times men and women appear to follow different motivational routes to white-collar crime. Women may be less likely to take advantage of white-collar offending opportunities for several other reasons, such as greater self-control, a lower taste for risk, a perception that they are under greater scrutiny, or greater empathy with potential victims. At this point, it is not clear how much of the gender gap in offending is accounted for by occupational discrimination and how much by other social or psychological differences between men and women.

A similar situation confronts us with respect to race and white-collar crime. Whites are significantly overrepresented among serious white-collar offenders. As with the gender gap in white-collar offending, the racial gap is certainly largely due to disparities in access to the appropriate types of occupational positions. However, other differences may also be involved. It remains an open question whether African Americans who attain leadership positions in large organizations engage in white-collar crime at the same rate as whites or at a rate that is lower.

Finally, we add one caveat in regard to our discussion of victimization. It is important to keep in mind that for some forms of white-collar crime it may be misleading to think of victimization in individual terms. As Sutherland (1983) noted long ago, a distinguishing characteristic of white-collar crime is diffuse victimization. For example, the price-fixing case involving automobile parts discussed in Chapter 5 affected in one way or another virtually everyone who bought or used an automobile. It does not really make sense to think of this as a crime that affects one gender, race, or ethnic group more than another, except perhaps in the trivial sense that it affects automobile users more than those who rely on public transportation. The same is often true of some types of securities offenses, such as insider trading, stock manipulation, and accounting fraud. These offenses affect the general operation of the economy. Since everyone is affected to some degree by the ups and downs of the economy, everyone (even those who do not own stocks themselves) can be affected by these forms of white-collar crime.

In addition, for some types of white-collar crime, the real victim is a government program or another organization. Frauds committed against the Medicare and Medicaid programs, as well as other health insurers, are good examples of white-collar crimes that directly victimize organizations more so than individuals. Likewise, in the mortgage fraud scandal of 2008, fraudulent mortgage backed securities were not bought by individual investors, but rather by banks, insurance companies, and pension funds. That the victims of white-collar crime can be organizations, corporations, and the government itself has important implications for the control of these offenses. For one thing, unlike most individual crime victims, organizational victims have significant political and economic power that they can employ against their victimizers. Organizations have the economic and political wherewithal to file civil lawsuits, press for vigorous investigations, or even lobby for new laws and regulations. All of these activities can affect opportunity structures for white-collar crime.

Part V

Control, Prevention, and the Future of White-Collar Crime

It should no longer be necessary to argue that white-collar crime represents a grave threat to individuals and society. The devastating effects of what Sutherland (1940) called "crime in relation to business" have been repeatedly and publicly demonstrated in financial scandals that result in billion-dollar losses, in environmental disasters that cost billions to clean up, and in workplace catastrophes whose emotional and physical costs are so dreadful that it would be tactless to put a financial price on them. That white-collar crime is a serious social problem should be obvious to anyone who pays attention to the news. Given the size and gravity of the problem, one might assume that controlling white-collar crime would be a top priority at all levels of government, but that assumption would be wrong. More resources, indeed vastly more resources of every type, are devoted to controlling crime on the streets as opposed to crime in the suites.

Nevertheless, even though official responses to white-collar crime are perhaps best described as "limp" (Shover and Hochstetler, 2006), they are not entirely absent and are not entirely ineffective. In this final section of the book, we describe the divergent approaches that are taken toward controlling and preventing white-collar crime. That there are divergent approaches is significant, because it represents yet another way in which white-collar crime differs from other forms of crime. The control of street crime is largely, though not entirely, relegated to the criminal justice system. We expect the police to uncover and arrest those who perpetrate street crimes, courts to convict them, and the correctional system to incapacitate or rehabilitate them. All of these measures we hope will make us and our streets safer.

The criminal justice system also is involved in the control of white-collar crime, but for a variety of reasons the justice system is not and probably never will be exceedingly effective as a response to the perpetrators of white-collar offenses. There are, however, other approaches to white-collar crime control and prevention that hold more promise. These other approaches include regulation, the civil justice system, a variety of extralegal measures and situational crime prevention theory. Taken individually, none of these approaches is a panacea, but collectively they have made a difference in some areas. Following other commentators, we advocate here for a pluralistic approach to white-collar crime control and prevention.

9

LEGAL CONTROLS
The Criminal Justice, Regulatory, and Civil Justice Systems

Legal Remedies

Traditional street crimes are controlled almost exclusively by the criminal law, but in the case of white-collar crime, two other kinds of legal systems—regulatory and civil—can also come into play. These three systems operate in distinct ways, with different philosophical approaches, legal standards, policing, and sanctioning methods. In this section, we focus on these different legal systems and how each of them intersects with opportunity structures. We distinguish among the legal interventions and between different sanction targets (individuals versus organizations). We then discuss some of the failures and limits of law, especially the danger of over-criminalization (i.e., unnecessarily broadening the scope of the criminal law) and what some have called creative compliance (McBarnet, 2005) or cultures of resistance (Bardach and Kagan, 1982). If law is perceived as illegitimate, unnecessarily restrictive, or overly punitive, firms may "fight back" through noncompliance and challenge the legal system. On the other hand, because much of the regulatory arena is not black and white but shades of gray, companies may seek out legal gaps to exploit in their favor. We conclude this chapter with suggestions for how the legal systems could be changed to become more effective in the fight against white-collar and corporate crime.

The Criminal Justice System

It goes without saying that the prevention and control of crime are two of the primary objectives and functions of the criminal justice system. Like other types of offenders, white-collar criminals can be pursued through the process of criminal prosecution. The criminal law is used to punish violators and to convey the message that the behavior in question is harmful, morally repugnant, and not to be tolerated. Legal philosophers long have argued that law and punishment are part of the social contract in which individuals surrender a degree of freedom in exchange for protection against harm and the enjoyment of peace and safety (Beccaria, 1983). From this perspective, when individuals violate the law, they are acting against the common good, and therefore, society has both a need and a responsibility to punish them for their violations and deter them from future acts that would be harmful to others.

Punishment for legal transgressions is necessary to preserve and protect society, but it will operate effectively only within the context of a "reasoned" system of justice, that is, a system that is fair and not subject to abuse (Bentham, 1948). Because there is always the potential for abuse and corruption by law enforcers, society has put in place a number of safeguards to protect individual rights and freedoms. For example, the criminal law has high evidentiary standards. To be convicted of a crime, a defendant's guilt must be proved beyond reasonable doubt by evidence that has been gathered and handled in accordance with strict procedural rules. In addition, defendants have a number of legal rights to protect them against the misuse of authority by law enforcers. These rights include such fundamental principles as the right to an attorney, to trial by jury, to confront witnesses, and to not be compelled to incriminate oneself. Criminal law requires proof that an offender meant to commit the illegal act and did so with a guilty mind (*mens rea*). Further, the prosecution must prove and convince a jury or judge that the offender is guilty beyond a reasonable doubt.

While these legal safeguards protect everyone from abuse by criminal justice functionaries, they can be especially helpful to those who are accused of white-collar crimes. Defendants in white-collar cases benefit in particular from the requirement that prosecutors must prove beyond a reasonable doubt that the accused acted with criminal intent (Benson and

Kerley, 2000). In other words, the prosecutor must show that the defendant knew that what he or she was doing was illegal and intentionally went ahead and did it anyway. Of course, this legal standard applies to ordinary street criminals, but it is often much easier to meet in their cases because the crimes that street criminals commit, such as robbery, burglary, assault, and theft, involve physical actions that are obviously illegal. But this is not true in many white-collar cases. As we noted, for example, in our discussion of health care fraud, when a physician submits a fraudulent claim to Medicaid, the fact that it is fraudulent is not readily apparent because on the surface fraudulent claims look just like legitimate claims. The difficulty of uncovering the illegal act that is created by the superficial appearance of legitimacy in white-collar cases is a major constraint on the effectiveness of the criminal justice system in this area.

Even if a fraudulent claim by a physician is discovered, the physician can always say that he or she just made a mistake or that this was just a onetime accident made by someone else in the office. While this assertion of innocence can be defeated in court, it is not necessarily easy to do so. Rather it requires that prosecutors and investigators gather additional evidence that relates to the defendant's state of mind. This additional work takes time, effort, and resources. The inherent ambiguity in the state of mind of defendants in white-collar cases is exploited by defense attorneys who try to construct a favorable interpretation of the facts to present to a jury. A favorable interpretation is one in which the defendant's state of mind appears ambiguous, and the requirement of proof beyond a reasonable doubt cannot be met. Almost without exception, the defendant's state of mind is a critical and contested issue when white-collar cases are adjudicated in court (Benson, 1985; Benson and Kerley, 2000; Katz, 1979; Mann, 1985).

Even though white-collar cases raise special problems for investigators and prosecutors, successful prosecutions do happen regularly and when they do, they can send a powerful message of deterrence to others. For instance, in a recent criminal case against Gwendolyn Hemphill—the former executive assistant to the president of the Washington D.C. Teachers Union—for conspiracy, embezzlement, mail fraud, wire fraud, false statements, money laundering, and theft (to the tune of nearly $5 million over a 7-year period), the government needed to prove that she actually committed the crimes (*actus reus*) and that she did so intentionally and with knowledge that her behavior was unlawful (*mens rea*).

An ideal criminal case provides a clear evidence trail (physical evidence, witnesses, and the like) linking the accused to the illegal acts. In the Hemphill case, the government was successful in its prosecution (*Washington Times*, 2006). If Beccaria and Bentham are correct, the punishment levied against Ms. Hemphill will send a message of general deterrence to other potential offenders (e.g., fraud and embezzlement will result in criminal prosecution, time in jail, and stigmatic consequences) and to Ms. Hemphill specifically. Although she appealed, the appellate court ultimately upheld the decision of the district court and Hemphill went to prison to serve an 11-year sentence. By going to prison, other goals of the criminal law, such as incapacitation and retribution, were also achieved.

Although the criminal law was used successfully in the Hemphill embezzlement case, criminal prosecutions can be very challenging in a corporate context (Stone, 1975) where prosecutors confront another problem. Not only is it difficult to show that someone acted with criminal intent, it is often just as difficult to tell precisely who should be held responsible for decision making within firms. Decision making in organizations is often fragmented and not in the hands of any one single person. And decision makers can practice concerted ignorance to shield themselves from criminal liability (Katz, 1979). Consequently, it is the case that "individual accountability is frequently displaced by corporate liability, which now serves as a rough-and-ready catch-all device" (Fisse and Braithwaite, 1993, p. 1). When the defendant is an organization instead of an individual, it is frequently difficult to utilize the criminal law against the violator. As Celia Wells (1993, p. 15) observes, the language of the law "assumes that state coercion is to be exercised against an individual and that the harm which that individual might bring about will injure other specific individuals. Corporate activities do not fit that paradigm."

Although the criminal law has adopted the notion of corporate personhood to substitute for natural persons and has broadened the reach of the law through corporate liability, it is still difficult for prosecutors to challenge corporations in criminal court (Benson et al., 1998). It is not surprising then that criminal prosecutions of corporations are relatively rare. In recent years, the federal government has redirected its focus on the prosecution of responsible officers and managers with the goal of "enhanced deterrence." The U.S. Sentencing Commission has developed new and tougher guidelines for organizational sentencing, and the U.S. Department of Justice has established new guidelines for corporate prosecutions (Cullen et al., 2006), and as we discussed in Chapter 8, the Corporate Fraud Task Force did investigate and prosecute a number of individuals involved in the corporate accounting frauds of the early 2000s. Yet, even with this renewed attention on corporate decision makers, criminal prosecution of individuals within corporations is uncommon, expensive, and often unsuccessful. As Clinard and Yeager observe in the updated introduction to their classic book, *Corporate Crime*, criminal actions against those responsible for company oversight (i.e., board members) are highly unusual (Clinard and Yeager, 2006: xxxvi–xxxvii).

Oftentimes, a successful conviction against a major corporate crime figure is appealed (Martha Stewart is a notable exception, as she chose not to appeal and served her sentence) and sometimes reversed at the higher court. Indeed, many legal scholars believed that Enron's Jeffrey Skilling had a "reasonable" chance of overturning his 2006 conviction on some of the charges against him because the government failed to hand over evidence that would have aided his defense and because of other serious legal flaws in Skilling's conviction (Hawn, 2007). Skilling did appeal his case repeatedly and the government finally agreed to reduce his sentence from 24 to 14 years. In return for the sentence reduction, Skilling agreed to no longer challenge his conviction (Wilbanks, 2013). When the government sets its sights on the company as a criminal offender, most successful prosecutions do not land the big fish but instead capture smaller and relatively newer companies (Cullen et al., 2006, p. 360; U.S. Sentencing Commission, 1993–2004).

In summary, as a means of controlling white-collar and corporate crime, the criminal justice system is difficult to use and has not been exceedingly successful. The very legal safeguards that protect our individual freedom from government abuse and oppression ironically also make us more vulnerable to victimization by white-collar criminals. Despite these problems, however, the criminal justice system still can play an important role in the fight against white-collar crime. Much more so than the civil and regulatory systems that we will discuss below, the sanctions that the criminal justice system can impose are very stigmatizing—especially against offenders who tend to see themselves as highly conventional and law-abiding. The criminal law thus has the potential for great deterrent effects, but the empirical evidence on the subject is far from conclusive (Simpson et al., 2014).

Civil Law Enforcement

For the criminal law to work, people must believe that illegal behavior will be discovered and punished. In addition, the system must operate in an efficient and fair manner. Yet, as we have pointed out repeatedly, one of the distinguishing features of white-collar crime is that it is hard to detect, and even when wrongdoing is detected, it is often difficult to successfully prosecute the wrongdoer in white-collar cases—particularly when the wrongdoer is a powerful corporation. Because of these obstacles, legal redress is often sought through means other than criminal law. Civil law, for instance, is easier to use. It requires a lower standard of evidence to prove responsibility (i.e., a preponderance of evidence rather than proof beyond a reasonable doubt). Moreover, the punishments, although they can be economically costly to the defendant, do not involve deprivation of freedom. Consequently, defendants have fewer legal and due process protections. As we know from one of the most infamous cases of the late 20th century, former football player and actor O.J. Simpson was found not guilty in a criminal trial but was found responsible (and culpable) in a civil trial for the death of his ex-wife, Nicole Brown Simpson, and her companion, Ronald Goldman.

Although the Simpson murder tragedy differs substantially from the more common forms of white-collar crime, the process in civil court is similar. The government (as the moving agent) will elect to bring a civil case instead of a criminal one against a corporate offender. Our antitrust laws, for instance, have both criminal and civil provisions giving the government greater leeway to select the most appropriate justice process for the crime after taking into consideration the quality of the evidence and the perceived seriousness of the case. Civil law lacks the punitive and stigmatic capacity of criminal prosecution because it has a different goal. Rather than incapacitation, deterrence, and retribution, which are the main objectives of the criminal justice system, the goal of civil justice is to compensate and repair the damage to victims. This is achieved primarily through the use of fines.

Relative to criminal prosecution, corporate civil cases are sought more often by the state (not to mention individuals who seek tort actions against corporate offenders), and although the empirical evidence is sketchy, these cases may be more successful (see Simpson, 2002). The government needs to meet a much lower standard of evidence, and legal reforms make it easier to demand documents and compel information from offenders. Punitive sanctions (double and treble damages), when added to the civil remedies (such as fines and court injunctions), increase pressure on defendants to settle cases. Moreover, responsible individuals, whether they are operating outside of the organizational context (such as a credit card fraudster) or within it (such as an owner who fails to protect workers from exposure to dangerous substances), can be sued and sanctioned. Both the government and victims can bring a civil case, although it is much more difficult for individual claimants to challenge corporate defendants than it is for the government to do so on their behalf. Unfortunately, civil litigation may be unduly costly for individual plaintiffs, especially if they must also pay the court costs for the defendant if the case is lost.

In spite of the availability and appropriateness of civil actions, their use depends on victims' recognizing their own victimization and being able to identify those responsible for it. As we discussed earlier, this link is easier to make when the relationship between offender and victim is more direct. For example, a mechanic takes money to fix a problem that is not repaired. An embezzler steals money from her employer. A physician overcharges the Medicare program. A financial consultant fails to invest his client's money and pockets it instead. In these types of cases, it may take the victim some time to determine that she or he has been victimized, but once the offense comes to light, it is relatively easy to determine the perpetrator in each instance. This is one of the reasons that criminal prosecution is more common in white-collar cases that involve a direct interaction between an individual offender and a victim. When the perpetrator is a company, however, it is often more difficult to determine exactly who the victims are and exactly who is responsible for the harm.

The Regulatory Justice System

The regulatory justice system evolved in the United States to monitor and control the behavior of economic institutions. In the regulatory system, control tends to be more persuasive and less punitive (e.g., consent agreements not to violate the law again, recalls of products, monetary penalties or warnings) (Clinard and Yeager, 2006, p. xiii). The goal is to bring the offender into compliance with the law. Administrative law is the most common means of legal redress in the United States for corporate offenses, but it is far from a monolithic system. Many regulatory agencies have the authority to investigate criminal cases and pursue civil judicial sanctions against corporate offenders. Agencies typically refer criminal cases to U.S. attorneys for prosecution. Frank and Lombness (1988) suggest that there are four ways to view the regulatory justice system—each view has its own assumptions about how the system works. These different views include the justice model, the rational-legal model, the economic model, and the conflict model.

Adherents to the justice model assume that the primary goal of the regulatory justice system is the social control of economic institutions. Criminologists, in particular, draw from the work of Edwin Sutherland (1983), whose research on corporate offenders revealed that corporations generally operate outside the purview of criminal law. Instead, violators are subject to civil and regulatory statutes. Sutherland suggested that this difference was not due to any moral ambiguity about the harmfulness of white-collar crime compared with traditional street crime, or confusion over the culpability of white-collar offenders (1983, pp. 52–53). Rather, Sutherland believed that corporate crime cases were "administratively segregated" and processed differently because the offenders, who are rich and powerful, demand and receive preferential treatment (1983, p. 6). It is out of this tradition that criminologists study civil and regulatory law by taking a criminal justice point of view. "Studies within the justice model describe the processes of investigation, adjudication, and punishment, focusing on issues of discretion, due process, and effectiveness" (Frank and Lombness, 1988, p. 5). However, because the regulatory justice system differs in significant ways from the criminal justice system (inspectors versus police; administrative courts versus criminal courts; an emphasis on compliance versus punishment), the comparison is superficial at best (Garner, 2007; Scott, 1989).

The rational-legal model of regulation assumes that regulatory law is a response to a set of social problems, recognized and acted upon by legislators. Somewhat similar to how problem-oriented policing works, a particular problem is brought to the attention of lawmakers, who then create policies and laws to "solve" the problem. Obviously some problems are much easier to "legislate" than others (product safety laws versus global warming), and a critical challenge for lawmakers is to find the right balance between law and other societal strategies to problem-solve (such as public awareness campaigns). The rational-legal approach is liberal in the sense that it assumes that government imposed controls in the form of laws can improve social conditions.

Another model of regulation suggested by Frank and Lombness (1988) is the conflict model. Based on conflict theory, this approach assumes that society is composed of groups with competing and contradictory interests. The regulatory arena (agencies, laws, policies, processes, and outcomes) is just one of many sites wherein the power struggle among group interests is contested. In the competitive struggle among groups, the powerful typically win. Regulatory law, which may initially appear to be responsive to the interests of the less powerful in society (e.g., worker health and safety) is eventually usurped, perverted, and manipulated to protect the interests, rights, and privileges of business owners.

Last, for the past three decades, the most prominent model of regulation has been the economic model. This approach adopts a utilitarian "cost-benefit" strategy to assess whether, on balance, the benefits of regulation exceed its costs. Regulatory agencies are required to conduct cost-benefit analyses when major initiatives are proposed. However, it is far from clear whether it is possible to assess accurately the assorted costs and benefits of regulation (especially social costs that are not easily quantifiable). Recent attempts to quantify the costs of crime demonstrate both the utility and weaknesses of this approach (Cohen, 2000). Much of the contemporary regulatory debate has centered on whether regulation is "efficient." Anti-regulatory critics claim that business regulation (particularly in its "social" forms) is inefficient and generally costly to a free-market system

(Shover, Clelland, and Lynxwiler, 1986). An unfettered system—or at least one that has as few fetters as possible—will produce greater social good with fewer costs than a system that is stifled with legal restrictions. Critics on the other side of the debate assert that left to their own devices, corporations naturally pursue their own self-interest (profit seeking) with little regard for the common societal good. For the critics of the economic perspective, regulation of business is necessary to force corporations to behave properly and "do the right thing."

Whether regulation can be said to "work" as a means of controlling white-collar crime depends a great deal on one's perspective or model of the regulatory system. For example, from a justice model point of view, the regulatory system is supposed to catch and punish violators. From this perspective, regulatory control could reasonably be seen as a stark failure. On the one hand, there are far too few inspectors to "police" corporations and too much discretion in the application of the law; the sanctions levied are neither certain nor severe enough to deter corporate offenders, and cases rarely are nominated for more severe legal consequences (such as criminal enforcement referrals), although this may vary by type of offense (Simpson, Garner, and Gibbs, 2007). On the other hand, when they are challenged by charges that regulatory processes are unfair and biased, some regulators adopt a strict "legalistic" enforcement style. This style decreases discretion and the perception of unfairness, but it carries with it a lack of flexibility. All violators, regardless of circumstance, are treated in a similar manner (Bardach and Kagan, 1982). The end result is the meaningless enforcement of rules, not the control of serious white-collar violations.

Viewed from a rational-legal perspective, however, regulation can be said to have had some degree of success in that many socially costly corporate behaviors have been redefined as social problems with attached legal remedies that appear to have had a positive impact on the extent of the problem in question (e.g., accounting and stock fraud, health and worker safety, environmental pollution, consumer product safety). For example, even though the Occupational Safety and Health Administration is often criticized as being a weak and ineffectual agency, occupational safety regulations undoubtedly have had a positive effect on the lives and safety of workers. Fifty years ago, workers were injured at a rate that is estimated to have been three times higher than the injury rate now (Cullen et al., 2006, p. 298). However, redefining harmful corporate behavior as a social problem is a difficult undertaking, one that can have unintended negative consequences. If the government unilaterally redefines some formerly legal activity as now illegal, and if it does so without the support and concurrence of the regulated entities, this action can increase the likelihood of deception, concealment, and conspiracy by companies. Subterranean resistance such as this is especially likely to happen if regulators adopt a legalistic approach to enforcement (Makkai and Braithwaite, 1994). Oppositional and criminogenic business subcultures develop that "facilitate the sharing of knowledge about methods of legal resistance and counterattack" (Braithwaite, 1989).

This problem is not unique to regulatory justice and can be a problem for criminal law as well (see Simpson, 2002). Similarly, the economic approach also may facilitate defiance and resistance if companies and their supporters believe that regulations are overly restrictive and inefficient. Corporations learn to "game" regulators, taking advantage of the shades of gray in regulations while appearing to be socially responsible (McBarnet, 2005).

According to the conflict approach, regulation is a contested terrain. Powerful corporations utilize political supporters to push their own legislative agenda. Pro- and anti-regulation forces engage in a battle of scientific wits, both utilizing their own cost-benefit assessments and scientific experts to demonstrate the "truth" of their positions. For example, one anti–climate change bureaucrat was recently quoted as saying, "You've got your science, I've got mine" (Simpson, 2006). When there is a lack of agreement among businesses, regulators, corporations, and the general public regarding normative standards and the moral wrongfulness of behaviors, then regulation as a means of control is likely to be ineffectual.

Like the criminal justice system, the regulatory system has both strengths and weaknesses as a means of controlling white-collar and corporate crime. Compared with the criminal justice system, three aspects of the regulatory system are particularly important: its proactive nature, specialized expertise, and fewer legal constraints.

In our legal tradition, the criminal justice system is conceived to be primarily a reactive force of control. When someone breaks the law, then the police can spring into action to find and bring the lawbreaker to justice. With only a few exceptions, such as vice crimes, the police generally do not enforce the law by actively seeking out offenses. Rather, they wait until someone files a complaint and then they react. Regulatory agencies, however, are expected to prevent harms from happening in the first place, not just to react to them after they have occurred. OSHA inspectors, for example, can require business owners to remedy dangerous work conditions even though no one may actually have been harmed. As we explain in more detail in the next chapter, the proactive nature of the regulatory system makes it at times more suitable for situational crime prevention than the criminal justice system.

A second advantage of the regulatory system is that regulatory agencies and their agents typically have specialized expertise in a particular area of business activity. For example, the EPA focuses on the potential harmful effects of manufacturing processes on the environment, while OSHA concentrates on workplace safety, and the SEC applies itself to securities. Specialized expertise enables regulatory agents to detect and understand complex corporate offenses better than can most criminal justice personnel.

A final advantage that regulatory agents have over the police is that they are not subject to the same legal constraints regarding their interactions with regulated entities. For example, before the police can conduct a search of a business, they must obtain a search warrant based upon a demonstration of probable cause that a crime has been committed there. Regulatory agents, on the other hand, have the authority to enter business premises and conduct inspections within their area of expertise to look for violations. Because they can enter and inspect businesses without having to get a search warrant, regulatory agents can act to prevent harm before it actually occurs rather than having to wait until something bad happens. Depending on the agency involved, the ability of regulatory agents to inspect is not limited to physical searches of premises. Rather, their powers often extend to searches of records, files, and other types of documentary evidence.

Unfortunately, regulatory agencies are often unable to make much use of the investigatory and preventive advantages that they have over criminal justice agencies, because they are understaffed and underfunded compared with the size of the regulated community. The failure of governments to allocate sufficient resources to regulatory agencies has been and remains a fundamental weakness of regulation as a means of controlling white-collar and corporate crime. It is one thing to establish an agency to protect, for instance, worker safety, but it is quite another to give it enough resources to provide the credible oversight needed to actually achieve that goal.

Another fundamental weakness of regulation is inadequate sanctioning power. The sanctions that regulatory agencies can impose simply do not have the same deterrent power as criminal sanctions. Depending on the circumstances, agencies can impose large fines, issue cease and desist orders, or force expensive recalls. However, in the eyes of businessmen and women, the threat imposed by these sanctions is trivial compared with the threat of conviction for a crime and incarceration. Simply put, for a multibillion-dollar company, a multimillion-dollar fine most of the time is nothing to really be concerned about.

Summary

The criminal justice, civil justice, and regulatory systems represent different approaches to controlling harmful conduct by businesses and professionals. None of these approaches can serve as a panacea to the problem of white-collar crime. Each approach has its strengths and weaknesses, but taken together they represent the traditional lines of defense against white-collar and corporate crime. And they have had some success. As we noted above, while injuries and deaths have not been entirely eliminated from the workplace, they have been significantly reduced in number, at least in the United States and other developed nations. This is progress that should be built on in the future and extended to developing countries.

Although we have presented the three systems of legal control separately, there is no reason why they cannot work together in practice. This possibility is especially true for the regulatory and criminal justice systems. As John Braithwaite and others have persuasively argued, legal responses to corporate wrongdoing can and should be organized in a hierarchical fashion, with criminal sanctions being used as a last resort for particularly egregious offenses involving particularly intransigent offenders.

However, while recognizing that progress has been made in some areas, there is still a long way to go in others. Particularly in regard to evolving and changing forms of financial fraud, legal controls often seem to be behind the curve, as the accounting frauds of 2001 and the mortgage fraud scandals of 2008 clearly revealed. The increased use of computer technology to facilitate white-collar crime is also on the rise. So, new approaches need to be considered. In the next chapter, we attempt to do that through an examination of the potential effectiveness of extralegal controls on corporate wrongdoing and the applicability of situational crime prevention theory to white-collar and corporate crime.

1 0

OPPORTUNITIES AND SITUATIONAL PREVENTION OF WHITE-COLLAR CRIME
Combining Legal and Extralegal Controls

Opportunities, Criminal Laws, and Regulations

From an opportunity perspective, laws and regulations are best viewed as tools that can be used to shape and control white-collar crime opportunities. Recall that white-collar crimes have certain characteristics (the offender's legitimate access to the victim, a physical separation between the offender and victim, and the superficial appearance of legality). These characteristics give rise to the use of particular criminal techniques (e.g., deception, abuse of trust, concealment, conspiracy). One way in which regulatory law affects white-collar crime opportunities is by setting the parameters of "legitimate" access. So, for instance, many professions require a degree or certification for an individual to offer services. Businesses often must be registered with a state or local authority before they can open their doors. There are age restrictions regarding who can enter into a contract, and so forth. In effect, these regulations limit who can have legitimate access to particular types of victims. Though such regulations do not stop those who have legitimate access from abusing their positions, they at least make it more difficult for the criminally motivated to get legitimate access.

Regulations can also be used to make it more difficult or riskier for potential offenders to deceive potential victims. For example, regulations that require contractors to provide written estimates for proposed work make it more difficult (but certainly not impossible) for them to promise one thing and do another. The passage of the Sarbanes-Oxley (SOX) Act in the wake of the Enron scandal provides another example. One part of the SOX Act requires chief executive officers and chief financial officers to certify their company's financial records (Cullen et al., 2006, p. 323). Failure to do so or certifying false financial statements can expose the executives to criminal penalties. In effect, this new requirement makes it more difficult for corporate executives to feign ignorance as a way of avoiding being held responsible for fraudulent accounting. There are other examples, such as the labeling that is required on appliances regarding energy efficiency or the nutritional labels on food products. Manufacturers and retailers can try to lie and cheat, of course, on these labels. However, it seems likely that they face a greater risk that their deception will be exposed than they would face if there were no legally required labels. In general, one of the best ways that regulations can help reduce white-collar crime is by increasing transparency, making it harder for potential offenders to deceive consumers and other victims.

The Limits of the Law and Legal Controls

Christopher Stone (1975), one of the first critics to call attention to the multiple ways in which law fails to control corporate misconduct, acknowledged the burdens of applying traditional legal forms to corporations. However, Stone's observation is also relevant for other (noncorporate) kinds of white-collar offenses. Some white-collar crimes emerge as new technologies develop. For instance, there was no such thing as Internet fraud until the Internet was developed. For this reason, law needs to be flexible and adaptable when new opportunities emerge. The common law is impressively adjustable to changing social conditions, but when developments (like the Internet) are truly innovative, the common law cannot adapt rapidly enough to the potential risks posed by such a new and expansive global phenomenon.

> [T]he rapidity with which changes occur in the digital age . . . makes the conventional processes of law reform cumbersome. Introducing a legislative change to accommodate the latest development in computer user authentication technologies, for

example, may take years, by which time the technological development in question may be outmoded and the reform no longer applicable.

(Grabosky, Smith, and Dempsey, 2001, p. 185)

Referencing the Enron case, Malcolm S. Salter (as quoted in Hawn, 2007) suggests that many of the acts were innovative "new ideas and new financial instruments for which there is not established accounting, or that don't conform with old principles."

Confirming what we noted in the preceding chapter that the law often seems to trail behind technological developments, these criticisms suggest that law, in its many forms, is—at best— marginal in its ability to restrict white-collar crime opportunities and may, on occasion, increase offending opportunities either through its limitations (gray areas) or how it affects perceptions. In the next section, we discuss some alternative remedies for the control of white-collar crime that rely on extralegal strategies.

Extralegal Remedies

Strategies to prevent white-collar crime that are not centered in legal controls focus mainly on reducing criminal opportunity. Routine activity theory suggests that crime results from three interrelated events that occur at the same time, in the same place: a motivated offender, a suitable target, and the lack of a capable guardian (Cohen and Felson, 1979). From this point of view, crime can be prevented by somehow decreasing the suitability of the target or increasing the level of guardianship. The suitability of a target can be reduced by target hardening (i.e., making it harder to get at the target). Guardianship can be increased by providing more, or more effective, surveillance. Prevention efforts can also focus on the motivated offender, but these may be more difficult to accomplish than increasing guardianship and hardening the crime target. From a practical point of view, however, situational crime prevention theory predicts that any intervention that disrupts the crime triad will reduce crime.

The risk of many traditional forms of white-collar crime can be mitigated by increasing public awareness about crime risks and enhancing victim protection. For instance, after Hurricane Katrina, the Department of Justice issued a warning to citizens regarding fraudulent relief efforts.

Credit card companies now require card recipients to call and "activate" their cards before use and, when using the card remotely, to report the security code on the back of the card. Consumers are encouraged not to use debit cards to purchase items remotely over the telephone or Internet, because it is easier for fraudsters to gain unwarranted access to bank account information. Anyone who has an e-mail account is familiar with the common warnings about e-mail scams, and for those who use the Internet, we are warned not to respond to or give out any personal information (such as bank account information or social security numbers) in response to "phishing" expeditions. With respect to white-collar crime control, consumer education is a form of target hardening.

To guard against employee (and consumer) theft, department stores at the turn of the 20th century implemented a number of new ways to display merchandise (locked in glass cabinets) that provided better control (Abelson, 1989). Today, businesses utilize cameras, alarms, security codes, and guards; they limit access to sensitive information and products; potential employees are interviewed, psychologically tested, and assessed before employment to determine crime risks (among other things). Employees are watched by their colleagues, and suspect behavior can be anonymously reported to "hotlines." Randomized audits of accounts, expense statements, legally sanctioned policies and procedures, coupled with other types of surveillance, affect both objective and perceptual opportunities for crime.

There are obviously many creative strategies to prevent white-collar crime, ranging from the simple (computer passwords) to the sophisticated (tracking data to pick up any unusual activity). For example, the Securities and Exchange Commission (SEC) regularly tracks the buying and selling of stocks, looking for unusual patterns that may indicate some form of insider trading or other stock fraud. At the Federal Trade Commission (FTC), the Bureau of Consumer Protection maintains a website where consumers can file complaints about deceptive or fraudulent businesses practices. These complaints are shared with law enforcement and, at the end of the year, the FTC issues a report to consumers that documents the kinds and number of complaints received. These kinds of prevention programs are flexible and timely, capable of responding quickly to new forms of white-collar crime. They also extend beyond the reach of our justice systems and, as such, are a broader and more comprehensive way to reduce white-collar crime opportunities. However, they tend to neglect the motivated offender.

In *Crime, Shame, and Reintegration*, John Braithwaite (1989) argues that the key to crime control rests in a society's capacity and ability to communicate the wrongfulness of behaviors to citizens and respond to the act in a manner that shames but reintegrates the offender. Although his argument focuses more on recidivism than on the initial decision to offend, his main point (which he shares with Bentham) is that there are alternatives to formal justice that carry tremendous potential for controlling all types of crime. These alternatives build around the notion that individuals are generally embedded in some kind of social network (religious organizations, families, neighborhoods, corporations, professional associations) that can impose shame and punishment outside of (or in conjunction with) the legal process. The effectiveness of these controls, like the legal process, will affect white-collar crime opportunities.

Extralegal social controls can take many different forms. The most basic form is socialization (by parents, peers, schools, churches, and businesses) that emphasize the right norms and values. Ethical standards are the backbone of a social control system that promotes pro-social behavior in children and adults. Even under the best of circumstances, socialization can fail. And in the case of white-collar crime, there are challenges to standards of right and wrong that do not exist for traditional crime. For instance, surveys suggest that although rape, murder, robbery, and burglary rank consistently high in crime seriousness surveys, white-collar crime (with the exception of corporate offenses that lead to death and injury) is not viewed as seriously by the general public (for a summary, see Simpson, 2002). Although assessments of white-collar crime seriousness appear to have increased over the past 30 years, public perceptions are fickle—easily influenced by the most recent sensational case or Wall Street scandals. This fact, coupled with the *mala prohibita* nature of many corporate offenses, suggests that society has not successfully communicated the seriousness and consequences of these types of crime.

Criminologists know that the greatest risk of crime rests with those offenses around which there is little moral consensus. After the stock market scandals of the 1980s (often perpetrated by highly credentialed

MBAs), several well-regarded and influential graduate programs adopted ethics training modules within traditional classes or added specific classes in business ethics as a way to introduce future managers to the kinds of ethical (and legal) dilemmas they were apt to face in the workplace. Similarly, many companies incorporated ethics codes and ethics training as integral parts of their internal compliance programs. Although the jury is still out on whether training programs have had any impact on offending (Schell-Busey, 2009)—in part because it is debatable whether those who implement the programs are "serious" about ethics—it is clear that this type of intervention has grown in popularity and legitimacy. Nevertheless, some respected scholars regard the whole business ethics movement as a failure (Clinard and Yeager, 1980).

Because most white-collar crime occurs within organizations, it is important to consider how social control systems within organizations can affect white-collar crime opportunities. Braithwaite (1989, p. 143) suggests that the organizational environment can effectively shame offenders when punishment for white-collar crime "maximizes the sense of shame [and] . . . communicates the message that white-collar crime is as abhorrent to the community as crime in the streets." Of course, having the potential to shame is not the same as actually shaming the offender. So, what kinds of practices are effective for corporate shaming? One of the more effective ways to sanction individual and corporate offenders is through negative publicity (Fisse and Braithwaite, 1983). One way to tell that publicity is an effective tool is to observe how corporate public relations departments go on the offensive after a negative incident (consider, for example, the infamous Exxon Valdez case). However, managers also fear discovery of their illicit activities by significant others, such as family, friends, and business associates. In fact, Simpson's research shows that intended illegal corporate activity by managers was significantly inhibited by the potential informal sanctions brought by significant others—and this effect is equal to or actually greater than the threat of formal legal sanctions (Simpson, 2002; Simpson, Garner, and Gibbs, 2007).

Smith, Simpson, and Huang (2007) suggest that informal sanctions and formal sanctions interact to lower corporate crime offending risk. Managers' perceptions of negative informal consequences (outcome expectancies) affect their perceptions of formal sanction threats, which in turn lower their willingness to engage in three types of corporate offenses (price fixing, Environmental Protection Agency offenses, and bribery). Thus, as Ayres and Braithwaite (1992) argue, prevention and control of white-collar crime will be accomplished best through a pyramid of enforcement. Informal controls and sanctions operate at the base of the pyramid as the first (and most important set of controls), followed up the pyramid with more punitive and "formal" kinds of interventions.

Situational Crime Prevention Theory

Situational crime prevention theory (SCPT) focuses on ways to make criminal opportunities less attractive to potential offenders. It takes an exceedingly pluralistic approach toward this objective. By pluralistic, we mean that SCPT holds that when it comes to crime control, we should not put all our eggs in one basket, regardless whether it is the criminal justice system, the regulatory system, the market, or any other legal or extralegal mechanism of control. Rather, we should recognize and take advantage of the usefulness of all of these mechanisms in different combinations depending on the situation confronting us.

To prevent any particular type of white-collar crime, we need to understand its opportunity structure and then figure out a way to intervene in and modify that specific structure. From the perspective of both SCPT and potential offenders, criminal opportunities have five dimensions or characteristics (Cornish and Clarke, 1986):

1. the effort required to carry out the offense;
2. the risks of detection associated with committing the offense;
3. the rewards to be gained from the offense;
4. situational conditions that may encourage criminal actions; and
5. excuses offenders can use to justify their actions.

In short, from the offender's point of view, crimes, including white-collar crimes, are more attractive if they are easy to commit, have low risks of detection, offer attractive rewards, are encouraged by the immediate environment, and are easy to justify (Benson, Madensen, and Eck, 2009). As we hope was made clear by our analysis of specific types of white-collar crime in Chapters 5 and 6, these conditions are often met for people who are contemplating committing a white-collar offense.

Before going on to discuss how SCPT may be applied to white-collar crime, we need to address one other important and distinctive aspect of opportunity structures for white-collar crimes. The term "opportunity structure" suggests something that is solid or fixed in place. For example, a house that is known to be unoccupied at night and that does not have an alarm system presents a fixed opportunity. From the perspective of a potential burglar, the target is sitting there waiting for him or her to take advantage of it. However, in regard to white-collar crime, opportunity structures are almost always not like this. That is, the opportunity is not present because a physical object has been left unguarded. Rather, the opportunity arises out of some sort of legitimate business activity or process. From our perspective, processes create opportunities. The procedure by which health care practitioners submit claims to health care insurers is a perfect example of a process that creates criminal opportunities.

Thus, white-collar crime opportunities almost always involve the intersection of two processes. The first is a legitimate process that is typically followed in the world of business or government, and the second is an illegitimate process that is parasitical on the first process. Recall, for instance, the cases of fraud that emerged out of the victim assistance opportunities that were put into place for persons and businesses damaged by Katrina and the BP oil spill. From a broad strategic point of view, prevention requires making adjustments to the legitimate process that make it difficult for individuals to act parasitically in relation to the legitimate process. Thus to prevent white-collar crimes, we need to develop legitimate processes that are difficult to copy or that raise the likelihood that an illegitimate use of the process will be detected. To put this in the conceptual framework that we have used throughout this book, prevention involves making it hard or complicated for white-collar offenders either to maintain the superficial appearance of legitimacy or to appear to have an ambiguous state of mind or both (Benson et al., 2009; Benson and Madensen, 2007).

To accomplish these objectives, we can draw from and extend the basic principles of situational crime prevention theory (Clarke, 1983). SCPT recommends that to reduce any particular type of white-collar crime, we should try to modify its opportunity structure so that it:

1. requires more effort to commit the offense;
2. raises the risk of detection for committing the offense;
3. reduces the rewards associated with the offense;
4. reduces any situational provocations for the offense; and
5. makes it more difficult to justify or excuse the offense (Benson and Madensen, 2007).

Depending on the type of crime under consideration, some of these objectives may be easier to meet than others, and it is not necessary to meet all of these objectives in every case.

As we demonstrated in Chapters 5 and 6, white-collar crimes take a variety of different forms. Fraud in health care is not carried out in the same way as mortgage fraud. We need to be sensitive to these differences and focus on highly specific forms of crime (Benson and Madensen, 2007). What may work to reduce fraud in health care may be useless in the case of mortgage fraud because the two offenses have different opportunity structures.

In the case of ordinary street crime, the effort required to commit the offense is usually increased by trying to block the offenders' access to the crime target. Because white-collar crimes are based on specialized access, simply blocking access is not an option for many types of white-collar crime, especially when the offense is based on the misuse of a legitimate occupational role. However, there are some instances in which variations on this strategy can be used to a degree. For example, laws and regulations that require practitioners to obtain licenses or certifications before they can practice a certain profession, in effect, block access to the target. Granted, those who have the license can misuse it, but licensing requirements, nevertheless, put limits on the number and type of people who can practice a particular line of work. They increase the effort for would-be offenders (Benson and Madensen, 2007).

With regard to consumer-related frauds, the effort required to commit an offense can also be increased through a form of target hardening. For consumer frauds to work, the offender must somehow fool the victim into thinking that he or she is legitimate. The victim must accept the offender's advantageous distortion of reality. This happened often during the early 2000s when predatory mortgage brokers and bankers talked eager home buyers into taking out loans with terms that were very unfavorable to them (Nguyen and Pontell, 2010). However, to the extent that consumers can educate themselves so that they become harder to deceive, the offender's job becomes all that much more difficult. Individuals who can spot distortions of reality can avoid many forms of white-collar crime victimization. Simple things such as knowing who you are dealing with when you buy a product or service, getting recommendations from friends and neighbors, and checking references or the Better Business Bureau can help you avoid coming into contact in the first place with someone intent on defrauding you and can help you recognize when someone is trying to deceive you.

Raising the risk of detection is particularly important with respect to white-collar crime, because once the crime is exposed, it is usually relatively straightforward to identify the responsible persons or organizations (Braithwaite and Geis, 1982). Exposure is threatening to white-collar offenders. Having their names linked with anything that appears untoward or disreputable is troubling for white-collar offenders because of their public persona and self-image as upstanding, moral, and law-abiding citizens. The threat of potential negative publicity can act as a deterrent even in cases where formal sanctions are never actually administered (Fisse and Braithwaite, 1983).

In order to raise the risk of detection, however, we need to think beyond just hiring more regulators or police officers. We need to think creatively and design strategies that are focused on particular opportunity structures. A good example of thinking creatively can be found in the enforcement of the Federal Crop Insurance Program (FCIP). The FCIP is supposed to insure farmers against risks such as floods and natural disasters. Significantly, it also insures farmers against crop failures. A simple scheme used by some farmers to take advantage of this program is to insure field A against failure. The farmer then takes the harvest from field A and records it as coming from field B, and then submits a claim to the FCIP to be indemnified for the "failure" of field A (Shover and Hochstetler, 2006). In effect, the farmer gets paid twice for the harvest of field A—once from the FCIP and once from the marketplace. White-collar crime in the FCIP program depends on the claim's appearing normal and on the inability or unwillingness of the program managers to distinguish between valid and invalid claims. The offenders attempt to create applications that look normal. They hope that their fraudulent applications will blend in with all of the legitimate applications. Because there may be only a few fraudulent applications scattered among the many legitimate applications, it may not be cost-effective to examine individual applications to determine their credibility. According to Shover and Hochstetler (2006, p. 102–103), the federal Risk Management Agency (RMA) figured out a more effective approach. In 2001, the RMA developed a computer program to identify FCIP claims filed for crop failures that came from producers located in counties where most other farmers were successful. The producers with the suspicious claims were sent letters informing them that a federal fraud investigation was being initiated. A year later, indemnity payouts to these farmers went down dramatically. The mere threat of exposure seemed to work as a deterrent.

Advances in computer hardware and software, coupled with the rise of data analytics, represent another way to raise the risk of detection. For example, the detection of certain types of securities cases such as insider trading and market manipulation often depends on uncovering hidden connections between people and identifying aberrant behavior patterns (Robinson, 2013). For the SEC, uncovering connections in insider trading cases almost always involves phone records. Less than a decade ago, it might have taken SEC investigators months to analyze phone records to determine whether two or more individuals were communicating, but now software is available that allows investigators to determine much more quickly if different phone numbers called the same phone line (Partnership for Public Service, 2013). Data analytics can also be used to identify "aberrational performance" such as, for example, if a hedge fund reports significantly better performance than its competitors during both good and bad markets (Robinson, 2013). Once the unusual pattern is identified, it can be investigated to see whether fraud or some other type of white-collar crime is involved. The general point here is that data analytics is a tool that can be used to help the SEC detect illegal activity much more quickly and easily than in the past (Partnership for Public Service, 2013). Of course, as with any enforcement tool, data analytics is not self-activating. Agency personnel must be empowered by institutional leaders to use it, and their results must be acted on to make the risk of detection palpable to potential offenders.

Other types of offenses will require other strategies. For example, some crimes, such as most antitrust offenses, are based on conspiracies inside or between organizations. They can be very difficult to detect because they are hidden behind a corporate veil of secrecy. Only insiders have knowledge of them. Laws that promote and protect whistle-blowers, such as the U.S. Whistleblower Protection Act of 1989, can be potentially helpful in these cases. They raise the likelihood that someone inside an organization will break ranks and bring information about the illegal activity outside of the organization. Of course, how well such laws work is an empirical question, and they certainly do not work perfectly. Organizations retaliate against individual whistle-blowers, and sometimes these individuals pay a heavy price (Miethe and Rothschild, 1994; Rothschild and Miethe, 1999). Nevertheless, the important lesson here is that the threat of exposure is something to which white-collar offenders are sensitive. It's a tool that can be used to society's advantage.

Reducing the rewards of crime can be a very effective way of preventing ordinary street crimes. For example, so-called "smart objects" that require a code or password in order to be used can make a seemingly valuable object virtually worthless to a thief. It is pointless to steal a CD player from an automobile if it won't work after it has been taken out. Because most white-collar crimes do not involve objects, this strategy may not be applicable in many cases. However, in some situations, this strategy may work. For example, to prevent embezzlement or the misappropriation of property, organizations often require multiple signatures on checks or transactions that are valued above a certain amount. Though it might be possible for an individual employee or executive to use his or her position to steal a relatively small amount of money from his or her company, trying to take a big amount is made harder and riskier by the multiple-signature requirement. In effect, the potential reward for misappropriation has been reduced.

Television crime shows often portray criminal offenders as cold, calculating predators who stalk innocent victims. In reality, however, many crimes result from what is perceived by the offender as some sort of provocation by the victim (Felson, 2002). From the offender's point of view, the crime may represent a way to get even for a previous slight or transgression by the victim (Black, 1983). Crime control specialists have learned that to prevent ordinary street crimes, it is helpful to reduce the situational provocations that may encourage criminal activity (Benson and Madensen, 2007). For example, not allowing bars to serve drinks at two-for-one prices during happy hours may reduce the number of people who get drunk on Friday and end up in fights.

Unlike some street crimes, most white-collar crimes are not driven by spontaneous emotions. Because of their complexity, they require planning on the part of the perpetrator and are not the result of impulsive decision making. Thus, the idea of reducing provocations may not work in regard to many types of white-collar crime. Nevertheless, there are some forms of white-collar crime that may result from perceived provocations by the victim. For example, embezzlers are sometimes motivated by the feeling that they have been mistreated by their employers and really deserve the money they take (Cressey, 1953). Similarly, doctors who cheat health insurers may feel justified in doing so because they think that insurers are not being fair to them or that inefficiency in the system makes the reimbursement procedures overly arduous (Vaughan, 1983). To counteract these feelings, both Medicare and Medicaid have tried to design claims-processing systems that are simple, easy, and fast for physicians. By making it easy to file legitimate claims, the programs hope to reduce the number of illegitimate claims filed out of frustration and stress.

The lesson to be learned from the experience of Medicare and Medicaid is that whenever large corporate entities interact with individuals in a way that is perceived as unfair, they open themselves up to the possibility of retaliation. Individuals may try to cheat or otherwise offend against large organizations because they feel frustrated and because offending against an organization as opposed to another individual is more excusable (Coleman, 1982). Organizations that fail to treat people fairly should not be surprised to find themselves victimized by the white-collar crimes of their employees, clients, and customers.

Finally, removing excuses should be another area of focus. Because white-collar offenders think of themselves as moral and upstanding citizens, they cannot easily engage in activities that are obviously illegal. White-collar offenders are loath to think of themselves or their behavior as criminal (Benson, 1985). They simply do not want to see that what they are doing is wrong. In their eyes, whatever they do is justified, and they are very creative at finding justifications for their misconduct (Box, 1983; Geis, 1977; Shover, 2007). They have to be, because the excuses and justifications are necessary conditions in the causal chain leading to the offense. Thus, white-collar offenders must not only perceive a criminal opportunity, they must be able to define the opportunity in morally acceptable terms.

This feature of the psychological makeup of white-collar offenders presents both an opportunity and an obstacle for control via the criminal law. To the extent that the criminal law can be used to convey to potential white-collar offenders that a particular form of behavior is morally wrong, it may reduce that particular type of white-collar crime. If white-collar offenders cannot define their behavior in morally acceptable terms, then they are unlikely to engage in that behavior. We need to foster cultures of compliance rather than subcultures of resistance to the law (Braithwaite, 1989). Unfortunately, as we showed in Chapter 7, white-collar offenders are very adept at avoiding or deflecting the moral strictures of the criminal law. In addition, as Sutherland pointed out long ago, one of the reasons why white-collar crime flourishes is that American society suffers from a conflict of standards in regard to the control of business (Sutherland, 1983). The seemingly never-ending conflict between the business community and those who would regulate its harmful behavior prevents the development of a strong public consensus against white-collar crime. We need also to recognize that the values that lie at the heart of American culture, such as the pursuit of wealth and individualized success, provide a constant source of motivation for white-collar crime (Messner and Rosenfeld, 1997; Weisburd et al., 1991; Wheeler, 1992). Thus, although it has potential, the strategy of removing excuses is one that is not likely to provide a quick fix.

Summary

In this chapter, we have discussed how legal and extralegal factors and processes can influence white-collar crime opportunities. We see how different legal systems (civil, criminal, and regulatory) have different relationships with white-collar crime opportunities. We also showed that extralegal factors, especially in conjunction with justice processes, can lower the risk of white-collar crime through their impact on opportunities. Although it should be abundantly clear that the control of white-collar crime is a difficult and never-ending task, we need also to note that it is not a hopeless one. Just as ordinary street crime will never be completely eliminated, neither will white-collar crime ever disappear, but specific forms and types can be reduced at some times and in some places. In the next chapter, we summarize our main arguments and conclusions regarding white-collar crime and opportunities.

11

OPPORTUNITIES AND THE FUTURE OF WHITE-COLLAR CRIME

As others have noted, the concept of white-collar crime has been ambiguous and problematic since its inception (Croall, 2001, pp. 143–144; Weisburd et al., 1991, p. 170). In some ways, the conceptual ambiguity surrounding white-collar crime has only gotten worse as time has passed. When Sutherland first introduced the term, the debate regarding white-collar crime focused primarily on whether it should be restricted strictly to activities that were encompassed by criminal legislation or more broadly construed to include activities that were illegal in the sense that they violated regulatory, but not necessarily criminal, codes (Sutherland, 1945; Tappan, 1947). It was a debate about what should count as crime and as the legitimate object of study for the criminologist. In the ensuing years, arguments have arisen regarding who the offender is or even *what* the offender is. Should the focus of study be limited to individuals or does it make sense to conceive of organizations themselves as offenders (Braithwaite and Fisse, 1990; Cressey, 1989)? In regard to individuals, there is disagreement over who should be included in the white-collar criminal category. Should it be restricted only to people of "respectability and high social status," or should we acknowledge, in light of a host of recent research findings, that many people who do not have high social status commit offenses that for all intents and purposes seem to be white-collar crimes (Benson and Moore, 1992; Croall, 1989; Weisburd et al., 1991).

Thus, the debate over the concept of white-collar crime has broadened from a focus on what should count as crime to a consideration of who or what the offender is. As Croall (1989, p. 145) has noted, it is a bit odd that criminologists have spent so much time debating the status of white-collar crime, because "crime" itself is a socially constructed and ambiguous construct.

In this book, we have tried not to get too bogged down in these debates and have opted for a more inclusive approach, one that recognizes offenders at all levels of the class structure and offenses of differing levels of illegality. This approach has the advantage of permitting more comparisons between different groups of offenders and offenses. It also enables us to analyze a very broad range of opportunities to engage in illegality and to explore how these opportunities are related to occupations, organizations, and the class structure of American society. But the main reason for adopting an inclusive approach to white-collar crime is that it permits us to focus on what we think is a more important issue: opportunities to use deception, abuse of trust, concealment, and conspiracy as techniques in criminal offending.

Thus, instead of trying to decide who is or is not the white-collar offender or what should or should not count as white-collar crime, we argued in Chapter 1 that it is more useful to focus on how occupations, organizations, industries, and government programs create situations in which some people can deceive or abuse the trust of other people or organizations for their own advantage. Although we really cannot prove the point empirically here, we expect that the use of these techniques is more common among middle-and upper-class individuals than it is among individuals from less advantaged socioeconomic backgrounds. To use a thought experiment, imagine we could assemble in one place all of the people who committed a criminal offense in one year. Then imagine that we could divide the offenders into low, middle, and high socioeconomic status. Then within each status group, we divide the offenders further into two categories based on whether their offenses involved the use of deception or the use of some sort of physical force, including but not limited to interpersonal violence. If we were able to carry out such an experiment, we strongly expect that in the middle-and upper-status groups, the proportion in the deception category would be substantially larger than the proportion of the lower-status group in that category. How big the difference would be is an open question. People of low socioeconomic status can use deception to cheat on taxes, welfare benefit applications, and in many other ways. So, we should not assume that the lower-class group would consist only of those who used force in their offending. Likewise, people of middle and upper socioeconomic status do occasionally commit crimes of violence and force. But the relative proportion of offenses that involve deception, we think, would rise as socioeconomic status rises. In other words, there is a strong link between social status and what we typically think of as white-collar crime, but the link between status and crime is better thought of as a continuum than as a dichotomy.

In this concluding chapter, we review the major themes that motivated this book, focusing primarily on the topic of opportunities and how these are shaped by the structure of occupational activities and organizations. Of course, it is important to recognize that opportunity structures for white-collar crime change constantly. New products, new services, new forms of business are constantly evolving or being invented, and technological change seems to be endless. All of these developments and changes create new opportunities for deception and, to be fair, new opportunities for controlling deception. Thus, what we have to say here will eventually become dated as new forms of white-collar crime arise. Although it is always risky to speculate about the direction of future trends, we nevertheless take that risk and address what we think will be some of the future directions of white-collar crime. Finally, we conclude with some thoughts on the policy implications of our perspective.

The Many Facets of Deception

All white-collar crimes are in some way based on deception. That is, the offender in some way tries to hide the crime itself. However, the nature of the deception varies in terms of its intended longevity, potential targets, and form. Sometimes the deception is meant or intended by the perpetrator to be permanent. The offender endeavors to design or commit the crime in such a manner that it will never be discovered. Non-self-revealing frauds in the health care system are textbook examples, and many other white-collar offenses, such as insider trading and price fixing, also are based on the idea of permanent deception. However, not all white-collar crimes are intended to remain hidden forever. In some cases, the offender aspires only to fool the victim long enough to get whatever it is that the offender wants from the victim and then get away. The rent-a-patient scam discussed in Chapter 5 is an example. The perpetrators of these scams understand that eventually their schemes will be exposed. Accordingly, they tend to move around and not stay put in one place too long. By the time Medicaid officials become aware of the pattern of suspicious claims arising from an area or neighborhood, those involved hope to have long since moved on to another location.

The targets of deception in white-collar crime vary from individuals to other organizations to government programs and to the community in general. The target sometimes is a specific individual whom the offender has somehow identified as a potential victim and who is approached directly by the offender. Some investment scams are like this. At other times, the victims may be individuals, but they are not individually targeted by offenders. False advertising is a classic example. Here the offender advertises some product or service in a misleading manner, hoping that someone will be fooled by the come-on. It does not really matter who falls for the scam as long as there are enough people who do, so that the scheme becomes profitable for the offender.

The victims of white-collar crime, however, are not always individuals. Some of the most profitable targets for white-collar offenders are actually government programs. These programs, such as the federal Medicare and Medicaid programs, distribute enormous sums of money. They make very attractive targets for those who wish to pick up some easy cash. Like government programs, business organizations can be targeted by individuals or other businesses. For example, in certain antitrust conspiracies, the victims are really other businesses who have to pay more for the products or services that they need because of price fixing among their suppliers. Consider here the price fixing among Japanese automobile parts suppliers mentioned in Chapter 5 (Trop, 2013).

Finally, for some white-collar crimes, there really may be no specific identifiable targets or victims. The target is the system of economic exchange itself. Consider, for example, insider trading, whereby a corporate insider makes some sort of advantageous stock trade on the basis of inside information. The offender uses the inside information to exploit or take advantage of the naturally occurring fluctuations in the price of stocks. The offender is not really out to hurt any particular other stock trader or organization or government program. Rather, he or she is making a trade based on superior information about what is likely to happen in the future. Other investors may, of course, be hurt if they happen to be the ones who bought or sold the stock that the offender is involved with, but they are not specifically targeted by the offender, and they may have made the same decision to buy or sell regardless of what the inside trader did. As Sutherland and so many other white-collar crime scholars have noted, a characteristic feature of some white-collar crimes is diffuse victimization.

Deception can take different forms or, to put it another way, deception can be achieved in different ways. Recall that deception is the advantageous distortion of perceived reality (Bowyer, 1982). It is a relational concept that always involves two organisms or entities—a deceiver and a deceived. Deception occurs when one person or entity (the deceiver) somehow defeats the ability of another person or entity (the deceived) to perceive reality as it really is. How the deceiver goes about accomplishing this objective depends in part on who or what the victim is and on what the offender is trying to do to or get from the victim. The cases that we have reviewed throughout this book suggest that there are three general forms or ways in which deception in white-collar crime is achieved: embellishing, mimicking, and hiding.

Consider first the strategy of embellishing. In many consumer and investment frauds, the offender tries to lure the victim into buying a product or service or investing in a project by somehow suggesting that the product or service is like others in its category—only better. The investment scheme is presented as solid and reliable, like other good investments, but better because it has a higher or more consistent rate of return. The example of Bernie Madoff clearly fits here. The fraudulent home repair contractor who does shoddy work or uses substandard materials presents himself as competent and reliable, like other good contractors, but better because he is cheaper. Offenders who use embellishment hope to entice victims by making them think that buying a product or investing in a scheme is in their best interests when it really is not. Embellishment depends on that part of human nature that always seems to be looking for a good deal or something for nothing. It is a good strategy for white-collar offenders to use, because the line between being justifiably proud of your product and lying about it is often not clear. Distinguishing between the person who is presenting his or her product in the best possible light and the person who is an outright liar is the problem for both victims and law enforcers.

Whereas successful embellishment depends on making something stand out from the ordinary and thereby bringing attention to yourself, mimicking depends on doing just the opposite. The object is to make something appear normal rather than exceptional. Fraud in the federal Medicare and Medicaid systems is a perfect example. In these frauds, a physician or other type of health care professional submits an unjustified claim for reimbursement to the Medicaid program. To be successful, the offender must make his or her claim appear to be normal and legitimate. The idea is not to draw attention but rather to blend in by mimicking the millions of other legitimate claims that are paid every day. Fraud in other government programs works in much the same way. The government provides a benefit to some qualified group. The trick for the white-collar offender is to appear to be qualified for the benefit. Recall the Federal Crop Insurance Program (FCIP) discussed in Chapter 10. Besides fraud in government programs, there are other white-collar offenses that depend on mimicking (e.g., some types of insider trading in the stock market). Recall that it is perfectly legal for insiders to buy or sell stock in their companies. It becomes illegal only if the decision to buy or sell is made on the basis of information that is not available to the market in general. Successful inside traders are those who make their moves appear to be part of normal market activity.

Hiding is another strategy that white-collar offenders use. It often underlies some of the more serious forms of white-collar crime. Consider, for example, the environmental and workplace safety offenses discussed in Chapter 6. In many of these crimes, offenders try to hide their illegal activities from outside observers. They do not try to entice potential victims into spending their money, nor do they try to obtain money illegally from government programs. Rather, offenders engage in clandestine activities that are to their financial benefit but are also illegal and potentially harmful to others. The Mazza case is a perfect example of this. This case involved several firms that conspired, over a 5-year period, to illegally dump asbestos-contaminated waste on its own property where it would be difficult if not impossible for outsiders to see. Similarly, behind the closed doors of its pipe manufacturing factories, McWane Incorporated routinely violated occupational safety rules and illegally exposed its workers to the risk of serious injuries or death. Massey mining operations in West Virginia were cited by inspectors for hundreds of violations (including those that were life-threatening) in the year before explosions and a fire killed miners at two Massey-owned mines. Yet the mines, thought by many to be unsafe, continued to operate. Hiding is also obviously a part of conspiratorial crimes such as bid rigging and price fixing, as well as those that involve the abuse of trust.

The Characteristics of White-Collar Crime

Regardless of the form it takes—embellishment, mimicking, or hiding—deception is intended to help the offender maintain the superficial appearance of legitimacy. This is one of the distinguishing features of white-collar crime and one that makes white-collar crime so difficult to control. Unlike most so-called traditional street crimes, such as robbery, burglary, auto theft, and assault, white-collar crimes are not obvious. They often do not leave visible traces of their occurrence. Even the victims may not be aware that a crime has taken place, let alone law enforcers. Efforts to control white-collar crime, therefore, must start with the problem of detection, finding the offense.

A second important feature of white-collar crime is that the offender has legitimate access to the target or victim of the offense. In all of the white-collar crimes discussed in Chapters 5 and 6, the offenders do not have to worry about gaining access to the targets of their offenses. They have a legitimate right to be there and to be involved in the kinds of activities out of which their offenses arise. Physicians, for example, are supposed to treat patients and submit claims to health insurers. Mortgage brokers are supposed to help home buyers apply for loans, and bankers are supposed to make loans. Manufacturers and retail stores are supposed to advertise and promote their products. These are all normal and expected economic activities, and they provide the basis for white-collar crime opportunities. White-collar offenders use their occupational positions to take advantage of these legitimate activities in illegal ways.

As with the superficial appearance of legitimacy, specialized access also complicates the control of white-collar crime in a couple of ways. For one, it makes it difficult to use a standard crime prevention tool—blocking the offender's access to the target, as we discussed in Chapter 10. Many conventional crimes can be prevented simply by making it difficult for the offender to gain access to the crime target. Although there are exceptions, in general this approach cannot be used to prevent white-collar crimes. Specialized access also complicates control in another way. Whatever mechanisms are put in place to control the illegal activity of white-collar offenders will necessarily affect the legal activities of their law-abiding counterparts. To use health care fraud as an example, one way to try to control it better would be for the Medicare and Medicaid programs to take more time reviewing claims before paying. Doing so would probably help the programs identify fraudulent claims more effectively, but it would also slow down the speed with which honest physicians get reimbursed. It seems likely that honest physicians will not be happy with that state of affairs and, as Sparrow (1996, 1998) notes, companies that handle claims are under pressure to process them quickly. Thus, because white-collar crimes are embedded in legitimate activities, the benefits of using any particular control measure always have to be balanced against the costs that its use would impose on the aspirations and creativity of those who are law-abiding (Weisburd et al., 1991, p. 191–192).

Although offenders have legitimate access to the location or target of their offenses, they are often spatially separated from the actual victims. The company owner who decides not to invest in required safety equipment may never even visit the plant in which workers are injured. The executives who conspire to fix prices never actually deal with the people who have to pay extra. Physicians who cheat Medicaid do so via computer networks and are located hundreds if not thousands of miles away from the program's main office. Spatial separation facilitates the invisibility of white-collar crime and white-collar offenders. It makes it difficult to see the crime, because the crime does not happen at a particular time and place, nor does it involve a visible interaction between an offender and a victim. The separation of offender and victim is yet another feature of white-collar crime that distinguishes it from the stereotypical image of crime.

Problems and Possibilities for Control

In some ways, it is surprising that white-collar crime is such a problem, because the people who commit white-collar offenses are assumed to be highly rational and sensitive to the pain and stigma of criminal sanctions. They are certainly much more afraid of being caught and sent to prison than ordinary street offenders (Braithwaite and Geis, 1982). The possibility of being publicly stigmatized as a criminal should act as a strong deterrent for people who have a stake in conformity and care about their public personae (Geerken and Gove, 1975; Zimring and Hawkins, 1973). Thus, the threat of punishment ought to deter the types of people who commit white-collar crimes. Yet, white-collar crime seems to be ubiquitous. Why is it so hard to control?

Certainly, a major problem is what Shover and Hochstetler (2006) call a lack of "credible oversight." Many of those who commit white-collar crimes simply do not think they will be caught and punished. There are several reasons why this is often a safe assumption on their part. For starters, the crimes themselves are difficult to detect. Done correctly, many white-collar crimes blend into the ongoing flow of economic transactions. They do not stand out as being unusual or a cause for concern. Hence, the whole criminal justice process may never get started. There are other factors as well that work against the establishment of credible oversight.

One very important factor is the influence that white-collar offenders have over the law itself. Unlike ordinary street criminals, the people and organizations that commit white-collar crimes play an active role in shaping the laws that govern their behavior. Businesses fight whenever state or federal governments attempt to impose stricter controls or harsher penalties on their misconduct. They hire lobbyists and call legislators to do whatever they can to weaken the imposition of controls. For example, the current General Motors case has exposed a culture of secrecy at the company in which cars with defective ignition switches knowingly were sold to consumers. As the case continues to unfold, it is unclear how many employees knew about the defect. Current CEO Mary Barra, in her report to Congress, has claimed that only one engineer knew about the problem (Vlasic and Ivory, 2014). Yet, in the face of numerous consumer injuries and death, GM chose not to recall the effected automobiles. This case parallels one in the late 1980s and early 1990s, where the Firestone Tire Company manufactured a defective tire that was used on Ford Explorers. The tire had a disturbing tendency to shred at high speeds, causing rollovers that killed hundreds of people and injured many others (Cullen et al., 2006). When it came to light that both Ford and Firestone knew about the problems with the tire but did not recall them or notify owners of the dangers they faced, the public was outraged. Members of the U.S. Congress were also outraged. Hearings were held, executives were publicly castigated, and a law was proposed that would have made it a crime to manufacture and sell a vehicle with a serious safety defect. However, that law was never enacted because of strenuous lobbying by the U.S. Chamber of Commerce, the tire industry, the auto industry, and other manufacturers (Cullen et al., 2006). This story, unfortunately, has a long history. Sutherland, himself, as well as many other white-collar crime scholars, noted that business corporations almost always resist the imposition of criminal law as a control (Sutherland, 1983). Because the GM case is ongoing, we do not know whether new laws might be proposed that criminalize this kind of behavior, but past experience does not promote optimism.

Corporations, of course, are not always successful in their attempts to avoid the criminalization of their conduct. There are many laws against white-collar crimes, but the enforcement of these laws is not as strong as it could be. Because of their hidden nature and complexity, white-collar crimes are difficult to investigate and prosecute (Benson, 2001a; Benson and Cullen, 1998; Braithwaite and Geis, 1982). The cases are expensive and time-consuming to bring to court. Prosecutors must be selective in deciding which cases are worth the effort and which are not (Benson, 2001b; Benson et al., 1990; Maakestad et al., 1987). Hence, the criminal law is not activated against white-collar crime as often as or as effectively as it could be.

Besides the criminal law, there are other forms of legal control, including regulatory codes and the civil law. As a means of control, regulation has both strengths and weaknesses. Perhaps the most important strength of regulation, and a major difference between it and the criminal law, is that regulations are proactive. They seek primarily to prevent harms from happening in the first place rather than reacting to offenders after they have broken the law, as the criminal justice system is constrained to do. On the downside, regulatory sanctions do not carry the bite and deterrent power of criminal justice sanctions, and the whole regulatory system is subject to even greater influence by corporations than is the criminal justice system. Corporations can influence both the way in which regulations are written and the way in which they are enforced. Nevertheless, because of their proactive nature, regulatory controls accord better with our opportunity perspective than the criminal law. From an opportunity perspective, the most effective way to control any type of crime, including white-collar crime, is not to catch and punish offenders severely. Rather, it is more effective and less costly to modify opportunity structures so as to make the crimes themselves less attractive to potential offenders. Regulations can help do this by making it more difficult for white-collar offenders to conceal their activities or to engage in deception.

The Future of White-Collar Crime

We began this book by noting that what we today call "white-collar crime" is really nothing new. Evidence of it or something very much like it can be found throughout the historical record, dating back to biblical times and probably long before that. Although it would be impossible to prove, we suspect that it is very likely that the use of fraud and deception in transactions arose simultaneously with the invention of trade itself and perhaps even earlier, with the evolution of social interaction among humans and our ancestor primate species. Indeed, evolutionary theory would suggest that deception as a technique of both survival and predation must go back nearly to the origin of life itself (Dawkins, 2004). Yet, despite its long historical pedigree, white-collar crime has always seemed less important, less threatening than the traditional forms of predatory street crime, except perhaps to a few criminologists like us who write books on the topic. There is certainly a great deal of evidence that many people think that white-collar crime is less serious and important. Sometimes statements to that effect are made directly (Wilson, 1975; Wilson and Herrnstein, 1985). However, the real evidence comes from the amount of money, time, and effort devoted to controlling and researching ordinary street crime and street offenders compared with white-collar crime. We take it as self-evident that they differ by many orders of magnitude and will continue to do so for a long time. Nevertheless, the threat posed by white-collar crime is likely to remain a significant social problem for the future. There are several reasons for our pessimism.

First, because of changes in the nature of work, more people than ever before have access to the "white-collar world of paper fraud" (Weisburd et al., 1991, p. 183). The explosive growth in the use of computers, fax machines, scanners, copiers, the Internet, and all sorts of other electronic information-processing technologies in all industries and occupations has given more and more ordinary people access to the basic tools of white-collar crime. These are the tools that can be used to deceive others and to create an advantageous distortion of reality.

Second, another condition that fosters white-collar crime has been the tremendous growth in state largesse that has come in the wake of the welfare state (Shover and Hochstetler, 2006; Weisburd et al., 1991). In Chapter 5, we concentrated on fraud against the Medicare and Medicaid programs, because they are the largest and probably most important sites for fraud in government programs. However, it would be naive to think that fraud is limited just to federal health care programs. There are hundreds, if not thousands, of other government programs that distribute financial and other types of benefits to millions of people and organizations. For example, millions of college students apply annually for government-backed student loans, and as we noted earlier in Chapter 10, some American farmers, those historical icons of the American way, are not above trying to cheat the government in the FCIP program. All of these programs depend on paper applications, and all of them must guard against fraudulent ones.

In the modern world, the social status of people is evaluated on the basis of their credentials (Collins, 1979). Our value as persons is determined not by our personal values or characteristics but rather by the educational degrees, awards, accomplishments, skills mastered, and prior experiences listed on our resumes, what economists call human capital. Not surprisingly, this situation creates pressure to inflate or doctor credentials so as to make ourselves look better on paper, and pressure to cheat in order to improve our chances of obtaining credentials in the first place (Weisburd et al., 1991).

The rise in agent–client relationships also has contributed to the expansion of white-collar crime opportunities. Increasingly, we must hire or depend on experts to help us navigate the world. Specialization is the order of the day. We cannot do it all ourselves. We find ourselves having to trust doctors, financial advisors, mechanics, insurance agents, pension fund managers, mortgage brokers, and a host of other professionals (Shapiro, 1990). All of these agent–client relationships carry with them the possibility of the abuse of trust. As more people enter into more agent–client relationships, an increase in abuses of trust is almost guaranteed.

A buzz word of the modern world is globalization. It represents a political, economic, and social reality that increasingly influences our lives in myriad ways. For our purposes, the aspect of globalization that is most important involves the development of a global system of production and exchange. As we are sure you know, the label "Made in America" applies to only a small percentage of the goods—and increasingly even the services—that we use in our daily lives. From automobiles to banking to pharmaceuticals to toys to wrapping paper to technical support for all of our electronic devices, much of what we buy comes from other countries. From the perspective of our opportunity theory of white-collar crime, this development makes oversight and control more difficult (Grabosky, 2009; Shover and Hochstetler, 2006). All of the laws and regulations that we have developed to control how goods are designed, tested, manufactured, and distributed and that govern how workers are treated lose much if not all of their force when companies locate outside our borders. For transnational corporations, opportunities to exploit workers, to pollute the environment, and to manufacture faulty and dangerous products are always available somewhere. Some developing nation is always willing to trade safety for jobs and capital investments. Indeed, as Shover and Hochstetler (2006, p. 105) nicely put it, "lax oversight is a developmental tool for some nations."

However, as Grabosky (2009) points out, globalization is not all bad when it comes to white-collar crime control. International agreements between nation-states on shared regulatory frameworks are now common in many areas of economic and productive activity. Thus, the possibility of "transnational" corporate crime control in response to transnational corporate crime is no longer just a fantasy but rather increasingly it is becoming a reality (Braithwaite and Drahos, 2000). This is a positive development.

One of the most disturbing aspects of the Enron case and the others like it in the most recent round of corporate frauds in accounting and the mortgage industry was that the frauds involved were new. The complex accounting schemes created by Enron's executives represented new and creative ways of hiding information (McLean and Elkind, 2003; Swartz, 2003). These new forms of fraud allowed Enron's leaders to avoid detection and the frauds to persist for several years. More recently, the mortgage industry has been the site of new forms of mortgage fraud (Gibeaut, 2007; Vickers and Burke, 2006). In the 1980s, many of the offenses that were committed in the savings and loan debacle represented new forms of bank fraud (Calavita and Pontell, 1990). All of these cases should remind us of an important point regarding white-collar crime: It evolves and changes with the times (Sparrow, 1996).

White-collar crime, of course, is not unique in this regard. Ordinary street criminals change with the times as well (Felson, 2002). Train robbery, safe cracking, and pickpocketing have all but disappeared as crimes, while credit card theft and now identity theft have risen in popularity. Nevertheless, we suspect that white-collar crime techniques evolve more continuously and with greater rapidity than ordinary street crime. Mainly this happens because white-collar crimes are always based on some type of legitimate economic activity, and the legitimate economic world is constantly changing and evolving. Hence, white-collar offenders always have new material to work with.

Because white-collar crime continuously changes and evolves, we should not be overly optimistic regarding our ability to control or reduce it. Besides its ever-changing nature, there are other reasons why the development of white-collar crime control policies should be approached cautiously. We need to recognize that policy changes always carry risks. They can have unintended consequences and negative side effects (McGarrell and Gibbs, forthcoming; Weisburd et al., 1991, p. 190). This can be especially true with respect to white-collar crime control, because white-collar offenses are always based in some sort of legitimate economic activity. The policies that we institute to control illegal or harmful activities in an industry may inadvertently make it more difficult and costly to conduct legal activities while at the same time giving rise to additional illicit opportunities. So, to put it simply, the problem of white-collar crime control is complex. But we do not wish to leave the reader with the impression that it is, therefore, hopeless and that nothing can be done. By focusing on specific crimes or specific forms of harm, improvements can and have been made. Being realistic about the limits to our ability to prevent white-collar crime is not the same as being fatalistic. The important thing is to continue to study the problem of white-collar crime and to continually search for new ways to respond to it.

Summary

In this final chapter, we have summarized our main arguments and attempted to draw out some of their implications in regard to the future of white-collar crime and its control. White-collar crimes are based on deception, and we have shown how deception can be achieved in a variety of different ways. White-collar crimes have special characteristics that facilitate the use of deception. These characteristics include specialized access to the victim or target of the crime, the superficial appearance of legitimacy, and a spatial separation from the victim or target. These characteristics make the control of white-collar crime different in a number of ways from the control of ordinary street crime. The main difference is that for white-collar crime, the problem is to find the offense rather than the offender, as is the case for ordinary street crime. Just because we do not see a crime, we cannot assume that therefore there is no crime (Sparrow, 1998). The problem, as Malcom Sparrow astutely notes, is always larger than you think it is. The key to white-collar crime control depends on understanding how legitimate economic activities create opportunities to deceive, abuse trust, and conspire against others and an ability to marshal multiple tools in an arsenal of control.

Because the world of legitimate economic activities evolves continuously, we need to accept the fact that white-collar crime will also continue to evolve. As technology, markets, and industries change and develop, new forms of white-collar crime will arise. Technological and economic change always create new opportunities. This means that our strategies and mechanisms of control must also change in order to keep pace, and we need to view white-collar crime control as an ongoing arms race between offenders and society.

Appendix
Annotated Websites for Further Exploration

There are a number of governmental websites relevant to white-collar crime and an increasing number of non-governmental sites as well. We have listed here some of the more prominent ones, many of which we consulted as we prepared this second edition. Each listing includes a description of the content as well as a URL that was accurate and working at the time we prepared the appendix. We hope that both students and instructors will find this additional material useful for their own research and exploration of white-collar crime.

Official Data Sources

FBI: Reports and Publications on White-Collar Crime
(www.fbi.gov/stats-services/publications)
The Federal Bureau of Investigation (FBI) compiles reports on a number of crimes, including several different types of white-collar crime. This website will give you access to a number of reports from the FBI, including reports on financial crimes in general, financial institution fraud and failures, insurance fraud, mass-marketing fraud, mortgage fraud, money laundering, and securities fraud.

Financial Crimes Report to the Public (2005–2011)

The FBI compiles reports of fraud, theft, or embezzlement occurring within or against the national and international financial community. These crimes are identified through the Financial Crimes Section (FCS) at the FBI. Each year (from 2005 to 2011), the FCS releases a general report regarding these different federal crimes, such as Corporate Fraud, Securities and Commodities Fraud, Health Care Fraud, Mortgage Fraud, Financial Institution Fraud, Financial Institution Failures, Insurance Fraud, Mass Marketing Fraud, Asset Forfeiture/Money Laundering, as well as reports about the Forensic Accountant Program, and the Financial Intelligence Center. The information included in the reports generally follows this pattern: a general overview of the crime, overall accomplishments and pending cases, and significant cases.

Financial Institution Fraud and Failure Reports (2000–2007)

The FBI compiled data about Financial Institution Fraud (FIF), with the goal to identify, target, disrupt, and dismantle criminal organizations and individual operations engaged in fraud schemes that target the country's financial institutions. This unit focuses primarily on the the crimes of mortgage and loan fraud, insider fraud, check fraud, counterfeit negotiable instruments, check kiting, and financial institution failures. In these reports, there is data regarding the year-to-year counts of financial institution failures, major cases under investigation by year, and accomplishments from FBI investigations.

Insurance Fraud: Program Overview and Consumer Information

This report contains a brief overview of what insurance fraud is, the costs associated with this kind of fraud, the common schemes associated with insurance fraud (such as premium diversion, fee churning, asset diversion, and worker's compensation fraud), and a list of resources regarding insurance fraud. The list of resources provided includes the National Insurance Crime Bureau (NICB), Coalition Against Insurance Fraud (CAIF), and the National Association of Insurance Commissioners (NAIC).

Mass Marketing Fraud: A Threat Assessment, June 2010

This report contains a brief overview of the nature, scope, and impact of Mass-Marketing Fraud, as well as describing some of the methods and techniques of mass-marketing fraud. It outlines, in detail, how mass-marketing fraud is defined, how it is implemented, how big of a problem it is, the risks involved, and the specific methods used by fraudulent mass-marketing perpetrators.

Mass Marketing Fraud: Awareness and Prevention Tips

This report is supplemental to the Mass-Marketing Fraud: A Threat Assessment. This report outlines the common schemes of mass-marketing fraud (including Foreign Lotteries, Nigerian Letter Scams, Credit and Loan Scams, Overpayment Scams, and Charity Scams), how you can protect yourself from mass-marketing fraud, and a list of resources where you can report mass-marketing fraud (including the Federal Trade Commission, Internet Crime Complain Center, the Internal Revenue Service, and the Better Business Bureau).

Mortgage Fraud Reports (2006–2010)

These yearly reports outline the extent and nature of mortgage fraud for that fiscal year. In each report, there are sections describing the perpetrators of mortgage fraud, the impact of this kind of fraud, the number of mortgage loan delinquencies, defaults, and foreclosures, and where mortgage fraud takes place, the schemes and techniques of mortgage fraud. This report also includes information about legislative issues surrounding mortgage fraud, and the FBI's response.

National Money Laundering Strategy

This report outlines the goals of the National Money Laundering Strategy, and the use of the U.S. Money Laundering Threat Assessment. The U.S. Money Laundering Threat Assessment is an analysis of money laundering in the United States, and includes the common schemes of money laundering, including schemes conducted through banking, money services businesses, online payment systems, informal value transfer systems, bulk cash smuggling, trade-based money laundering, insurance companies, shell companies and trusts, and casinos. This report also includes statistics on money laundering, a list of law enforcement data and intelligence centers, and the strategic use of asset forfeitures.

Securities Fraud Awareness and Prevention Tips

This report provides a basic overview of the extent and nature of securities fraud. Provided in this report is a definition of securities fraud, common scams (including high yield investment frauds, Ponzi and pyramid schemes, and advance fee schemes), how to avoid being a victim of securities fraud, and where you can report scams. This report also includes some statistics from the FBI covering accomplishments in prosecuting securities fraud by the FBI.

Federal Bureau of Investigation—Health Care Fraud
(www.fbi.gov/about-us/investigate/white_collar/health-care-fraud)

The FBI gathers information on health care fraud in the United States. On this webpage, the FBI provide information on the estimated health care fraud costs, as well as links to additional resources that cover fraud prevention, and the 2012 health care fraud report. The website also provides information on the FBI's most wanted for crimes related to health care fraud.

FBI/Department of Justice Report: The Measurement of White-Collar Crime Using Uniform Crime Reporting Data (Barnett, 2003)
(www.fbi.gov/stats-services/about-us/cjis/ucr/nibrs/nibrs_wcc.pdf)

This report discusses the utility and applicability of using the FBIs Uniform Crime Report data in measuring white-collar crime.

Department of Justice: United States Attorneys' Annual Statistical Report
(www.justice.gov/usao/reading_room/foiamanuals.html)

This website provides access to the annual reports of the United States Attorneys' Offices (1959–2012). Each of these statistical reports outlines the mission of the U.S. Attorneys, criminal prosecutions that year, asset forfeiture litigations, civil litigations, and appeals. These reports include information about Federally prosecuted crimes, including white-collar crimes.

Department of Justice: Criminal Division Organizations
(www.justice.gov/criminal/about/graphic.html)

This website provides you with information about the Department of Justice's different criminal division organizations. These organizations include the Office of the Assistant Attorney General, Administration, Appellate Section, Asset Forfeiture and Money Laundering Section, Computer Crime and Intellectual Property Section, Fraud Section, Human Rights and Special Prosecution Sections, International Criminal Investigative Training Assistance Program, Office of Enforcement Operations, Office of International Affairs, Office of Policy and Legislation, and the Office of Overseas Prosecutorial Development, Assistance & Training.

Asset Forfeiture and Money Laundering

This website provides centralized management for the Department Of Justice's asset forfeiture program to ensure its integrity and maximize its law enforcement potential. The Asset Forfeiture and Money Laundering Section (AFMLS) prosecutes and coordinates complex multi-district, and international money laundering and asset forfeiture investigations; provide legal and policy assistance and training to federal, state, and local prosecutors and law enforcement personnel; develop and review legislative, regulatory, and policy initiatives; and distributes forfeited assets to domestic and foreign law enforcement agencies within the United States. There are five units within AFMLS: forfeiture unit, international unit, money laundering and bank integrity unit, policy and training unit, and the program operations unit.

Computer Crime and Intellectual Property

This website provides information on the Computer Crime and Intellectual Property Section (CCIPS). This section is responsible for implementing the Department of Justice's national strategies in combating computer and intellectual property crimes worldwide. The CCIPS prevents, investigates, and prosecutes computer crimes by working with other government agencies, the private sector, academic institutions, and foreign counterparts. The website also provides links to the annual DOJ and FBI reports for intellectual property crimes.

Fraud

This website provides information on the DOJ's Fraud Section. This section acts as a rapid response team for investigating and prosecuting complex white-collar crimes in the United States. The fraud section acts in conjunction with the United States Attorneys' Office to combat white-collar crimes. The website offers a wide range of information, from governmental reports on the activities conducted through the fraud section, and information regarding identity theft and mass-marketing fraud.

U.S. Sentencing Commission's Annual Report and Sourcebooks
*(www.ussc.gov/Research_and_Statistics/Annual_Reports_and_*
Sourcebooks/index.cfm)

The United States Sentencing Commission is tasked with establishing sentencing policies and practices for courts at the federal level, including sentencing guidelines that outline the appropriate form and severity of punishment for offenders convicted in federal courts. The Commission also advises the executive, legislative, and judicial branches of government in effective and efficient crime policies. Finally, the Commission collects, analyzes, researches, and distributes information on federal crime and sentencing issues. On this website, you can find the Commission's Annual Report, as well as the Annual Sourcebook of Federal Sentencing Statistics. In the both of these reports, you can find information regarding the Primary Offense and Offender Characteristics (e.g., distribution, age, race, gender, education, citizenship in each primary offense category).

In the Annual Report, under the Research section, you can find information regarding the Commission's findings. The report includes information on the offenders, and their characteristics, as well as their primary offense. Under the Sourcebook section, there is information regarding the primary offense and offender characteristics as well.

National White-Collar Crime Center
(www.nw3c.org/docs/ic3-annual-reports/
2012-Internet-crime-report.pdf?sfvrsn=5)

The National White-Collar Crime Center supports and assists law enforcement agencies, helping them to better understand and utilize tools to combat Internet and white-collar crimes. This website will bring you to the Internet Crime Complaint Center report. In it, you can find information on the type of complaints, the frequency and total monetary losses attributed to Internet crimes.

Internet Crime Report

The Internet Crime Report is an annual report from the national White Collar Crime center (NW3C). In the report, it provides information on how to file a claim with the Internet Crime Complaint Center, demographic information about complaintants, reported Internet crimes, a number of case highlights, and announcements and tips aimed at preventing Internet crime. This report also has a number of statistics by state and of complaintants overall. Complainant demographics include age, race, gender, estimated loss, and other information.

Regulatory Agency Websites

Securities and Exchange Commission (www.sec.gov/News/Article/Detail/Article/1356125787012#.Uvjm7PldXzg)

The United States Securities and Exchange Commission is an agency that monitors and enforces law regarding securities and exchanges violations. The SEC is capable of filing civil actions in federal court against individuals that have violated securities laws. This website brings you to the SEC's information page, which provides information regarding common violations that lead to SEC investigations, as well as information regarding civil and administrative actions the SEC can file in federal court.

Occupational Health and Safety Administration (www.osha.gov/oshstats/est1def.html)

The Occupational Safety and Health Administration (OSHA) is a branch of the U.S. Department of Labor that specifically regulates the health and safety of workplace conditions in the United States. This website will bring you to a page with information regarding inspections, violations, and accidents. The Inspection tab provides information about data collected from inspected sites. The Violation tab provides information regarding the specific violations, including dollar amounts, cited by OSHA. The Accident tab provides information about accident and injury information. There is also a link on this page to Data and Statistics from OSHA.

National Labor Relations Board
(www.nlrb.gov/what-we-do/investigate-charges/
10j-injunctions/section-10j-categories)

The National Labor Relations Board is a federal agency created to enforce the National Labor Relations Act, which grants the right of employees to form or join unions, or engage in protected activities to improve working conditions. This website brings you to the Board's section outlining what violates the National Labor Relations Act. This section includes information on each category under the Labor Relations Board Section 10(j).

Food and Drug Administration
(www.fda.gov/ForConsumers/ConsumerUpdates/ucm049070.htm)

The U.S. Food and Drug Administration is tasked with protecting public health by ensuring the safety of human and veterinary drugs, biological products, medical devices, the nation's food supply, and products that emit radiation. This webpage brings up information regarding product recalls. This website also provides information regarding the first alert process, how the agency alerts the public, and how the agency decides when a recall is considered complete. This webpage also provides information regarding the classifications of recalls.

Federal Trade Commission
(www.ftc.gov/enforcement/anticompetitive-practices)

The Federal Trade Commission is a regulatory agency that prevents business practices that are anticompetitive and deceptive to consumers, to enhance informed consumer choice of the competitive process without unduly harming legitimate business activities. This webpage contains the FTC's definition of anticompetitive practices. The page provides information regarding Horizontal Conduct, Single Firm Conduct, as well as statutory descriptions of competitive practices.

Federal Reserve System/Federal Deposit Insurance Corporation
(www.federalreserve.gov/apps/enforcementactions/)

The Federal Reserve supervises state member banks, bank holding companies and their subsidies, edge and agreement corporations, branches and agencies of foreign banking organizations that are operating within the United States, as well as any officers, directors, or employees of these organizations. This website provides information on the organizational responsibilities of Federal Reserve and Federal Deposit Insurance Corporation (FDIC) and the violations that both organizations deal with.

Consumer Protection Safety Commission
(www.cpsc.gov//Global/About-CPSC/Reports/
Annual-Reports/FY12AnnualReport.pdf)

The Consumer Protection Safety Commission (CPSC) is a regulatory agency whose task it is to protect individuals from unreasonable risks of injuries and illnesses associated with consumer products. This website contains the Commission's Annual Report (Fiscal Year 2012) submitted to the President and Congress. The report provides information about hazard identification and monitoring practices, safety standards, compliance and enforcement actions, public outreach, and coordination with other governmental agencies.

Environmental Protection Agency
(www2.epa.gov/enforcement)

The Environmental Protection Agency (EPA) is tasked with ensuring that all Americans are protected from risks to human health and the environment where they live, learn, and work, as well as enforcing laws regarding environmental protection. This website contains the EPA's enforcement page, which provides information regarding enforcement actions that reduce air pollution, waste and chemical cleanup, water protection, and criminal enforcement of environmental law violators. The website also provides information about the enforcement process in general, enforcement initiatives, cases and settlements, enforcement data and results, federal facility enforcement, and policies and guidelines.

Nongovernmental Websites on White-Collar Crime

White-Collar Crime Prof Blog
(http://lawprofessors.typepad.com/whitecollarcrime_blog/)

The White-Collar Crime Prof Blog is edited by Ellen S. Podgor, Solomon L. Wisenberg, and Lawrence S. Goldman, who all practice in the field of white-collar crime law. This blog provides information regarding court cases dealing with white-collar crimes, and in-depth analysis on how these rulings will affect future court rulings.

FBI's 10 Most Wanted White-Collar Criminals
(www.cnbc.com/id/101253928)

This website was created by CNBC and lists the Federal Bureau of Investigation's top 10 most wanted white-collar criminals. Each entry consists of the fugitive's name, sex, height, weight, and hair and eye color, as well as the crimes for which he or she is being sought.

American Greed: The Fugitives (Case Files)
(www.cnbc.com/id/101078365)

American Greed: The Fugitives is a television show produced by CNBC that features interviews with victims of white-collar criminals and law enforcement agents who track them down. Each link to the different episodes also has information (such as letters, wanted posters, etc.) specific to that case.

White-Collar Crime Case Studies
(http://whitecollarcrimecasestudies.com/public/)

The White-Collar Crime Case Studies website provides information on specific cases regarding white-collar crimes. The website also includes links to definitions and cases of: Securities Fraud; Money Laundering; Insurance Fraud; Bank Fraud; and Other Financial Crime. The webpage is great for finding out more information relating to fraud, money laundering, and financing terrorism, as well as other white-collar crimes.

National Health Care Anti-Fraud Association
(www.nhcaa.org/resources/health-care-anti-fraud-resources/
the-challenge-of-health-care-fraud.aspx)

The National Health Care Anti-Fraud Association (NHCAA) is an organization that focuses exclusively on issues regarding health care fraud in the United States. The website brings you to a consumer alert page that outlines what the NHCAA does and how health care fraud impacts the public with both the dollar amount spend on health care fraud and the costs of health care fraud for each individual with health insurance. The consumer alert also gives examples of what health care fraud is, how it is prosecuted, and what the public can do to avoid and prevent health care fraud.

REFERENCES

Abelson, Elaine S. 1989. *When Ladies Go a-Thieving: Middle-Class Shoplifters in the Victorian Department Store*. New York: Oxford University Press.

Ackman, Dan. 2005. "Bernie Ebbers Guilty." *Forbes*. Retrieved October 30, 2007 (www.forbes.com/2005/03/15/cx_da_0315ebbersguilty.html).

Adler, Freda. 1975. *Sisters in Crime: The Rise of the New Female Criminal*. New York: McGraw-Hill.

Akpinar, Tim. 2010. "The Seaman's Manslaughter Statute." Retrieved July 2, 2014 (www.workboat.com/newsdetail.aspx?id=4294987724).

Albanese, Jay S. 1995. *White-Collar Crime in America*. Englewood Cliffs, NJ: Prentice Hall.

Alexander, Cindy R., Jennifer Arlen, and Mark A. Cohen. 2001. "Evaluating Data on Corporate Sentencing: How Reliable Are the U.S. Sentencing Commission's Data?" *Federal Sentencing Reporter*, Vol. 13, p. 108. Available at SSRN: http://ssrn.com/abstract=269356 or http://dx.doi.org/10.2139/ssrn.269356 Revised, April 2001.

Anonymous. 2007. "Medicare Fraud Strike Force Convicts Owner of Miami Durable Medical Equipment Company of Defrauding Medicare." Retrieved September 10, 2008 (www.usdoj.gov/criminal/pr/press_releases/2007/06/06-28-07gvalladares-convict.pdf).

Arlen, Jennifer. 2012. "The Failure of the Organizational Sentencing Guidelines." Law & Economics Research Paper Series Working Paper No. 11-12. Retrieved July 2, 2014 (http://papers.ssrn.com/sol3/papers.cfm?abstract_id=1903975).

Associated Press. 2014. "Turkey Mine Disaster: 2 More Arrested after 301 Killed." Retrieved July 2, 2014 (www.cbc.ca/news/turkey-mine-disaster-2-more-arrests-after-301-killed-1.2647141).

Atkinson, Phyllis. 2006. "Women and White-Collar Crime." Deloitte & Touche South Africa. Retrieved September 9, 2008 (www.deloitte. com/dtt/press_release/0,1014,cid%3D135645%26pv%3DY,00.html).

Ayres, Ian and John Braithwaite. 1992. *Responsive Regulation.* Oxford: Oxford University Press.

Babiak, Paul and Robert Hare. 2006. *Snakes in Suits: When Psychopaths Go to Work.* New York: Regan Books.

Babiak, Paul, Craig Newmann, and Robert Hare. 2010. "Corporate Psychopathy: Talking the Walk." *Behavioral Sciences and the Law* 28:174–93.

Bardach, Eugene and Robert A. Kagan. 1982. *Going by the Book.* Philadelphia: Temple University Press.

Barlow, Hugh D. 1993. "From Fiddle Factors to Networks of Collusion: Charting the Waters of Small Business Crime." *Crime, Law and Social Change* 20:319–37.

Barnett, Cynthia. 2003. *The Measurement of White-Collar Crime Using Uniform Crime Reporting (UCR) Data.* U.S. Department of Justice, Federal Bureau of Investigation, Criminal Justice Information Services Division. Retrieved September 12, 2014 (www.fbi.gov/stats-services/about-us/cjis/ucr/nibrs/nibrs_wcc.pdf).

Barnett, Harold C. 2013. "And Some with a Fountain Pen: Mortgage Fraud, Securitization, and the Subprime Bubble." Pp. 104–29 in *How They Got Away with It: White-Collar Criminals and the Financial Meltdown,* edited by Susan Will, Stephen Handelman, and David C. Brotherton. New York: Columbia University Press.

Barrett, Paul M. 2014. "Who Runs Freedom Industries? West Virginia's Chemical Spill Mystery." *Bloomberg Business Week*, January 30. Retrieved September 10, 2014 (www.businessweek.com/articles/2014-01-30/west-virginia-chemical-spill-mystery-who-runs-freedom-industries).

Barstow, David and Lowell Bergman. 2003. "At a Texas Foundry, an Indifference to Life." *New York Times,* January 8, 2003, A1.

Beccaria, Cesare. 1983. *An Essay on Crimes and Punishment.* Boston: Branden Books.

Benson, Michael L. 1984. "The Fall from Grace: Loss of Occupational Status among Convicted White Collar Offenders." *Criminology* 22:573–93.

———. 1985. "Denying the Guilty Mind: Accounting for Involvement in a White-Collar Crime." *Criminology* 23:583–608.

———. 2001a. "Investigating Corporate Crime: Local Responses to Fraud and Environmental Offenses." *Western State University Law Review* 28:87–116.

———. 2001b. "Prosecuting Corporate Crime: Problems and Constraints." Pp. 381–91 in *Crimes of Privilege: Readings in White-Collar Crime,* edited by Neal Shover and John P. Wright. New York: Oxford University Press.

Benson, Michael L. and Francis T. Cullen. 1988. "The Special Sensitivity of White-Collar Offenders to Prison: A Critique and a Research Agenda." *Journal of Criminal Justice* 16:207–15.

———. 1998. *Combating Corporate Crime: Local Prosecutors at Work.* Boston: Northeastern University Press.

Benson, Michael L., Francis T. Cullen, and William J. Maakestad. 1990. "Local Prosecutors and Corporate Crime." *Crime and Delinquency* 36:356–72.

Benson, Michael L. and Kent R. Kerley. 2000. "Life Course Theory and White-Collar Crime." Pp. 121–36 in *Contemporary Issues in Crime and Criminal Justice: Essays in Honor of Gilber Geis,* edited by Henry N. Pontell and David Shichor. Upper Saddle River, NJ: Prentice Hall.

Benson, Michael L., William J. Maakestad, Francis T. Cullen, and Gilbert Geis. 1998. "District Attorneys and Corporate Crime: Surveying the Prosecutorial Gatekeepers." *Criminology* 26:505–18.

Benson, Michael L. and Tamara D. Madensen. 2007. "Situational Crime Prevention and White-Collar Crime." Pp. 609–26 in *International Handbook of White-Collar and Corporate Crime*, edited by Henry N. Pontell and Gilbert Geis. New York: Springer.

Benson, Michael L., Tamara D. Madensen, and John E. Eck. 2009. "White-Collar Crime from an Opportunity Perspective." Pp. 175–94 in *The Criminology of White-Collar Crime* edited by Sally S. Simpson and David Weisburd. New York: Springer.

Benson, Michael L. and Sarah L. Manchak. 2014. "The Psychology of White-Collar Crime," in *Oxford Handbooks Online in Criminology and Criminal Justice*. New York: Oxford University Press.

Benson, Michael L. and Elizabeth Moore. 1992. "Are White-Collar and Common Offenders the Same? An Empirical and Theoretical Critique of a Recently Proposed General Theory of Crime." *Journal of Research in Crime and Delinquency* 29:251–72.

Benson, Michael L. and Esteban Walker. 1988. "Sentencing the White-Collar Offender." *American Sociological Review* 53:294–302.

Bentham, Jeremy. 1948. *An Introduction to the Principles of Morals and Legislation*. New York: Macmillan.

Birnbaum, S. Elizabeth and Jacqueline Savitz. 2014. "The Deepwater Horizon Threat." *New York Times*. Retrieved July 2, 2014 (www.nytimes.com/2014/04/17/opinion/the-deepwater-horizon-threat.html).

Black, Donald. 1983. "Crime as Social Control." *American Sociological Review* 48:34–45.

Black, William K. 1983. *The Best Way to Rob a Bank Is to Own One: How Corporate Executives and Politicians Looted the S&L Industry*. Austin, TX: University of Texas Press.

Blickle, Gerhard, Alexander Schlegel, Pantaleon Fassbender, and Uwe Klein. 2006. "Some Personality Correlates of Business White-Collar Crime." *Applied Psychology: An International Review* 55(2):220–233.

Blumstein, Alfred, Jacqueline Cohen, Jeffrey A. Roth, and Christy A. Visher, eds. 1986. *Criminal Careers and Career Criminals*, Vol. 1. Washington, DC: National Academy Press.

Boudette, Neal E. and Andrea Fuller. 2014. "General Motors Recall: A Burden of Proof." *Wall Street Journal*. Retrieved July 2, 2014 (http://online.wsj.com/articles/general-motors-recall-a-burden-of-proof-1403478781).

Bowyer, J.B. 1982. *Cheating: Deception in War & Magic, Games & Sports, Sex & Religion, Business & Con Games, Politics & Espionage, Art & Science*. New York: St. Martin's Press.

Box, Steven. 1983. *Power, Crime, and Mystification*. London: Tavistock Publications.

Braithwaite, John. 1981. "The Myth of Social Class and Criminality Reconsidered." *American Sociological Review* 46:36–57.

———. 1984. *Corporate Crime in the Pharmaceutical Industry*. London: Routledge & Kegan Paul.

———. 1985. "White Collar Crime." *Annual Review of Sociology* 11:1–25.

———. 1989. "Criminological Theory and Organizational Crime." *Justice Quarterly* 6:333–58.

Braithwaite, John and P. Drahos. 2000. *Global Business Regulation*. Cambridge: Cambridge University Press.

Braithwaite, John and Brent Fisse. 1990. "On the Plausibility of Corporate Crime Control." *Advances in Criminological Theory* 2:15–37.

Braithwaite, John and Gilbert Geis. 1982. "On Theory and Action for Corporate Crime Control." *Crime & Delinquency* 28:292–314.

Branham, Vernon C. and Samuel B. Kutash. 1949. *Encyclopedia of Criminology*. New York: Philosophical Library.

Brickey, Kathleen. 2008. Major Corporate Fraud Prosecutions, March 2002–July 2007. Private data used with permission.

Brodeur, Paul. 1985. *Outrageous Misconduct*. New York: Pantheon.

Brook, Yaron and Alex Epstein. 2002. "Paralyzing America's Producers: The Government's Crackdown on American Businessmen Is Devastating Our Economy." *Capitalism Magazine*. Retrieved December 20, 2007 (www.capmag.com/article. asp?id=2093).

Brown, Phil and Edwin J. Mikkelsen. 1990. *No Safe Place: Toxic Waste, Leukemia, and Community Action*. Berkeley: University of California Press.

Bullard, Robert. 1990. *Dumping in Dixie: Race, Class, and Environmental Quality*. Boulder, CO: Westview.

———. 2000. "Anatomy of Environmental Racism." Pp. 223–31 in *Environmental Discourse and Practice: A Reader*, edited by Lisa M. Benton and John R. Short. Oxford: Blackwell Publishers.

Burns, Ronald G. and Michael J. Lynch. 2004. *Environmental Crime: A Sourcebook*. New York: LFB Scholarly Publishers.

Calavita, Kitty. 1983. "The Demise of the Occupational Safety and Health Administration: A Case Study in Symbolic Interaction." *Social Problems* 30:437–48.

Calavita, Kitty and Henry N. Pontell. 1990. "'Heads I Win, Tails You Lose': Deregulation, Crime, and Crisis in the Savings and Loan Industry." *Crime & Delinquency* 36:309–41.

Calem, Paul S., Jonathan E. Herschaff, and Susan M. Wachter. 2004. "Neighborhood Patterns of Subprime Lending: Evidence from Disparate Cities." *Housing Policy Debate* 15(3):603–22.

Calhoun, Craig and Henryk Hiller. 1992. "Insidious Injuries: The Case of Johns-Manville and Asbestos Exposure." Pp. 259–84 in *Corporate and Governmental Deviance: Problems of Organizational Behavior in Contemporary Society*, 4th ed., edited by M.D. Ermann and Richard J. Lundman. New York: Oxford University Press.

Carson, Rachel. 1962. *Silent Spring*. Boston: Houghton Mifflin.

Catalyst. 2006. "2005 Catalyst Census of Women Corporate Officers and Top Earners of the Fortune 500." Retrieved September 5, 2014 (www.catalyst.org/knowledge/2005-catalyst-census-women-corporate-officers-and-top-earners-fortune-500).

Catan, Thomas, Jeffrey A. Trachtenberg, and Chad Bray. 2012. "U.S. Alleges E-Book Scheme." *Wall Street Journal*. Retrieved May 16, 2014 (http://online.wsj.com/news/articles/SB10001424052702304444604577337573054615152.).

Checker, Melissa. 2005. *Polluted Promises: Environmental Racism and the Search for Justice in a Southern Town*. New York: New York University Press.

Chesney-Lind, Meda. 1989. "Girls' Crime and Woman's Place: Toward a Feminist Model of Female Delinquency." *Crime and Delinquency* 35:10–27.

Chibnall, Steven and Peter Saunders. 1977. "Worlds Apart: Notes on the Social Reality of Corruption." *British Journal of Sociology* 28:138–54.

Christensen, Ronald. 1967. *Projected Percentage of U.S. Population with Criminal Arrest and Conviction Records*. Washington, DC: U.S. Government Printing Office.

Clarke, Ronald V. 1983. "Situational Crime Prevention: Its Theoretical Basis and Practical Scope." Pp. 225–56 in *Crime and Justice: An Annual Review*, edited by Michael Tonry and Norval Morris. Chicago: University of Chicago Press.

Cleveland, Cutler J. 2013. "Deepwater Horizon Oil Spill." Retrieved July 2, 2014 (www. eoearth.org/view/article/161185/).

Click On Detroit. 2014. "GM CEO Mary Barra Testifies Again on Capitol Hill about Ignition Recall." Retrieved July 2, 2014 (www.clickondetroit.com/news/gm-ceo-mary-barra-to-testify-again-on-capitol-hill-about-ignition-recall/26532480).

Clinard, Marshall B. and Richard Quinney. 1973. *Criminal Behavior Systems: A Typology.* New York: Holt, Rinehart, and Winston.

Clinard, Marshall B. and Peter C. Yeager. 1980. *Corporate Crime.* New York: Free Press.

——. 2006. *Corporate Crime.* New Brunswick, NJ: Transaction Publishers.

Coffee, John C., Jr. 2002. "Understanding Enron: It's about the Gatekeepers, Stupid." *The Business Lawyer* 57:1–2.

Cohen, Lawrence E. and Marcus Felson. 1979. "Social Change and Crime Rate Trends: A Routine Activity Approach." *American Sociological Review* 44:588–608.

Cohen, Mark A. 1998. "Sentencing the Environmental Criminal." Pp. 229–52 in *Environmental Crime: Enforcement, Policy, and Social Responsibility.* Gaithersburg, MD: Aspen Publications.

——. 2000. "Measuring the Costs and Benefits of Crime and Justice." Pp. 263–316 in *Measurement and Analysis of Crime and Justice.* Washington, DC: National Institute of Justice.

Coleman, James S. 1982. *The Asymmetric Society.* Syracuse, NY: Syracuse University Press.

Coleman, James W. 1987. "Toward an Integrated Theory of White-Collar Crime." *American Journal of Sociology* 93:406–39.

——. 1989. *The Criminal Elite.* New York: St. Martin's Press.

Collins, Judith M. and Frank L. Schmidt. 1993. "Personality, Integrity, and White Collar Crime: A Construct Validity Study." *Personnel Psychology* 46:295–311.

Collins, Randall. 1979. *The Credential Society: An Historical Sociology of Education and Stratification.* New York: Academic Press.

Commoner, Barry. 1971. *The Closing Circle: Nature, Man, and Technology.* New York: Knopf.

Congressional Research Service. 2014. "*Deepwater Horizon* Oil Spill: Recent Activities and Ongoing Developments." Retrieved September 12, 2014 (http://fas.org/sgp/crs/misc/R42942.pdf).

Conklin, John E. 1977. *Illegal but Not Criminal: Business Crime in America.* Englewood Cliffs, NJ: Prentice-Hall.

Cornish, Derek B. and Ronald V. Clarke. 1986. "Opportunities, Precipitators, and Criminal Decisions: A Reply to Wortley's Critique of Situational Crime Prevention." *Crime Prevention Studies* 16:41–96.

Cressey, Donald. 1953. *Other People's Money.* New York: The Free Press.

——. 1989. "The Poverty of Theory in Corporate Crime Research." Pp. 31–55 in *Advances in Criminological Theory,* edited by William S. Laufer and Freda Adler. New Brunswick, NJ: Transaction.

Croall, Hazel. 1989. "Who Is the White-Collar Criminal?" *British Journal of Criminology* 29:157–74.

——. 2001. *Understanding White Collar Crime.* Buckingham, Open University Press.

——. 2009. "White-Collar Crime, Consumers, and Victimization." *Crime, Law and Social Change* 51:127–46.

Cullen, Francis T., Gray Cavender, William J. Maakestad, and Michael L. Benson. 2006. *Corporate Crime under Attack: The Fight to Criminalize Business Violence.* Newark, NJ: LexisNexis Matthew Bender.

Daly, Kathleen. 1989. "Gender and Varieties of White-Collar Crime." *Criminology* 27:769–94.

———. 1994. *Gender, Crime, and Punishment.* New Haven, CT: Yale University Press.

Davidoff, Steven M. 2013. "Why So Few Women Reach the Executive Rank." *NY Times. com.* Retrieved July 2, 2014 (http://dealbook.nytimes.com/2013/04/02/why-so-few-women-reach-the-executive-rank/).

Dawkins, Richard. 2004. *The Ancestor's Tale: A Pilgrimage to the Dawn of Evolution.* Boston: Houghton Mifflin.

Dowie, Mark. 1987. "Pinto Madness." Pp. 13–29 in *Corporate Violence,* edited by Stuart L. Hills. Totowa, NJ: Rowman & Littlefield.

Downes, John and Jordan Elliot Goodman. 2006. *Dictionary of Finance and Investment Terms.* 7th ed. Hauppauge, NY: Barron's.

Durkheim, Emile. 1951. *Suicide, a Study in Sociology.* New York: Free Press.

Dyck, Alexander, Adair Morse, and Luigi Zingales. 2013. "How Pervasive is Corporate Fraud?" Rotman School of Management Working Paper No. 2222608. Retrieved July 2, 2014 (http://papers.ssrn.com/sol3/papers.cfm?abstract_id=2222608).

Economist. 2005. "The Conundrum of the Glass Ceiling—Women in Business." *The Economist,* July 23, 2005, p. 64(US). *Expanded Academic ASAP.* Retrieved May 22, 2014 (http://go.galegroup.com/ps/i.do?id=GALE|A134340782&v=2.1&u=ucinc_main& it=r&p=EAIM&sw=w&asid=d522bd92eeb686701c7f141f0f268902).

Edelhertz, Herbert. 1970. *The Nature, Impact and Prosecution of White-Collar Crime.* Washington, DC: U.S. Department of Justice.

Eichenwald, Kurt. 2002. "White-Collar Defense Stance: The Criminal-Less Crime." *New York Times,* March 3, 2002. Retrieved September 10, 2014 (www.nytimes.com/2002/03/03/weekinreview/the-nation-white-collar-defense-stance-the-criminal-less-crime.html).

Epstein, Joel and Theodore M. Hammett. 1995. *Law Enforcement Responses to Environmental Crime.* Washington, DC: National Institute of Justice.

Ermann, M. David and Richard J. Lundman, eds. 1978. *Corporate and Governmental Deviance: Problems of Organizational Behavior in Contemporary Society.* New York: Oxford University Press.

Faber, Jacob. 2013. "Racial Dynamics of Subprime Mortgage Lending at the Peak." *Housing Policy Debate* 23(2):328–49.

Felson, Marcus. 2002. *Crime and Everyday Life.* Thousand Oaks, CA: Sage Publications.

Felson, Richard B. 1996. "Big People Hit Little People: Sex Differences in Physical Power and Interpersonal Violence." *Criminology* 34:433–52.

Financial Crimes Enforcement Network. 2006. "Mortgage Loan Fraud: An Industry Assessment Based upon Suspicious Activity Report Analysis, November 2006. Retrieved September 12, 2014 (file:///C:/Users/bensonm/Documents/Current%20 Projects/WCC%202nd%20Edition/2nd%20Edition/Articles/FINCEN%20 mortgage_fraud112006.pdf).

Fisk, Margaret Cronin. 2014. "Ex-BP Engineer Wins New Trial in Oil Spill Evidence Case." *World Oil News Center.* Retrieved July 2, 2014 (www.worldoil.com/Ex-BP-Engineer-wins-new-Trial-in-oil-spill-evidence-case.html).

Fisse, Brent and John Braithwaite. 1983. *The Impact of Publicity on Corporate Offenders.* Albany: State University of New York Press.

———. 1993. *Corporations, Crime, and Accountability.* Cambridge, New York: Cambridge University Press.

Frank, Nancy. 1985. *Crimes Against Health and Safety.* New York: Harrow and Heston.

———. 1993. "Maiming and Killing: Occupational Health Crimes." *Annals* 525:107–18.

Frank, Nancy and Michael Lombness. 1988. *Controlling Corporate Illegality: The Regulatory Justice System.* Cincinnati, OH: Anderson.

Friedman, Hershey H. 1980. "Talmudic Business Ethics: An Historical Perspective." *Akron Business and Economic Review* 11:45–49.

Friedrichs, David O. 2002. "Occupational Crime, Occupational Deviance, and Workplace Crime: Sorting Out the Difference." *Criminal Justice* 2:243–56.

———. 2010. *Trusted Criminals: White Collar Crime in Contemporary Society.* 4th ed. Belmont, CA: Thomson Wadsworth.

Fuchs, Victor R. 2013. "The Gross Domestic Product and Health Care Spending." *New England Journal of Medicine* 369:107–109. Retrieved March 6, 2014 (www.nejm.org/doi/full/10.1056/NEJMp1305298).

Garner, Joel. 2007. "Understanding the Nature and Context of Local Environmental Enforcement: What We Learned from Interviews with Inspectors." *Why Do Corporations Obey Environmental Law?*, edited by Sally S. Simpson, Joel Garner, and Carole Gibbs. Washington, DC: National Institute of Justice, U.S. Department of Justice.

Geerken, Michael R. and Walter R. Gove. 1975. "Deterrence: Some Theoretical Considerations." *Law & Society Review* 9:497–514.

Geis, Gilbert. 1977. "The Heavy Electrical Equipment Antitrust Cases of 1961." Pp. 117–32 in *White-Collar Crime: Offenses in Business, Politics, and the Professions,* edited by Gilbert Geis and Robert F. Meier. New York: The Free Press.

———. 1988. "From Deuteronomy to Deniability: A Historical Perlustration on White-Collar Crime." *Justice Quarterly* 5:7–32.

———. 1996. "Definition in White-Collar Crime Scholarship: Sometimes It Can Matter." Pp. 159–211 in *Definitional Dilemma: Can and should there be a Universal Definition of White-Collar Crime? Proceedings of the Academic Workshop,* edited by James Helmkamp, Richard Ball, and Kitty Townsend. Morgantown, WV: National White-Collar Crime Center.

———. 2000. "On the Absence of Self-control as the Basis for a General Theory of Crime: A Critique." *Theoretical Criminology* 4:35–53.

Geis, Gilbert and Colin Goff. 1983. Introduction to *White-Collar Crime: The Uncut Version* by Edwin H. Sutherland. New Haven, CT: Yale University Press.

Gerber, Jurg and Susan L. Weeks. 1992. "Women as Victims of Corporate Crime: A Call for Research on a Neglected Topic." *Deviant Behavior* 13:325–47.

Gibbs, Carole, Meredith L. Gore, Edmund F. McGarrell, and Louie Rivers III. 2010. "Introducing Conservation Criminology: Towards Interdisciplinary Scholarship on Environmental Crimes and Risks." *British Journal of Criminology* 50:124–44.

Gibeaut, J. 2007. "Mortgage Fraud Mess." *ABA Journal* 93:50–56.

Gilligan, Carol. 1993. *In a Different Voice: Psychological Theory and Women's Development.* Cambridge, MA: Harvard University Press.

Gioia, Dennis A. 1992. "Pinto Fires and Personal Ethics: A Script Analysis of Missed Opportunities." *Journal of Business Ethics* 11:379–89.

Glass Ceiling Commission. 1995. *Good for Business: Making Full Use of the Nation's Human Capital: A Fact-Finding Report of the Federal Glass Ceiling Commission*. Washington, DC: U.S. Government Printing Office.

Gold, Stuart. 1989. "Occidental Petroleum: Politics, Pollution, and Profit." *Multinational Monitor*. Retrieved September 11, 2008 (http:// multinationalmonitor.org/hyper/issues/1989/07/gold.html).

Gorman, Elizabeth H. and Julie A. Kmec. 2009. "Hierarchical Rank and Women's Organizational Mobility: Glass Ceilings in Corporate Law Firms." *American Journal of Sociology* 114:1428–74.

Gottfredson, Michael R. and Travis Hirschi. 1990. *A General Theory of Crime*. Stanford, CA: Stanford University Press.

Grabosky, Peter N. 2009. "Globalization and White-Collar Crime." Pp. 129–51 in *The Criminology of White-Collar Crime*, edited by Sally S. Simpson and David Weisburd. New York, NY: Springer.

Grabosky, Peter N., Russel G. Smith, and Gillian Dempsey. 2001. *Electronic Theft: Unlawful Acquisition in Cyberspace*. Cambridge: Cambridge University Press.

Gross, Edward. 1978. "Organizational Crime: A Theoretical Perspective." Pp. 55–85 in *Studies in Symbolic Interaction*, edited by Norman Denzin. Greenwich, CT: JAI Press.

——. 1980. "Organization Structure and Organizational Crime." Pp. 52–76 in *White-Collar Crime: Theory and Research*, edited by Gilbert Geis and Ezra Stotland. Beverly Hills, CA: Sage.

Hagan, John. 1994. *Crime and Disrepute*. Thousand Oaks, CA: Pine Forge Press.

Hagan, John L. and Ilene H. Nagel. 1982. "White-Collar Crime, White-Collar Time: The Sentencing of White-Collar Offenders in the Southern District of New York." *American Criminal Law Review* 20:259–89.

Hagan, John, Ilene H. Nagel (Bernstein), and Celesta Albonetti. 1980. "The Differential Sentencing of White-Collar Offenders in Ten Federal District Courts." *American Sociological Review* 45:802–20.

Hammett, Theodore M. and Joel Epstein. 1993. *Local Prosecution of Environmental Crime*. Washington, DC: U.S. National Institute of Justice.

Hare, Robert. 1993. *Without Conscience: The Disturbing World of the Psychopaths among Us*. New York: Pocket Books.

Harris, Anthony R. 1976. "Race, Commitment to Deviance, and Spoiled Identity." *American Sociological Review* 41:432–42.

——. 1977. "Sex and Theories of Deviance: Toward a Functional Theory of Deviant Typescripts." *American Sociological Review* 42:3–16.

——. 1991. "Race, Class, and Crime." Pp. 95–120 in *Criminology: A Contemporary Handbook*, edited by Joseph F. Sheley. Belmont, CA: Wadsworth.

Harris, Anthony R. and G.D. Hill. 1982. "The Social Psychology of Deviance: Toward a Reconciliation with Social Structure." *Annual Review of Sociology* 8:161–86.

Harris, Anthony R. and James A.W. Shaw. 2000. "Looking for Patterns: Race, Class, and Crime." Pp. 129–64 in *Criminology: A Contemporary Handbook*, edited by Joseph F. Sheley. Belmont, CA: Wadsworth/Thompson Learning.

Hast, Robert H. 2000. "Health Care Fraud: Schemes to Defraud Medicare, Medicaid and Private Health Care Insurers: Statement of Robert H. Hast, Associate Comptroller, General for Special Investigations, Office of Special Investigations, before the Subcommittee on Government Management, Information and Technology, Committee on Government Reform, House of Representatives." GAO/T-OSI-00–15:10.

Hawkins, Keith. 2002. *Law as Last Resort: Prosecution Decision-Making in a Regulatory Agency.* New York: Oxford University Press.

Hawn, Carleen. 2008. "Enron's Skilling Sprung? It Could Happen This Week." *Financial Week,* June 9, 2008. Retrieved September 10, 2014 (www.financialweek.com/article/20080609/REG/806090322/-1/FWIssueAlert01).

Helmkamp, James, Richard Ball, and Kitty Townsend, eds. 1996. *Definitional Dilemma: Can and Should There Be a Universal Definition of White-Collar Crime? Proceedings of the Academic Workshop.* Morgantown, WV: National White-Collar Crime Center.

Henriques, Diana B. 2011. *The Wizard of Lies: Bernie Madoff and the Death of Trust.* New York: Times Books.

Herbig, F.J.W., and S. J. Joubert. 2006. "Criminological Semantics: Conservation Criminology—Vision or Vagary?" *Acta Criminologica* 19:88–103.

Hirschi, Travis. 1969. *Causes of Delinquency.* Berkeley: University of California Press.

Hirschi, Travis and Michael Gottfredson. 1987a. "Causes of White-Collar Crime." *Criminology* 25:949–74.

———. 1987b. "Toward a General Theory of Crime." Pp. 8–26 in *Crime & Capitalism,* edited by Wouter Buikhuisen and Sarnoff Mednick. Leiden: Brill.

Hochstetler, Andrew and Heith Copes. 2001. "Organizational Culture and Organizational Crime." Pp. 210–21 in *Crimes of Privilege: Readings in White-Collar Crime* edited by Neal Shover and John Paul Wright. New York: Oxford University Press.

Holtfreter, Kristy. 2005. "Is Occupational Fraud 'Typical' White-Collar Crime? A Comparison of Individual and Organizational Characteristics." *Journal of Criminal Justice* 33:353–65.

Howe, Michelle. 2003. "Gender, Morality, and Corporate Crime." Unpublished master's thesis, University of Maryland, Department of Criminology and Criminal Justice. College Park.

Huffington Post. 2014. "David Rainey, Former BP Executive, Given More Time for Gulf Oil Spill Trial." Retrieved July 2, 2014 (www.huffingtonpost.com/2013/07/04/david-rainey-bp-gulf-oil-spill_n_3543426.html).

Ingels, Steven J., Elizabeth Glennie, Eric Lauff, and John G. Wirt. 2012. "Trends among Young Adults over Three Decades, 1974–2006 (NCES 2012–345)." U.S. Department of Education, National Center for Education Statistics. Washington, DC. Retrieved July 2, 2014 (http://nces.ed.gov/pubs2012/2012345.pdf).

International Committee in Solidarity with the Victims of Nemagon. 2008. Webpage. Retrieved September 11, 2008 (www.opticalrealities.org/Nicaragua/ NemagonAction. html).

Jesilow, Paul, Gilbert Geis, and Henry Pontell. 1991. "Fraud by Physicians Against Medicaid." *Journal of the American Medical Association* 266:3318–24.

Kalev, Alexandra. 2009. "Cracking the Glass Cages: Restructuring and Ascriptive Inequality at Work." *American Journal of Sociology* 114(6):1591–1643.

Katz, Jack. 1979. "Concerted Ignorance: The Social Construction of Cover-up." *Urban Life* 8:295–316.

———. 1980. "The Social Movement Against White-Collar crime." *Criminology Review Yearbook* 2:161–84.

Klenowski, Paul M., Heith Copes, and Christopher W. Mullins. 2011. "Gender, Identity, and Accounts: How White-Collar Offenders Do Gender when Making Sense of Their Crimes." *Justice Quarterly* 28(1):46–69.

Kmietowicz, Z. 2013. "Johnson & Johnson to Pay $2.2bn to Settle Charges of False Marketing on Three Drugs." *British Medical Journal* 347:f6696. Retrieved July 2, 2014 (www.bmj.com/content/347/bmj.f6696?tab=citation).

Lasley, James R. 1988. "Toward a Control Theory of White-Collar Offending." *Journal of Quantitative Criminology* 4:347–62.

Lee, Matthew T. and M.D. Ermann. 1999. "Pinto 'Madness' as a Flawed Landmark Narrative: An Organizational and Network Analysis." *Social Problems* 46:30–47.

Leeth, John D. and John Ruser. 2006. "Safety Segregation: The Importance of Gender, Race, and Ethnicity on Workplace Risk." *Journal of Economic Inequality* 4:123–52.

Lister, S. 2005. "Secrets and Lies of Beauty Industry Laid Bare by Advertising Watchdog." *The Times* [of London], January 28, p. 11.

Lydon, James. 2012. "Justice Department Defends Role of Deferred Prosecution Agreements in Corporate Crime Enforcement." Constitutional Rights, Sentencing, U.S. Attorney's Office. Retrieved July 2, 2014 (www.thewhitecollarblog.com/2012/10/17/justice-department-defends-the-role-of-deferred-prosecution-agreements-in-corporate-crime-enforcement/).

Maakestad, William J., Michael L. Benson, Francis T. Cullen, and Gilbert Geis. 1987. "Prosecuting Corporate Crime in California." Unpublished manuscript, presented at Symposium '87: White-Collar and Institutional Crime. Berkeley, CA.

MacLaury, Judson. 2008. "The Occupational Safety and Health Administration: A History of the First Thirteen Years, 1971–1984." Retrieved March 26, 2008 (www.dol.gov/oasam/programs/history/mono-osha13introtoc. htm).

Maher, Lisa. 1997. *Sexed Work: Gender, Race, and Resistance in a Brooklyn Drug Market.* New York: Clarendon Press.

Makkai, Toni and John Braithwaite. 1994. "The Dialectics of Corporate Deterrence." *Journal of Research in Crime and Delinquency* 31:347–73.

Mann, Kenneth. 1985. *Defending White-Collar Crime: A Portrait of Attorneys at Work.* New Haven, CT: Yale University Press.

Maruna, Shadd and Heith Copes. 2005. "What Have We Learned from Five Decades of Neutralization Research?" *Crime and Justice* 32: 221–320.

Mayer, Robert N. 2012. "The U.S. Consumer Movement: A New Era amid Old Challenges." *Journal of Consumer Affairs* 46:171–89.

McBarnet, Doreen. 2005. "After Enron: Corporate Governance, Creative Compliance and the Uses of Corporate Social Responsibility." Pp. 205–22 in *Governing the Corporation,* edited by Justin O'Brien. New York: John Wiley.

McGarrell, Edmund and Carole Gibbs. Forthcoming. *Conservation Criminology.* Oxford Handbooks Online

McLean, Bethany and Peter Elkind. 2003. *The Smartest Guys in the Room: The Amazing Rise and Scandalous Fall of Enron.* New York: Penguin Group.

McMullen, Troy. 2010. "Dannon to Pay $45 Billion to Settle Yogurt Lawsuit." *ABC News.* Retrieved July 2, 2014 (http://abcnews.go.com/Business/dannon-settles-lawsuit/story?id=9950269).

Meier, Robert F. and Gilbert Geis. 1982. "The Psychology of the White-Collar Offender." Pp. 85–102 in *On White-Collar Crime,* edited by Gilbert Geis. Lexington, MA: Lexington Books.

Merton, Robert K. 1938. "Social Structure and Anomie." *American Sociological Review* 3:672–82.

Merton, Robert K. 1964. "Anomie, Anomia, and Social Interaction: Contexts of Deviant Behavior." Pp. 213–42 in *Anomie and Deviant Behavior: A Discussion and Critique,* edited by M.B. Clinard. New York: The Free Press.

Messner, Steven and Richard Rosenfeld. 1997. *Crime and the American Dream.* Belmont, CA: Wadsworth.

———. 2013. *Crime and the American Dream.* 5th ed. Belmont, CA: Wadsworth.

Miethe, Terance D. and Joyce Rothschild. 1994. "Whistleblowing and the Control of Organizational Misconduct." *Sociological Inquiry* 64:322–47.

Miller, George A. 1987. "Meta-analysis and the Culture Free Hypothesis." *Organization Studies* 8(4):309–326.

Miller, Jody. 2001. *One of the Guys: Girls, Gangs, and Gender.* New York: Oxford University Press.

Miller, Matthew. 2006. "A Visual Essay: Post-Recessionary Employment Growth Related to the Housing Market." *Monthly Labor Review,* October, pp. 23–34.

Mintz, Morton. 1995. "Corporate Greed, Women, and the Dalkon Shield." Pp. 191–99 in *White-Collar Crime: Classic and Contemporary View,* 3rd ed., edited by Gilbert Geis, Robert F. Meier, and Lawrence M. Salinger. New York: The Free Press.

Moffat, Susan. 1993. "Brothers Enter Guilty Pleas in Massive Insurance Fraud." *Los Angeles Times,* March 17, p. 12.

Mullins, Christopher and Richard Wright. 2003. "Gender, Social Networks, and Residential Burglary." *Criminology* 42:911–40.

National Academy of Engineering. 2011. *Macondo Well Deepwater Horizon Blowout: Lessons for Improving Offshore Drilling Safety. National Research Council.* Washington, DC: National Academies of Science.

National White-Collar Crime Center. 2009. "Disaster Fraud." Retrieved September 10, 2014 (file:///C:/Users/bensonm/Documents/Current%20Projects/WCC%202nd%20 Edition/Articles/NW3C-%20disaster_fraud.pdf).

New York Times. 2006. "The Sago Mine Disaster." January 5. Retrieved July 2, 2014 (http:// query.nytimes.com/gst/fullpage.html?res=9E0CEFD71130F936A35752C0A9609 C8B63&module=Search&mabReward=relbias%3Aw%2C[%22RI%3A6%22%2C% 22RI%3A17%22]).

Nguyen, Tomson H. and Henry N. Pontell. 2010. "Mortgage Origination Fraud and the Global Economic Crisis: A Criminological Analysis." *Criminology and Public Policy* 9(3):591–612.

Partnership for Public Service. 2013. "Helping the SEC Crack Securities Fraud Cases Using Cutting-Edge Technology and Data Analysis." *The Washington Post.* Retrieved June 25, 2014 (www.washingtonpost.com/politics/federal_government/ helping-the-sec-crack-securities-fraud-cases-using-c-utting-edge-technology-and- data-analysis/2014/05/13/9c99de8a-daa5–11e3-b745–87d39690c5c0_story.html).

Partnoy, Frank. 2003. *Infectious Greed: How Deceit and Risk Corrupted the Financial Markets.* New York: Times Books.

Passas, Nikos. 1990. "Anomie and Corporate Deviance." *Contemporary Crises* 14:157–78.

Paternoster, Raymond and Sally Simpson. 1993. "A Rational Choice Theory of Corporate Crime." Pp. 37–58 in *Routine Activity and Rational Choice,* edited by Ronald V. Clarke and Marcus Felson. New Brunswick, NJ: Transaction.

Perez, Zathrina, Eric Cochran, and Christopher Sousa. 2008. "Securities Fraud." *American Criminal Law Review* 45:923–94.

Perri, Frank. S. 2013. "Visionaries or False Prophets?" *Journal of Contemporary Criminal Justice* 29:331–50.

Pike, Luke O. 1873. *A History of Crime in England: Illustrating the Changes of the Laws in the Progress of Civilisation.* London: Smith, Elder & Co.

Piquero, Alex R. 2008. "Taking Stock of Developmental Trajectories over the Life Course." Pp. 23–78 in *The Long View of Crime: A Synthesis of Longitudinal Research,* edited by A. Liberman. New York: Springer.

Piquero, Nicole Leeper and David Weisburd. 2009. "Developmental Trajectories in White-Collar Crime." Pp. 153–74 in *The Criminology of White-Collar Crime,* edited by Sally S. Simpson and David Weisburd. New York: Springer.

Podgor, Ellen S. 1999. "Criminal Fraud." *American Law Review* 48:730–70.

Pollock, Otto. 1950. *The Criminality of Women.* Philadelphia: University of Pennsylvania Press.

Pontell, Henry and Gilbert Geis. 2014. "The Trajectory of White-Collar Crime Following the Great Economic Meltdown." *Journal of Contemporary Criminal Justice* 30(1):70–82.

Portney, Paul R. 2000. "EPA and the Evolution of Federal Regulation." Pp. 11–30 in *Public Policies for Environmental Protection,* edited by Paul R. Portney and R.N. Stavisn. Washington, DC: Resources for the Future.

Preston, Ivan. 1975. *The Great American Blow Up: Puffery in Advertising and Selling.* Madison, WI: University of Wisconsin Press.

Reasons, Charles E., Lois L. Ross, and Craig Paterson. 1981. *Assault on the Worker: Occupational Health and Safety in Canada.* Toronto: Butterworths.

Rebovich, Donald J. 1992. *Dangerous Ground: The World of Hazardous Waste Crime.* New Brunswick, NJ: Transaction Press.

Reed, Gary E. and Peter C. Yeager. 1996. "Organizational Offending and Neoclassical Criminology: Challenging the Reach of a General Theory of Crime." *Criminology* 34:357–82.

Reichman, Nancy. 1993. "Insider Trading." *Crime and Justice* 18:55–96.

Reiman, Jeffrey H. 1979. *The Rich Get Richer and the Poor Get Prison.* New York: John Wiley & Sons.

———. 1990. *The Rich Get Richer and the Poor Get Prison: Ideology, Class, and Criminal Justice.* New York: Macmillan.

Reiss, Albert J. and Albert D. Biderman. 1981. *Data Sources on White-Collar Law-Breaking.* Washington, DC: U.S. Dept. of Justice, National Institute of Justice.

Reuter, Peter. 1993. "The Cartage Industry in New York." *Crime and Justice* 18:149–201.

Robb, George. 2006. "Women and White-Collar Crime: Debates on Gender, Fraud and the Corporate Economy in England and America, 1850–1930." *British Journal of Criminology* 46:1058–72.

Robinson, Ken. 2013. "The Role of Data Analytics in SEC Fraud Investigations." Retrieved June 25, 2014 (http://blogs.cfainstitute.org/marketintegrity/2013/10/23/the-role-of-data-analytics-in-sec-fraud-investigations).

Rorie, Melissa and Sally S. Simpson. n.d. "'The American Dream Gone Wrong': Criminogenic Tiers in America's Mortgage Market." Unpublished manuscript.

Rosoff, Stephen, Henry N. Pontell, and Robert Tillman. 2013. *Profit without Honor: White-Collar Crime and the Looting of America.* Upper Saddle River, NJ: Prentice Hall.

Ross, Edward A. 1977. "The Criminaloid." Pp. 29–37 in *White-Collar Crime,* revised, edited by Gilbert Geis and Robert F. Meier. New York: Macmillan.

Rothman, Martin L. and Robert P. Gandossy. 1982. "Sad Tales: The Accounts of White-Collar Defendants and the Decision to Sanction." *Pacific Sociological Review* 25:449–73.

Rothschild, Joyce and Terance D. Miethe. 1999. "Whistle-Blower Disclosures and Management Retaliation: The Battle to Control Information about Organizational Corruption." *Work and Organizations* 26:107–28.

Rowland, Christopher. 2005. "US Fraud Inquiry Targets Fresenius: Probe Comes 5 Years After Dialysis Chain Settled Medicare Case." *Boston Globe,* April 7, 2005. Retrieved September 10, 2014. (www.highbeam.com/doc/1P2-7895826.html)

Rue, Loyal. 1994. *By the Grace of Guile: The Role of Deception in Natural History and Human Affairs.* New York: Oxford University Press.

Rushe, Dominic. 2013. "Deepwater Trial: U.S. Lawyers Say BP Ignored Warnings on 'Well from Hell' "*The Guardian.* Retrieved July 1, 2014 (www.theguardian.com/environment/2013/feb/25/deepwater-trial-justice-bp-warnings).

Salinger, Lawrence M., ed. 2005. *Encyclopedia of White-Collar and Corporate Crime.* Thousand Oaks, CA: Sage.

Scalia, John. 1999. "Federal Enforcement of Environmental Laws, 1997." NCJ175686:1–10.

Schell-Busey, Natalie. 2009. The Deterrent Effects of Ethics Codes for Corporate Crime: A Meta-analysis. Dissertation. Digital Repository at the University of Maryland, College Park. Retrieved July 2, 2014 (http://hdl.handle.net/1903/9289).

Scott, Donald. 1989. "Policing Corporate Collusion." *Criminology* 27:559–87.

Scott, Marvin B. and Stanford M. Lyman. 1968. "Accounts." *American Sociological Review* 33:46–62.

Sealock, Miriam D. and Sally S. Simpson. 1998. "Unraveling Bias in Arrest Decisions: The Role of Juvenile Typescripts." *Justice Quarterly* 15:427–57.

Seidler, Lee J., Frederick Andrews, and Marc J. Empstein, eds. 1977. *The Equity Funding Papers: The Anatomy of a Fraud.* New York: John Wiley and Sons.

Senderdem, Enis. 2014. "Turkey's Mining Safety: Bleak Track Record." *BBC Turkish Service.* Retrieved July 2, 2014 (www.bbc.com/news/world-europe-27414972).

Shapiro, Susan P. 1984. *Wayward Capitalists: Target of the Securities and Exchange Commission.* New Haven, CT: Yale University Press.

———. 1985. "The Road Not Taken: The Elusive Path to Criminal Prosecution for White-Collar Offenders." *Law and Society Review* 19:179–217.

———. 1990. "Collaring the Crime, Not the Criminal: Reconsidering the Concept of White-Collar Crime." *American Sociological Review* 55:346–65.

Sharp, Kathleen. 2011. "To Save on Health Care, First Crack Down on Fraud." *New York Times.* Retrieved March 6, 2014 (www.nytimes.com/2011/09/27/opinion/to-save-on-health-care-first-crack-down-on-fraud.html?_r=0).

Shover, Neal. 2007. "Generative Worlds of White-Collar Crime." Pp. 81–97 in *International Handbook of White-Collar and Corporate Crime,* edited by Henry N. Pontell and Gilbert Geis. New York: Springer.

Shover, Neal, Donald A. Clelland, and John Lynxwiler. 1986. *Enforcement or Negotiation.* Albany, NY: State University of New York Press.

Shover, Neal and Andrew Hochstetler. 2006. *Choosing White-Collar Crime.* New York: Cambridge University Press.

Silberman, Charles E. 1978. *Criminal Violence, Criminal Justice.* New York: Random House.

Simon, David R. and Stanley D. Etizen. 1990. *Elite Deviance.* Boston: Allyn & Bacon.

Simon, Rita J. 1975. *Women and Crime.* Lexington, MA: Lexington Books.

Simpson, Sally S. 1986. "The Decomposition of Antitrust: Testing a Multilevel, Longitudinal Model of Profit-Squeeze," *American Sociological Review* 51:859–975.

———. 2002. *Corporate Crime, Law, and Social Control.* Cambridge: Cambridge University Press.

———. 2006. "Corporate Crime and Regulation." Pp. 63–90 in *Managing and Maintaining Compliance,* edited by H. Elffers, P. Verboon, and W. Huisman. The Hague: Boom Legal Publishers.

———. 2012. "Making Sense of White-Collar Crime: Theory and Research." *Ohio State Journal of Criminal Law* 8:481–502.

———. 2013. Illuminating the Dark Figure of White-collar Crime. Invited Keynote Lecture (June), Griffith University, Brisbane Australia.

———. 2013. "White-Collar Crime." *Annual Review of Sociology* 39:309–31.

Simpson, Sally S., Joel Garner, and Carole Gibbs. 2007. "Why Do Corporations Obey Environmental Law?" Washington, DC: National Institute of Justice.

Simpson, Sally S. and Nicole L. Piquero. 2002. "Low Self-Control, Organizational Theory, and Corporate Crime." *Law & Society Review* 36:509–48.

Simpson, Sally S., Melissa Rorie, Mariel Alper, Natalie Schell-Busey, William Laufer, and N. Craig Smith. 2014. *Corporate Crime Deterrence: A Systematic Review.* Campbell Systematic Reviews 2014.01 DOI 10.4073/csr.2014.4

Sinclair, Upton. 1906. *The Jungle.* New York: Doubleday.

Singh, B.K. and Larry D. Adams. 1979. "Variations in Self-Reported Arrests: An Epidemiological Perspective." *Criminal Justice Review* 4:73–83.

Smith, Douglas A. and Christy A. Visher. 1980. "Sex and Involvement in Deviance/Crime: A Quantitative Review of the Empirical Literature." *American Sociological Review* 45:691–701.

Smith, N.C., Sally S. Simpson, and Chun-yen Huang. 2007. "Why Managers Fail to do the Right Thing: An Empirical Study of Unethical and Illegal Conduct." *Business Ethics Quarterly* 17:633–67.

Smith, R. 2005. "Do the Determinants of Promotion Differ for White Men versus Women and Minorities?" *American Behavioral Scientist* 48: 1182–99.

Sparrow, Malcolm K. 1996. *License to Steal: Why Fraud Plagues America's HealthCare System.* Boulder, CO: Westview Press.

———. 1998. "Fraud Control in the Health Care Industry: Assessing the State of the Art." *Research in Brief.* Washington, DC: National Institute of Justice.

Steffensmeier, Darrell J. 1983. "Organization Properties and Sex Segregation in the Underworld: Building a Sociological Theory of Sex Differences in Crime." *Social Forces* 61:1010–32.

———. 1989. "On the Causes of 'White-Collar' Crime: An Assessment of Hirschi and Gottfredson's Claims." *Criminology* 27:345–58.

Steffensmeier, Darrell J. and Emilie Allan. 2000. "Looking for Patterns: Gender, Age, and Crime." Pp. 85–42 in *Criminology: A Contemporary Handbook,* edited by Joseph F. Sheley. Stamford, CT: Wadsworth/Thompson Learning.

Steffensmeier, Darrell J., Jennifer Schwartz, and Michael Roche. 2013. "Gender and Twenty-First-Century Corporate Crime: Female Involvement and the Gender Gap in Enron-Era Corporate Frauds." *American Sociological Review* 78(3):448–76.

Stempel, Jonathan. 2014. "Ex-BP Well Managers Must Face Gulf Spill Criminal Charges." *Reuters,* January 28. Retrieved September 11, 2014 (www.reuters.com/article/2014/01/28/us-bp-spill-charges-idUSBREA0R1H920140128).

Stewart, James B. 2011. *Tangled Webs: How False Statements Are Undermining America: From Martha Stewart to Bernie Madoff.* New York: Penguin Press.

Stone, Christopher D. 1975. *Where the Law Ends: The Social Control of Corporate Behavior.* New York: Harper & Row.

Stotland, Ezra. 1977. "White Collar Criminals." *Journal of Social Issues* 33:179–96.

Sutherland, Edwin H. 1940. "White-Collar Criminality." *American Sociological Review* 5:1–12.

———. 1941. "Crime and Business." *Annals of the American Academy of Political and Social Science* 217:112–18.

———. 1945. "Is 'White-Collar Crime' Crime?" *American Sociological Review* 10:132–39.

———. 1949. *White-Collar Crime.* New York: Holt, Rinehart and Winston.

———. 1983. *White-Collar Crime: The Uncut Version.* New Haven, CT: Yale University Press.

Swartz, Mimi. 2003. *Power Failure: The Inside Story of the Collapse of Enron.* New York: Doubleday.

Swigert, Victoria L. and Ronald A. Farrell. 1981. "Corporate Homicide—Definitional Processes in the Creation of Deviance." *Law & Society Review* 15(1):161–82.

Sykes, Gresham M. and David Matza. 1957. "Techniques of Neutralization: A Theory of Delinquency." *American Sociological Review* 22:664–70.

Szasz, Andrew. 1984. "Industrial Resistance to Occupational Safety and Health Legislation, 1971–1981." *Social Problems* 32:103–16.

Szockyj, Elisabeth. 1993. "Insider Trading: The SEC Meets Carl Karcher." *Annals of the American Academy of Political and Social Science* 525:46–58.

Szockyj, Elizabeth and James G. Fox. 1996. *Corporate Victimization of Women.* Boston: Northeastern University Press.

Tallmer, Matt. 1987. "Chemical Dumping as a Corporate Way of Life." Pp. 111–20 in *Corporate Violence,* edited by Stuart L. Hills. Totowa, NJ: Rowman & Littlefield.

Tappan, Paul W. 1947. "Who Is the Criminal." *American Sociological Review* 12:96–102.

Thompson, Richard and Claire Galofaro. 2013. "Defendants in BP Oil Spill Say Justice Department Scapegoating Them." *The Advocate,* December 5. Retrieved September 11, 2014 (http://theadvocate.com/news/7715100-123/defendants-in-bp-oil-spill).

Tillman, Robert. 1987. "The Size of the 'Criminal Population': The Prevalence and Incidence of Adult Arrest." *Criminology* 25:561–79.

Tillman, Robert H. and Michael H. Indergaard. 2005. *Pump and Dump: The Rancid Rules of the New Economy.* New Brunswick, NJ: Rutgers University Press.

Tittle, Charles R. 1991. "Review of *A General Theory of Crime.*" *American Journal of Sociology* 96:1609–13.

Tracy, Paul E. and James A. Fox. 1989. "A Field Experiment on Insurance Fraud in Auto Body Repair." *Criminology* 27:589–603.

Tracy, Paul, Marvin Wolfgang, and Robert Figlio. 1990. *Delinquency Careers in Two Birth Cohorts.* New York: Plenum.

Trefis Team. 2014. "BP's Oil Settlement Could Cost Over $15 Billion as the Court Upholds the Original Agreement." Retrieved July 2, 2014 (www.trefis.com/stock/bp/articles/222367/bps-oil-spill-settlement-could-cost-over-15-billion-as-the-court-upholds-the-original-agreement/2014-01-14).

Trop, Jaclyn. 2013. "Companies Admit They Fixed Prices of Car Parts." *New York Times.* Retrieved on June 3, 2014 (www.nytimes.com/2013/09/27/business/9-auto-parts-makers-plead-guilty-to-fixing-prices.html?pagewanted=all&_r=0) .

Trost, Cathy. 2008. "Good Neighbor Policy." Retrieved April 2, 2008 (www.aliciapatterson. org/APF0404/Trost/Trost.html).

USA Today. 2014. "Halliburton settles Deepwater Horizon claims for $1.1B." Retrieved September 15, 2104 (www.usatoday.com/story/money/business/2014/09/02/ halliburton-settles-gulf-explosion-claims/14958979/).

U.S. Bureau of Labor Statistics. 2013a. "The Editor's Desk: Changes in Men's and Women's Labor Force Participation Rates. Retrieved December 19, 2014 (www.bls.gov/ opub/ted/2007/jan/wk2/art03.htm) .

———. 2013b. "BLS Reports: Report 1040.Women in the Labor Force: A Databook." Retrieved December 19, 2014 (www.bls.gov/cps/wlf-databook-2012.pdf.) .

U.S. Department of Justice. 2014. "Deepwater Horizon (BP) Oil Spill Fraud." Retrieved July 2, 2014 (www.justice.gov/criminal/oilspill/).

U.S. Department of Justice, Environmental and Natural Resources Division. 2013. *ENRD Accomplishments Report Fiscal Year 2013.* Retrieved July 2, 2014 (www.justice.gov/enrd/ ENRD_Assets/ENRD_Accomplishments_Report_2013_2.pdf).

U.S. Environmental Protection Agency. 2001. "Pulping and Bleaching System NESHAP for the Pulp and Paper Industry: A Plain English Description." Retrieved July 2, 2014 (www.epa.gov/ttn/atw/pulp/guidance.pdf).

_____. 2013. "Enforcement Annual Results Numbers at a Glance for Fiscal Year (FY) 2013a." Retrieved July 2, 2014 (www2.epa.gov/enforcement/enforcement-annual-results-numbers-glance-fiscal-year-fy-2013).

_____. 2014. "Enforcement and Compliance History Online." Retrieved July 2, 2014 (http://echo.epa.gov/air_dashboard?state=National&view=activity).

U. S. Federal Bureau of Investigation. 2008. "Former Washington Teacher's Union Official Sentenced to 11 Years in Prison."

_____. 2009. "Financial Crimes Report." Retrieved on March 7, 2014 (www.fbi.gov/ stats-services/publications/financial-crimes-report-2009).

_____. 2010. "Members of Organized Crime Enterprises Charged with Federal Health Care Fraud Offenses." October 13, 2010. Retrieved September 12, 2014 (www.fbi.gov/ albuquerque/press-releases/2010/aq101310-1.htm).

_____. 2011. "Financial Crimes Report to the Public." Retrieved on March 7, 2014 (www.fbi.gov/stats-services/publications/financial-crimes-report-2010–2011/ financial-crimes-report-2010–2011#Health).

U.S. Federal Trade Commission. 2013. "Consumer Fraud in the United States, 2011. The Third FTC Survey." Staff Report of the Bureau of Economics, Federal Trade Commission. Retrieved July 2, 2014 (www.ftc.gov/sites/default/files/documents/reports/ consumer-fraud-united-states-2011-third-ftc-survey/130419fraudsurvey_0.pdf).

U.S. General Accounting Office. 2002. "Financial Statement Restatements: Trends, Market Impacts, Regulatory Responses, and Remaining Challenges." GAO-02–138.

U.S. Sentencing Commission. 1993–2004. "U.S. Federal Sentencing Guidelines." Washington, DC: U.S. Sentencing Commission.

_____. 2012. Interactive Sourcebook (isb.ussc.gov) Datafile, USSCFY2012.

_____. 2011. http://ussc.gov/sites/default/files/pdf/research-and-publications/annual-reports-and-sourcebooks/2011/assorted tables.

Vandenbergh, Michael P. 2001. "The Social Meaning of Environmental Command and Control." *Virginia Environmental Law Journal* 20:191–219.

Vaughan, Diane. 1983. *Controlling Unlawful Organizational Behavior.* Chicago: University of Chicago Press.

———. 1990. "The Macro/Micro Connection in 'White-Collar Crime' Theory." Pp. 124–45 in *White-Collar Crime Reconsidered,* edited by Kip Schlegel and David Weisburd. Boston: Northeastern University Press.

———. 2005. "The Normalization of Deviance: Signals of Danger, Situated Action, and Risk." Pp. 255–76 in *How Professionals Make Decisions,* edited by Henry Montgomery, Raanan Lipshitz, and Berndt Brehmer. Mahwah, NJ: Lawrence Erlbaum.

———. 2007. "Beyond Macro-and Micro-Levels of Analysis, Organizations, and the Cultural Fix." Pp. 3–24 in *International Handbook of White-Collar and Corporate Crime,* edited by Henry N. Pontell and Gilbert Geis. New York: Springer.

Vickers, M. and D. Burke. 2006. "The Bonnie and Clyde of Mortgage Fraud." *Fortune.* Retrieved April 18, 2008 (www.scopus.com/scopus/inward/record.url?eid=2-s2.0–35349031732&partnerID=40&rel=R7.0.0).

Vlasic, Bill and Danielle Ivory. 2014. "Barra Faces Scrutiny in House over G.M. Recalls." *New York Times.* Retrieved July 2, 2014 (www.nytimes.com/2014/06/19/business/house-hearing-on-general-motors-recalls.html?_r=0).

von Fritz, Kurt and Ernst Kapp. 1950. *Aristotle's Constitution of Athens and Related Texts.* New York: Hafner Publishing.

Washington Times. 2006. "Hemphill Given 11 Years for Union Embezzlement." Retrieved September 12, 2014 (www.washingtontimes.com/news/2006/may/22/20060522-111813-2310r/?page=all).

Weisburd, David and Elin J. Waring. 2001. *White-Collar Crime and Criminal Careers.* New York: Cambridge University Press.

Weisburd, David, Stanton Wheeler, Elin Waring, and Nancy Bode. 1991. *Crimes of the Middle Classes: White-Collar Offenders in the Federal Courts.* New Haven, CT: Yale University Press.

Wells, Celia. 1993. *Corporations and Criminal Responsibility.* Oxford: Clarendon Press.

Wheeler, Stanton. 1992. "The Problem of White-Collar Crime Motivation." Pp. 108–23 in *White-Collar Crime Reconsidered,* edited by Kip Schlegel and David Weisburd. Boston: Northeastern University Press.

Wheeler, Stanton, Kenneth Mann, and Austin Sarat. 1988b. *Sitting in Judgment: The Sentencing of White-Collar Criminals.* New Haven, CT: Yale University Press.

Wheeler, Stanton and Mitchell L. Rothman. 1980. "The Organization as Weapon in White-Collar Crime." *Michigan Law Review* 80:1403–26.

Wheeler, Stanton, David Weisburd, and Nancy Bode. 1982. "Sentencing the White-Collar Offender: Rhetoric and Reality." *American Sociological Review* 47:641–59.

Wheeler, Stanton, David Weisburd, Elin Waring, and Nancy Bode. 1988a. "White Collar Crime and Criminals." *American Criminal Law Review* 25:331–57.

Wilbanks, Charles. 2013. "Enron's Jeff Skilling May Get Early Release." *Moneywatch,* May 9, 2013. Retrieved September 12, 2014 (www.cbsnews.com/news/enrons-jeff-skilling-may-get-early-prison-release/).

Willott, Sara, Christine Griffen, and Mark Torrance. 2001. "Snakes and Ladders: Upper-Middle Class Male Offenders Talk about Economic Crime." *Criminology* 39(2):441–66.

Wilson, George. 2012. "Starting the Same . . . Finishing the Same? Race, Occupational Origins, and Mobility into Managerial Positions." *American Behavioral Scientist* 56(5):682–95.

Wilson, James Q. 1975. *Thinking about Crime.* New York: Basic Books.

Wilson, James Q. and Richard J. Herrnstein. 1985. *Crime and Human Nature.* New York: Simon and Schuster.

Wright, Erik O. 1997. *Class Counts: Comparative Studies in Class Analysis.* New York: Cambridge University Press.

Yang, Wan-Shiou and San-Yih Hwang. 2006. "A Process-Mining Framework for the Detection of Health Care Fraud and Abuse." *Expert Systems with Applications* 31:56–68.

Yeager, Peter C. and Gary E. Reed. 1998. "Of Corporate Persons and Straw Men: A Reply to Herbert, Green and Larragoite." *Criminology* 36:885–97.

Zietz, Dorothy. 1981. *Women Who Embezzle or Defraud: A Study of Convicted Felons.* New York: Praeger Publishers.

Zimring, Franklin E. and Gordon Hawkins. 1973. *Deterrence: The Legal Threat in Crime Control.* Chicago: University of Chicago Press.

INDEX